BUDDHIST METAPHYSICS AND ETHICS

Buddhist Metaphysics and Ethics

Buddhist Metaphysics And Ethics

H Prasad

MD Publications Pvt Ltd
New Delhi
www.mdppl.com

Published by :

MD Publications Pvt Ltd
"MD House", 11, Darya Ganj,
New Delhi - 110 002
Phone : +91-11- 45355555
E-mail : contact@mdppl.com
Website: www.mdppl.com

ISBN : 978-81-7533-351-2

Published and Printed by Mr. Pranav Gupta on behalf of **MD Publications Pvt Ltd** at Repro India Limited.

PREFACE

Buddhism is a religion and philosophy encompassing a variety of traditions, beliefs and practices, largely based on teachings attributed to Siddhartha Gautama, commonly known as the Buddha. The Buddha lived and taught in the northeastern Indian subcontinent some time between the 6th and 4th centuries BCE. He is recognized by adherents as an awakened teacher who shared his insights to help sentient beings end suffering (or dukkha), achieve nirvana, and escape what is seen as a cycle of suffering and rebirth.

The Buddha's main concern was to eliminate suffering, to find a cure for the pain of human existence. In this respect he has been compared to a physician, and his teaching has been compared to a medical or psychological prescription. Like a physician, he observed the symptoms - the disease that human kind was suffering from; next he gave a diagnosis - the cause of the disease; then he gave the prognosis - it could be cured; finally he gave the prescription - the method by which the condition could be cured. His first teaching, the Four Noble Truths, follows this pattern.

Another main teaching of Buddhist metaphysics is known as the Three Marks of Existence. The first is Anicca, impermanence: all things are transitory, nothing lasts. The second is Anatta, No-Self or No-Soul: human beings, and all of existence, are without a soul or self. The third mark of existence is that of Dukkha, suffering: all of existence, not just human existence but even the highest states of meditation are forms of suffering, ultimately inadequate and unsatisfactory. The three marks of existence can be seen as the basis for the four noble truths above; in turn the three marks of existence may be seen to come out of an even more fundamental Buddhist theory, that of Pratityasamutpada: Dependent Origination, or Interdependent Co-arising. This theory says that all things are cause and are caused by other things; all of existence is conditioned, nothing exists independently, and there is no First Cause. There was no beginning to the chain of causality; it is useless to speculate how phenomenal existence started.

Although there are many ethical tenets in Buddhism that differ depending on whether one is a monk or a layman, and depending on individual schools, the Buddhist system of ethics can always be summed up in the Eightfold Path. The purpose of living an ethical life is to escape the suffering inherent in (unenlightened) worldly life. Essentially, according to Buddhist teachings, the ethical and moral principles are governed by examining whether a certain action, whether connected to body or speech is likely to be harmful to one's self or to others and thereby avoiding any actions which are likely to be harmful. In Buddhism, there is much talk of a skilled mind. A mind that is skilful avoids actions that are likely to cause suffering or remorse.

I am very grateful to Mr. Pranav Gupta, Director of MD Publications Pvt Ltd, New Delhi, for his kind cooperation and support for this book.

H Prasad

CONTENTS

1

Lord Buddha and his Mystic Disciples

Having gained this doctrine the Buddha thought how difficult it would be for humanity to understand because of their attachments and lust. Trying to teach it to them would be vexation for him. However, the god Brahma asked him to teach the doctrine, because some people, who were not too impure, were falling away from not hearing the teachings. The Buddha in pity for beings surveyed their conditions and saw some of little impurity whom he could teach. At first he thought of his former teachers Alara Kalama and Uddaka, but in his clairvoyant awareness he realized that both of them had just died in the last few days. Then he decided to teach the five mendicants who had been with him in their striving.

Perceiving that they were in the deer park at Benares, he decided to go there. Along the way he met an Ajivika ascetic named Upaka, who when told of the Buddha's enlightenment, merely said that he hoped that it was so and went his way. When the five mendicants saw Siddartha Gautama, they thought they would not rise in respect but would offer him a seat. However, as the Buddha arrived, they spontaneously greeted him as a friend. They still criticized him for living in abundance, but the Buddha explained that he does not live in abundance. He spoke to them as one enlightened, and they had to agree that he never had spoken to them in that manner before. While he admonished two of them, the other three went off to collect alms; then he spoke with those three while the other two went for alms.

In this way all five soon attained insight and the supreme peace. In this deer park at Benares the Buddha gave his first sermon in which he explained that the two extremes are not to be practiced by the one who is enlightened - what is joined with the passions and luxury which is low, vulgar, common, ignoble, and useless, nor what is joined with self-torture which is painful, ignoble, and useless too. Avoiding these two extremes the enlightened follow the middle path which produces insight and knowledge and leads to peace, wisdom, enlightenment, and *nirvana*. The Buddha declared that Kaundinya had understood the doctrine, and he welcomed him as the first monk in the community by saying, "Come, monk, well proclaimed is the doctrine; lead a religious life for making a complete end of pain."

After further instruction the other four mendicants were also admitted into the community *(Sangha)*. Then the Buddha preached to the five that the body, perceptions, feelings, the mind, and even discriminating consciousness are not the self or soul. By turning away from the body, perceptions, feelings, mind, and discriminating consciousness, one becomes free from craving and emancipated. Life then becomes religious and is no longer under finite conditions.

Yasa, the son of a wealthy guildmaster, lived in luxury at Benares, and like Siddhartha he became disgusted with his palace attendants. After hearing the Buddha's doctrine he left home and became the first lay disciple in the new Community. The first women to become lay disciples were Yasa's mother and former wife. They were soon followed by four friends of Yasa and then fifty more. The Buddha then suggested that the sixty disciples wander around separately to preach the doctrine so that others may be liberated from the fetters of illusion, while he went to Uruvela in Magadha.

There thirty men of royal blood had entered the forest with their 29 wives and a courtesan for the one who was not married. When the courtesan ran off with their gold, silver, and gems, they all went to search for her and found the Buddha. He asked them if it was more important to seek for that woman or for themselves. When they agreed that their selves were more important, they sat down so that the Buddha could teach them how to seek within themselves. Sakyamuni was sitting under a banyan tree when a Brahmin named Drona approached him in awe, asking if he was a god. The Tathagata said no. The Brahmin asked if he were a kind of nature spirit *(gandharva* or *yaksha)*, but again the Buddha denied it. When he asked if he were a human, he denied that too. Finally Drona asked him if he was neither divine nor non-human nor human, then what he was. The reply was that he is Buddha (awake).

Shubha, a Brahmin student, asked the Buddha why humans differed so much in birth, intelligence, health, and so on. Sakyamuni explained that beings are heirs of karma, the consequences of their actions. Evildoers may experience happiness until their deeds ripen, and the good may experience bad things until their good deeds ripen. The pure and the impure create their own destinies; no one can purify another. Also living in this region were three Brahmin brothers of the Kashyapa family. They were ascetics with matted hair over the age of seventy and were the most respected religious leaders in Magadha with a total of about one thousand disciples. The Buddha spoke with the oldest, Uruvilva Kashyapa, but it was difficult for him to accept that such a young man could be so holy.

Finally the Buddha used his mystic powers, and convinced of the Buddha's superiority Uruvilva decided to follow him. The Buddha suggested that they ask his five hundred followers what they wanted to do and they all decided to join as well, shaving their hair and beards and throwing their ceremonial utensils into the river. The two Kashyapa brothers saw the implements in the river and eventually joined as well with their disciples. On the way to Rajagriha the Buddha and the thousand disciples saw the volcanic mountain Gayashirsa with its glowing fire. The Buddha preached his sermon on fire - how the sensations, perceptions, thoughts, and actions are burning with the poisons of covetousness, anger, and ignorance. At the capital he preached to King Bimbisara about the triple doctrine of almsgiving, precepts, and good works.

The king declared that all five of his wishes had been fulfilled - that he might be king, that a Buddha would come to his kingdom, that he would meet him, be instructed by him, and understand the teachings. After the sermon King Bimbisara donated a bamboo grove near the capital as a site for a monastery. Also at Rajagriha lived the agnostic Sanjaya, who also had many disciples under two named Sariputra and Maudgalyayana who were seeking enlightenment and a better teacher. Sariputra observed Assaji (one of the first five mendicants in the Community) begging and learned of the Buddha's teachings. He told Maudgalyayana, and they told the two hundred fifty disciples of Sanjaya. Even though Sanjaya tried three times to stop them from going away, they all went to find the Buddha, who greeted them with the revelation that these two would become his greatest disciples.

Within two weeks of joining the community both Sariputra and Maudgalyayana had become enlightened. In meditation Maudgalyayana had trouble with drowsiness and falling asleep. The Buddha suggested several remedies including lying down for a while to sleep before resuming meditation. The uncle of Sariputra was a skeptic like Sanjaya and told the Buddha that he could not accept any conclusive doctrine. Sakyamuni simply asked him if he recognized his own doctrine as conclusive. Caught in self-contradiction, he realized the weakness and limitation of skeptical philosophy. Then the Buddha explained the law of causation in human life. Having heard that his son had become a Buddha, King Suddhodana sent Udayin to invite Sakyamuni to the capital at Kapilavastu. Udayin was converted to the new religion, and Sakyamuni returned to his home town.

His father criticized him for begging for food when he was rich enough to feed thousands of followers. Sakyamuni replied that mendicancy was the correct custom for his line, by which he meant the line of Buddhas. Verbal discussions were not enough to win over people who had known him as a boy; so the Buddha used his mystical powers to convince them. Siddartha's half-brother Nanda was about to be declared crown prince and married to Sundari, the most beautiful woman in the kingdom, but he decided to join the community instead. However, he could not help thinking about Sundari; so the Buddha gave him a vision of hundreds of heavenly maidens, though this was later criticized by others as a wrong motivation for seeking enlightenment. Eventually Nanda repented of this motivation and asked the Buddha to dissolve his promise of these maidens, and Nanda attained enlightenment and became an *arhat* (a term meaning "worthy" or "honorable" used for disciples who attained the highest level of awareness).

Siddartha's son Rahula was also admitted to the community at the age of ten, but later a rule was made that minors under twenty could not join the community without permission from their parents. Many Sakya nobles also joined the community at this time (according to legend 80,000) including Ananda, Anuruddha, Devadatta, Bhaddiya, and Kimbila. On the way to Buddha they were accompanied by their barber and slave, UPali. They sent him back to Kapilavastu with their jewels, but afraid of the Sakyas' reaction, he put them on a tree and rejoined the five aristocrats. UPali, who was of the lowest caste, was ordained first giving him seniority over the nobles he had served so that their Sakya pride might be moderated. Like Mahavira, the Buddha taught in the ordinary language of the people rather than in the aristocratic Sanskrit.

Complaints that monks wandering around during the rainy season trampled the grass and destroyed living creatures led the Buddha to adopt the custom of staying in retreat during the three months of rain. After one of these retreats a wealthy householder from Sravasti, who became known as Anathapindada ("Giver of alms to the unprotected"), confessed to the Buddha that he enjoyed his investing and business cares. Sakyamuni suggested that he be a lay disciple and continue his work and use it as a blessing for other people. So Anathapindada invited the Buddha to spend the next rainy season at Sravasti, the chief city in Kosala, where he purchased and built the Jetavana Monastery. Later when Anathapindada was dying of a painful illness, Sariputra went and taught him the mental concentration for the avoidance of pain usually only taught to monks, and Anathapindada died in peace.

The Buddha liked the Jetavana Monastery to be quiet, for he once dismissed Yashoja and five hundred monks for talking too loudly after they arrived. However, they went to another place near Vaishali and made great spiritual gains. Later when the Buddha traveled to Vaishali he noticed that the area was illuminated. He told Ananda to invite Yashoja and the five hundred monks to the hall with the peaked roof. When they arrived, the Buddha was sitting in silent meditation; they too joined him in silent concentration. Every few hours Ananda approached the Buddha to ask him to greet these monks, but Sakyamuni remained silent and in the morning told Ananda that if he understood meditation better him would not have kept asking him to greet the monks, who were likewise sitting in immovable concentration.

A new monk once confessed to the Buddha for having eaten meat in his almsbowl, but the Buddha forgave those who ate meat that was not prepared for them. Their ethical principle was not to harm any living creature. Yet he criticized those who hunt and kill animals for sport and warned his followers not to accept any food from such blood-stained hands. After Sakyamuni's father died as a lay disciple, he declared that a lay disciple, whose mind is free from the poisons of lust, attachment, false views, and ignorance, is no different than anyone else who is free. Fearing a famine the Sakya warrior chiefs agitated for a war with the Kolyas over water rights to the Rohini River. The Kolyas had built a dike to conserve water; when they refused the Sakyas' demand to dismantle it, both sides prepared for war.

Just before the battle was to begin, the Buddha spoke to

both sides, asking them to compare the value of earth and water to the intrinsic value of people and the human blood they were about to spill. He told a parable about a decrepit demon, who fed on anger and took over a royal throne becoming stronger as more anger was directed at him until the true king came and calmly offered to serve the throne which led to the diminishment and disappearance of the anger demon. In this way the war was avoided. Krisha Gautami was stricken with grief when her only son died. Unable to find a physician who could bring him back to life, someone suggested that she go to the Buddha. He told her to get a handful of mustard seed in the city, but it must be from a house where no one has ever lost a child, spouse, parent, or friend. Eventually she came to realize how common death was and put aside her selfish attachment to her child.

Prajapati, the aunt and foster mother of Sakyamuni, asked to be admitted to the community. With Ananda acting as intermediary the Buddha established eight conditions for the admittance of nuns into the community. Nuns had to make obeisance to all the monks even the newest, and nuns were not allowed to criticize a monk, though monks criticized nuns. Although they were not treated equally, at least women were allowed to join the community. The sexism was also apparent when the Buddha told Ananda that the religious life would only last five hundred years instead of a thousand because women had been admitted. A legend tells how a disciple used magical power to get a sandalwood bowl that had been tied from the top of a bamboo pole as a kind of contest.

When the Buddha heard of it, he forbade those in the community to use such magical powers and had the bowl broken up and used as perfume. He suggested that his disciples only gain adherents by the miracle of instruction. In the ninth year after the enlightenment the Buddha was at Kaushambi, and the monk Malunkyaputra complained that the Buddha never explained whether the world is eternal or temporary, finite or infinite, or whether life and the body are the same or different, or whether *arhats* are beyond death or not. He even threatened to leave the community if the Buddha would not answer his questions. First the Buddha asked him if he had ever promised to explain these things; he had not.

Then he told the parable of a man who was pierced by a poisoned arrow, and his relatives summoned a doctor. Suppose, he said, the physician had said that he would not remove the arrow or treat the patient until his questions had been answered, such as who made the bow, what kind it was, all about the arrow, and so on. The man would die, and still the information would not be known. Then the Buddha told Malunkyaputra that a person would come to the end of one's life before those metaphysical questions he had asked could be answered by the Tathagata. Those questions do not tend toward edification nor lead to supreme wisdom. However, the Buddha's teaching regarding suffering, its cause, and the means of ending it is like removing the poisoned arrow.

A conflict arose in the community when a monk who refused to admit he had committed an offense was expelled. Some complained that this violated their principle that only evil deeds committed with conscious intent are morally reprehensible. However, the Buddha declared that the two greatest ways to obtain demerit are not to ask forgiveness after committing a wrong and not to forgive one who has confessed and asked for forgiveness. A Kalama nobleman from north of Kaushambi admitted that he had doubts because various teachers expressed contradictory views. The Buddha responded that he was wise not to believe everything but to question with reason and by experience. After thorough investigation whether the teachings are good, free from faults, praised by the noble, and when practiced lead to the welfare and happiness of oneself and other beings as well, then they may be accepted and lived.

At Asyapura they found Brahmin priests sacrificing horses, sheep, goats, cows, and other animals on bloody altars decorated with images of gods. The Buddha told his followers not to be deceived but to purify their hearts and cease to kill. They should not refuse to admit they are ascetics, who enjoy robes, bowl, bed, and medicine. In their simplified lives they learn how to calm their bodies and concentrate their minds to awaken the four religious qualities of loving friendship, compassion, altruistic joy, and equanimity. The Buddha also declared that in regard to this ascetic life all the castes are equal. A monk named Sona in the Sitavana Monastery at Rajagriha was so zealous in walking that his feet left a bloody trail. The Buddha asked him if his lute could be played well if the strings were too tight or too loose. Just so, excessive zeal may make the mind weary and one's thoughts irritable and uncertain. He suggested to Sona that gradual progress led to self-mastery and happiness rather than anxiety.

A young Brahmin named Vakula was so infatuated with the Buddha that he continually kept him in his sight. The Buddha explained that the one who sees the *dharma* (doctrine) sees the Buddha, but Vakula still always remained in his presence. Finally at the end of the rainy season the Buddha asked him to go away. Realizing that Vakula was climbing Vulture Peak to commit suicide, Sakyamuni went after him and called him back lest he destroy the conditions for winning great fruit. An ambitious disciple named Purna decided to spread the doctrine to the Shronaparantakas. The Buddha knowing that they were a dangerous people asked him what he would do if they insulted and abused him. Purna said he would consider them good and kind for not hitting him and throwing rocks at him. But what if they hit and throw rocks?

Then he would be glad they did not use clubs and swords. If they used clubs and swords, he would be glad they did not kill him; even if they kill him, they will have delivered him from his vile body. So equipped with patience and love Purna went to the Shronaparantakas and was about to be killed by a hunting archer for fun, when the hunter was so struck by how willing this person was to die that he stopped and eventually accepted the three refuges of the Buddha, the Doctrine, and the Community. Another monastery at Purvarama near Rajagriha was donated by Vishakha, the daughter of a rich man. Once at this monastery the Buddha remained silent on the moon day when the preaching service and confessions by the monks took place. Finally the Buddha said to Ananda that the assembly was not wholly pure. Maudgalyayana perceiving who the immoral person was, asked him to leave; when he refused to leave three times, he was escorted out of the hall by the arm.

The Tathagata thought it strange that he should wait until he was thrown out. Then the Buddha declared that he would no longer attend these sessions, but the monks would recite the regulations themselves. When Sakyamuni was about 55 his personal attendant at the time, Nagasamala, insisted on taking a different road than the Buddha advised and was beaten by robbers. At the Sravasti Monastery the Buddha announced that he wanted to have a permanent attendant. Sariputra volunteered, but the Buddha said his work was teaching. Maudgalyayana and others were also rejected. Ananda remained silent, but Sakyamuni asked him if he would find it a bother. Ananda said that it would not be bothersome, but he did not consider himself worthy.

Then he offered to do it on the following eight conditions: that he not have to accept gifts or alms given to the Buddha nor dwell in his chamber nor accept invitations offered only to him and that he may accompany the Perfect One when the monks are invited, that he may present him to those who come from a distance, that he may have access to him at all times, and that whatever teaching he missed by absence should be repeated to him by the Perfect One's own lips. The Buddha heartily agreed, and Ananda was his personal attendant for the rest of his life. Sakyamuni was able to tame a dangerous robber and admitted him into the community. He also bathed and treated a monk, who was suffering from dysentery and had been neglected by the other monks because he lay in his own excrement. On another occasion he found that a leper understood the doctrine very well as he explained that whatever has a beginning must have an end.

About 491 BC when Shayamuni was 72 a schism arose in the community, because his cousin Devadatta wanted to take over as head of the community; but Buddha refused saying that he would not even turn it over to Sariputra or Maudgalyayana much less to a vile one to be vomited like spit. Devadatta became resentful and used his magical powers to win the favor of Prince Ajatashatru, the son of King Shrenika Bimbisara. They plotted together to take over the kingdom of Magadha and the Buddhist community. Bimbisara and the Buddha were to be murdered, but since Bimbisara turned over his kingdom to his son he was merely put in prison where he soon died, though chronicles stated he was killed by his son. Hired killers were converted by the Buddha, but Devadatta tried to roll a huge boulder from Vulture Peak down upon the Buddha.

However, only Sakyamuni's foot was scratched. Yet spilling the blood of a Tathagata with murderous intent created terrible karma for Devadatta. When he had learned of his intent, the Buddha had already declared that Devadatta's words and actions were not to be considered as representing the community in any way. Although he had gained a few followers, these were persuaded to return to the real community after long sermons by Sariputra and Maudgalyayana when Devadatta fell asleep after his own talk. Abandoned and with his psychic powers destroyed by his evil intentions Devadatta soon became ill and died. King Ajatashatru, who had also listened to Mahavira, was eventually converted by the Buddha, but his previous evil intentions and actions prevented him from attaining the enlightenment he might have achieved in that life.

Ajatashatru married the daughter of the Kosala King Pasenadi, and Pasenadi's son married a maiden of the resentful Sakyas who was secretly of low birth. Her son, Vidudabha, swore revenge against the Sakyas. Pasenadi killed his powerful general and his sons, replacing them with the nephew Digha Karayana. While Pasenadi was listening to the Buddha, Digha hurried off and put Vidudabha on the throne. Pasenadi tried to get help from Ajatasatru but died of exposure on the way to Rajagriha. Surveying the world the Buddha became aware of Vidudabha's intention to attack the Sakyas and three times was able to convince him to turn back, but on the fourth time the Sakyas' karma for poisoning the river could not be averted, and they were massacred. Enough Sakyas remained, however, to accept a portion of Sakyamuni's relics after his death. When Sakyamuni was 79, both his chief disciples, Sariputra and Maudgalyayana, died. Sariputra died in the home where he was born, but Maudgalyayana was killed by robbers to balance karma from a former life.

At the age of eighty the vitality of the Tathagata's body seemed to diminish, and he declared that he had only three months to live. Ananda missed the opportunity to plead with him to stay until the end of the eon as Buddhas could do, and Ananda was later blamed for that by the Community. Finally Sakyamuni took his last meal, ordering a smith named Cunda to give him some mushrooms (literally pig's food or pork) and give the monks other food and then bury the rest of the mushrooms. Sharp sickness arose with a flow of blood and deadly pains, but the Buddha mindfully controlled them and declared that he would die in the third watch of the night. He sent word that Cunda was not to feel remorse but consider this giving of alms of the greatest merit.

Ananda asked the Buddha how he was to act toward women. The Buddha advised him not to see them; but if he saw them, not to speak to them; but if speaking, to exercise mindfulness. Then he said his burial was to be handled by the local Kshatriyas. That evening Ananda brought the local families to say goodby, and then the Buddha answered the questions of an ascetic named Subhadda. Before going through the four stages of higher awareness into *nirvana*, the last words of the Buddha were, "Decay is inherent in all component things. Work out your salvation with diligence."

2

Life of Nuns in Buddhist Monastries

Monasticism is the religious practice in which one renounces worldly pursuits in order to fully devote one's life to spiritual work. The origin of the word is from Ancient Greek, and the idea was originally related to Christian monks. In the Christian tradition, those pursuing a monastic life are usually called monks or brethren (brothers) if male, and nuns or sisters if female. Both monks and nuns may also be called monastics. Some other religions also include what could be described as "monastic" elements, most notably Buddhism, but also Taoism, Hinduism, and Jainism, though the expressions differ considerably. The order of Buddhist bhikkus (similar to monks) and original *Bhikkhunis* (similar to nuns) (*Sangha*) was founded by Gautama Buddha during his lifetime over 2500 years ago.

The Buddhist monastic lifestyle grew out of the lifestyle of earlier sects of wandering ascetics, some of whom the Buddha had studied under, and was initially fairly eremetic in nature. *Bhikkhus* and bhikkunis were expected to live with a minimum of possessions, which were to be voluntarily provided by the lay community. Lay followers also provided the daily food that *Bhikkhus* required, and provided shelter for *Bhikkhus* when they were needed. After the death of the Buddha, the Buddhist monastic order developed into a primarily cenobitic movement. The practice of living communally during the rainy vassa season, prescribed by the Buddha, gradually grew to encompass a settled monastic life centered on life in a community of practitioners.

Most of the modern disciplinary rules followed by *Bhikkhus* and *Bhikkhunis*-the *Patimokkha*-relate to such an existence, prescribing in great detail proper methods for living and relating in a community of *Bhikkhus* or *Bhikkhunis*. The number of rules observed varies with the order; Theravada *Bhikkhus* follow around 227 rules. There are a larger number of rules specified for *Bhikkhunis* (nuns). Buddhist monasticism with its tradition of councils, missions, and being a source of knowledge and literacy spread from India to the Middle East and eventually west, with Christian monasticism following in its footsteps in the areas where Emperor Ashoka sent missions.

The Buddhist monastic order consists of the male *Bhikkhu* assembly and the female *Bhikkhuni* assembly. Initially consisting only of males, it grew to include females after the Buddha's stepmother, Mahaprajapati, asked for and received permission to live as an ordained practitioner. *Bhikkhus* and *Bhikkhunis* are expected to fulfill a variety of roles in the Buddhist community. First and foremost, they are expected to preserve the doctrine and discipline now known as Buddhism. They are also expected to provide a living example for the laity, and to serve as a "field of merit" for lay followers-providing laymen and women with the opportunity to earn merit by giving gifts and support to the *Bhikkhus*.

In return for the support of the laity, *Bhikkhus* and *Bhikkhunis* are expected to live an austere life focused on the study of Buddhist doctrine, the practice of meditation, and the observance of good moral character. A *Bhikkhu* in Pali or Bhikshu in Sanskrit first ordains as a *Samanera* (novice) for a year or more. Novices often ordain at a very young age, but generally no younger than eight. *Samaneras* live according to the Ten Precepts, but are not responsible for living by the full set of monastic rules. Higher ordination, conferring the status of a full *Bhikkhu*, is usually given only to men who are aged

20 or older. *Bhikkhunis* follow a similar progression, but are required to live as *Samaneras* for a longer period of time-typically five years.

The disciplinary regulations for *Bhikkhus* and *Bhikkhunis* are intended to create a life that is simple and focused, rather than one of deprivation or severe asceticism. Celibacy is of primary importance in monastic discipline. The order of Buddhist monks and nuns was founded by Gautama Buddha during his lifetime over 2500 years ago.

The Buddhist monastic lifestyle grew out of the lifestyle of earlier sects of wandering ascetics, some of whom the Buddha had studied under. It was not really isolationist or eremetic: the *Sangha* was dependent on the lay community for basic provisions of food and clothing, and in return *Sangha* members helped guide laid followers on the path of Dharma. Individuals or small groups of monks - a teacher and his students, or several monks who were friends - traveled together, living on the outskirts of local communities and practicing meditation in the forests.

Monks and nuns were expected to live with a minimum of possessions, which were to be voluntarily provided by the lay community. Lay followers also provided the daily food that monks required, and provided shelter for monks when they were needed. During the Buddha's time, many retreats and gardens were donated by wealthy citizens for monks and nuns to stay in during the rainy season. Out of this tradition grew two kinds of living arrangements for monastics, as detailed in the Mahavagga section of the Vinaya and Varsavastu texts:

1. *Avasa*: a temporary house for monastics called a vihara. Generally more than one monk stayed in each house with each monk in his own cell, called a *parivena*.
2. *Arama*: a more permanent and more comfortable arrangement than the avasa. This property was generally donated and maintained by a wealthy citizen. This was more lavish (as suggested by the name - *Arama* means both pleasant and park). It generally consisted of residences within orchards or parks.

One of the more famous Arama is Anathapindika's, known as *Anathapindikassa arame*, built on Prince Jeta's grove. It had buildings worth 1.8 million gold pieces built in a beautiful grove, with the total gift worth 5.4 million gold pieces. After the pari*nirvana* of the Buddha, the Buddhist monastic order developed into a primarily cenobitic movement. The practice of living communally during the rainy vassa season, prescribed by the Buddha, gradually grew to encompass a settled monastic life centered on life in a community of practitioners. Most of the modern disciplinary rules followed by monks and nuns-the *Patimokkha*-relate to such an existing, prescribing in great detail proper methods for living and relating in a community of monks or nuns. The number of rules observed varies with the order; Theravada monks follow around 227 rules. There are a larger number of rules specified for *Bhikkhunis*.

MONASTICISM'S ROLE IN CREATING LITERATE SOCIETIES

Monastic institutions and missions became vehicles for the spread of literacy and culture throughout the ancient world and held an important place in promoting charitable causes, building libraries, hospitals, schools, and universities. We see this in the Mauryan, where Emperor Ashoka builds rest houses for weary travelers, free hospitals for both people and animals, and wells and helped monasteries become institutions of learning such as Nalanda University and Vikramshila. During the Tang Dynasty the monasteries fostered artistic creativity, cared for the sick, old, and orphaned, and ran community development projects such as developing roads and building bridges and wells.

Even today, in Southeast Asia, many monasteries serve as free accommodations, retirement homes, and homes for the homeless or chronically ill. Poor families frequently use monasteries as hostels. They serve as village libraries and centers of news and information, and the surplus money is used to make schools....as Buddhism spread literate culture into many societies in the process of political unification and organization, it is not surprising that the *Sangha* came to wield political influence, or even political power, in a number of countries. -*Peter Harvey, An Introduction to Buddhism*

MONASTIC LIFE

The Buddhist monastic order is theoretically divided into two assemblies, the male *Bhikkhu* (Pali, Skt. bhikshu) assembly, and the female *Bhikkhuni* (Skt. bhikshuni) assembly. Initially consisting only of men, the Buddha recognized women after his stepmother, Mahaprajapati, asked for and received permission to live as an ordained practitioner. Female monastic communities in the *Bhikkhuni* linneage were never established in the Vajrayana communities of Tibet and Nepal; Theravada communities formerly existed, but died out between the 11th and 14th century. Ordination in the *Bhikkhuni* linneage continues to exist among East Asian communities, and attempts have been made at a revival in Southeast Asia and Sri Lanka.

Monks and nuns are expected to fulfill a variety of roles in the Buddhist community. First and foremost, they are expected to preserve the doctrine and discipline now known as Buddhism. They are also expected to provide a living example for the laity, and to serve as a "field of merit" for lay followers, providing laymen and women with the opportunity to earn merit by giving gifts and support to the monks. In return for the support of the laity, monks and nuns are expected to live an austere life focused on the study of Buddhist doctrine, the practice of meditation, and the observance of good moral character. The relative degree of emphasis on meditation or study has often been debated in the Buddhist community. A *Bhikkhu* or *Bhikkhuni* first ordains as a *Samanera* (novice) for a year or more.

Male novices often ordain at a very young age, but generally no younger than 8. Women usually choose to ordain as adults, since there is no expectation that they do so in childhood. *Samaneras* live according to the Ten Precepts, but are not responsible for living by the full set of monastic rules, vinaya. Higher ordination, conferring the status of a full *Bhikkhu* or *Bhikkhuni*, is usually given only to those 20 or older. Women monastics follow a similar progression, but are required to live as *Samaneras* for a longer period of time, typically five years. In Thailand, monks are considered well supported by the community, and in return the monks offer guidance in life and in the Dharma. The disciplinary regulations for monks and nuns are intended to create a life that is simple and focused, rather than one of deprivation or severe asceticism. Celibacy is of primary importance in monastic discipline, seen as being the preeminent factor in separating the life of a monastic from that of a householder.

Depending on the tradition and the strictness of observation, monastics may eat only one meal a day provided either by direct donations of food from lay supporters, or from a monastery kitchen that is stocked (and possibly staffed) by lay supporters. Unlike Christian monastics, Buddhist monastics are not required to live a life of obedience to a superior. However, it is expected that monastics will offer respect to senior members of the *Sangha* (in Thai tradition, seniority is based on the number of rains retreats, vassas, that one has been ordained). The Buddha did not appoint a successor, nor did he specify rules mandating obedience in the monastic code. Individual groups of monastics are expected to make decisions collectively through regular gatherings of the community, at which decisions regarding violations of monastic rules and the dispositions of communal property are to be made.

Individual relationships of teacher/student, senior/junior, and preceptor/trainee may be observed among groups of monastics, but there are no formal positions, nor is there any authority to give orders or commands invested in senior monks. An abbess or abbot, typically a senior monastic still young enough to be active, is usually responsible for the day-to-day administration of the monastery, and may appoint others to assist with the work. In some traditions, the abbess/abbot is chosen by a vote of the monastics in a monastery. In other traditions (Thailand, for example), the abbot is chosen by the lay community.

LOCAL VARIATIONS

Monastic practices vary significantly according to location. In part, this can be attributed to differences in the scriptural and doctrinal traditions that were received in different parts of the Buddhist world. Additionally, local concessions to social, geographical, and climatic conditions have been adopted by most monastic orders in order to smooth the integration of monks into local communities, and to ensure that monks live in a safe and reasonable manner. In cold climates, for instance, monks are permitted to own and wear additional clothing not specified in the scriptures. In areas where begging rounds are impossible (due to traffic, geography, or disfavor by the lay community), monks more commonly employ a kitchen staff of monks or lay followers who are responsible for providing meals for the community.

TIBET

In Tibet, before the Communist invasion in the late 1940s and early '50s, more than half of the country's male population was ordained. Due to the oppression, and destruction of monasteries and libraries by the Chinese, this is no longer the case-the Chinese have historically justified this by the accusation that the Tibetan monks exploited the poor peasantry of Tibet for their sustenance. Hoping to find religious freedom, many Tibetan monks annually risk crossing the Himalayas, often trying to reach India. While generally adhering to a Mahayana tradition that advocates the virtues of vegetarianism, Tibetan monks generally eat meat as a concession to climatic conditions that make a plant-based diet largely unfeasible.

EAST ASIA

In East Asia, monastics live in greater isolation from the lay population than is observed in most Theravada countries. Because of local conditions of geography and climate, as well as local attitudes towards begging, monks generally do not make begging rounds in China, Korea, Vietnam and many parts of Japan. Instead, monasteries receive donations of bulk food (such as rice) and funds for the purchase of food that is then stored and prepared at the monastery. The management of the kitchen and monastery properties may be the purview of a specially designated layman, or a monk who has been given a special role by the abbot of the monastery.

Monastics in Japan are particularly exceptional in the Buddhist tradition because they generally marry after receiving their higher ordination. There had long been many instances of Japanese monks marrying, from the Heian period (794-1185) onward, but it was not predominante until a government initiative was passed during the Meiji Restoration that required monks to seek wives. While one of the four Tibetan monastic orders permits marriage, as well as some Korean orders, Japan is the only Buddhist country where the majority of religious specialists are married.

SOUTHEAST ASIA

In Thailand, Cambodia, Laos, and Myanmar, where the Theravada school is dominant, there is a long tradition of temporary ordination. During a school break, many young men usually ordain for a week or two to earn merit for loved ones and to gain knowledge of Buddhist teachings. In most countries, this temporary ordination occurs during the vassa retreat, which is regarded as a period of intensified spiritual effort by local Buddhists.

Men in Thailand typically ordain only before being married; men in Laos and Myanmar could traditionally return to the monastery from time to time after being married, provided that they secured their wives' permission. Theravada monks are also most likely to engage in traditional begging practices, although the urbanization of parts of Southeast Asian (particularly Thailand) has presented a challenge to this practice.

In Thailand, where the Buddhist institution has traditionally been closely associated with the government and the institution of kingship, a more hierarchical structure has evolved to deal with the administration and regulation of monasteries. This system initially stemmed from a system of royal patronage, in which monks who were appointed the abbots of 'royal monasteries' (those endowed and supported by members of the royal family) were accorded greater respect than those who headed more conventional monasteries. This system remained fairly unstructured until the modernisation efforts of the 19th Century, during which a more formal system of governance was created by the central government.

Modern Thai monks are ranked according to their ability to pass examinations in Buddhist doctrine and the Pali language, and are appointed to successively higher positions in the ecclesiastic hierarchy on the basis of these exams, as well as their support among influential members of the royal family and government. Local affairs continue to be handled primarily by the local monastic and lay community, but nationwide efforts (such as curriculum decisions for monastic schools and the authoritative form of scriptures and rituals) are typically made by the central hierarchy.

BHIKKHU

A *Bhikkhu* is a fully ordained male Buddhist monastic. Female monastics are called *Bhikkhunis*. *Bhikkhus* and *Bhikkhunis* keep many precepts: they live by the vinaya's framework of monastic discipline, the basic rules of which are called the *patimokkha*. Their lifestyle is shaped so as to support their spiritual practice, to live a simple and meditative life, and attain *Nirvana*. Bhiksu may be literally translated as "beggar" or more broadly as "one who lives by alms". It is philologically analysed in the Pali commentary of Buddhaghosa as "the person who sees danger (in *samsara* or cycle of rebirth)". He therefore seeks ordination in order to release from it. The Dhammapada states:

Not therefore is he a Bhikkhu

Merely because he begs from others

Not by adopting the outward form

Does one truly become a Bhikkhu

He who wholly subdues evil,

Both small and great,

Is called a monk (Bhikkhu)

Because he has overcome all evil - Dhammapada 266, 267

A *Bhikkhu* has taken a vow to enter the *Sangha* (Buddhist monastic community) and is expected to obey rules of conduct (typically around 227 for a male) as set out in the Vinaya, although there are considerable local variations in the interpretations of these rules. A novice monk or nun in the Tibetan tradition takes 36 vows of conduct. The minimum age to take *Bhikkhu* vows is 21 years (although this varies from country to country). In English literature prior to the mid-20th Century, Buddhist monks were often referred to by the term *bonze*, particularly when describing monks from East Asia and French Indochina. This term is derived via Portuguese and French from the Japanese word *bonsô* for a priest or monk, and has become less common in modern literature.

VOWS AND ORDINATION

Although the European concepts "monk" and "nun" are applied to Buddhism relatively unproblematically, the situation of 'ordination' is more complicated.

BECOMING A *BHIKKHU/BHIKKHUNI*

In Buddhism, monasticism is part of the system of "vows of individual liberation". These vows are taken by monks and nuns from the ordinary *Sangha*, in order to develop personal ethical discipline. In Mahayana Buddhism, the term "*Sangha*" is, in principle, often understood to refer particularly to the *Arya Sangha* (Tib. *mchog kyi tshogs*, pronounced *chokyi tsok*)) the "community of the noble ones who have reached the first bhumi. These, however, need not be monks and nuns. The vows of individual liberation are taken in four steps. A lay person may take the five *upasaka* (Pali and Sanskrit;

feminine: *Upasika;* Tibetan *dge snyan/dge snyan ma,* pronounced *genyen/genyenma,* "approaching virtue") vows.

The next step is to enter the pabbajja (Srt: *pravrajya,* Tib. *rab byung* pronounced *rabjung*), or monastic way of life, which includes wearing monk's or nun's robes. After that, one can become a *Samanera,* or novice monk/nun. The last and final step is to take all the vows of a *Bhikkhu/Bhikkhuni* a "fully ordained monk/nun." Monks and nuns take their vows for a lifetime, but they can "give them back" (up to three times in one life), a possibility which is actually used by many people. In this way, Buddhism keeps the vows "clean". It is possible to keep them or to leave this lifestyle, but it is considered extremely negative to break these vows. In Tibet, rabjung, getshül, gelong ordinations are usually taken at ages six, fourteen and twenty-one or older, respectively.

Robes

The special dress of ordained people, the robes, comes from the idea of wearing cheap clothes just to protect the body from weather and climate. They shall not be made from one piece of cloth, but mended together from several pieces. Since dark red was the cheapest colour in Kashmir, the Tibetan tradition has red robes. In the south, yellow played the same role, though the color of saffron also had cultural associations in India; in East Asia, robes are yellow, grey or black. The robes of getshül novices and gelong monks differ in various aspects, especially in the application of "holes" in the gelong dress.

Some monks tear their robes into pieces and then mend these pieces together again. The rabjung novices shall not wear the "chö-göö", the yellow tissue worn during Buddhist teachings by both getshüls and gelongs. In observance of the Kathina Puja, a special Kathina robe is made in 24 hours from donations by lay supporters of a temple. The robe is donated to the temple or monastery, and the resident monks then select from their own number a single monk to receive this special robe.

ADDITIONAL VOWS IN THE MAHAYANA AND VAJRAYANA TRADITIONS

In Mahayana traditions, a *Bhikkhu* may take additional vows not related to ordination, including the *Bodhisattva* vow, samaya vows, and others, which are also open to laypersons in most instances. In addition, there in various traditions there are other kinds of non-vinaya ordinations, the holders of which are not considered *Bhikkhu*s. These included ordination into the "white *Sangha*" lineage of Tibetan yogis, and all of the ordination lineages of the various Japanese traditions.

"Ordination" in Buddhism is a cluster of methods of self-discipline according to the needs, possibilities and capabilities of individuals. According to the spiritual development of his followers, the Buddha gave different levels of vows. The most advanced method is the state of a bhikshu (ni), a fully ordained follower of the Buddha's teachings. The goal of the bhikku (ni) in all traditions is to achieve liberation from suffering. The Teaching of the Buddha is concerned with more than intellectual knowledge for it needs to be experienced as truth in one's own life. The Buddha often called his teaching the Dhamma-Vinaya and when he passed away he left these as the guide for all of us who followed. As Venerable Thiradhammo writes:

In simple terms we could say that while "Dhamma represented the principles of Truth, the Vinaya represented the most efficacious lifestyle for the realization of that Truth. Or, the Vinaya was that way of life which enshrined the principles of Truth in the practicalities of living within the world."

For the *Bhikkhu*, the Vinaya helps to highlight actions and speech, and show up their significance. It brings an awareness of how he is intervening in the world, how he is affecting other people. Of course, such awareness is necessary for every human being, not just Buddhist monks. This is why the Buddha bequeathed to us the Five, the Eight and the Ten Precepts - as well as the *Bhikkhu*'s 227 rules of the Patimokkha.

These precepts and rules remain as pertinent today as they were 2,500 years ago for they restore the focus back to the human being, to how actions and words affect individuals and the world. While the particulars may have changed, the fundamentals remain the same.

Those who take the Buddha's teaching seriously become ever more aware of their actions and speech, and how they match up against the Five Precepts. They then might start to realize the advantage in occasionally keeping the Eight Precepts - perhaps on the weekly Observance Day - and become more interested in the *Bhikkhu*'s Rule and how its precepts come together into a whole way of life. This compilation, therefore, is for anyone interested in *Bhikkhus* and how to relate to them. Some might think that the Theravada lineage follows an overly traditionalist approach but then, it does happen to be the oldest living major tradition.

A slight caution therefore for anyone completely new to the ways of monasticism, for it is an approach to dealing with life that may appear radically different for this modern day and age. The best introduction, perhaps essential for a true understanding, is meeting with a practicing *Bhikkhu* who should manifest and reflect the peaceful and joyous qualities of the *Bhikkhu*'s way of life. Buddhist monks and nuns first received the going-forth into the Holy Life from the Buddha himself, more than two and a half thousand years ago in India. Since then, their influence has been felt over much of Asia. The countries of Sri Lanka and South East Asia have been profoundly affected by the Theravadin School of Buddhism, which looks back to the original Teachings as recorded in the Pali scriptures. Buddhism was often first introduced to a new country when *Bhikkhus* were invited to come and teach the new religion by the indigenous ruler.

This process now continues throughout the world, although the invitation nowadays comes more often from local Buddhists. Buddhism is justly admired for its appreciation of tolerance and broad-mindedness, with a history generally unblemished by heretical infighting. This has resulted in a wide spectrum of practices, from the old Theravada to the Zen of Japan and the Vajrayana of Tibet. Even between the different Theravadin countries and Schools there are slight variations in the ways the *Bhikkhus* understand and practice the Vinaya Rule. Such differences have sometimes confused lay devotees so this is also an attempt to offer a clearer understanding about the responsibilities of the Theravadin *Bhikkhu*'s life and those of the lay devotee.

When the Buddha was about to finally pass away and leave his followers, rather than appoint an individual to take his place he said this:

"Whatever Dhamma and Vinaya I have pointed out and formulated for you, that will be your Teacher when I am gone." (Mahaparinibbana Sutta, [D.16])

More than twenty-five centuries have now gone by; empires have come and gone, great movements and ideologies have flared up and been lost. Yet on a deeper level under all of this, the Dhamma and Vinaya have been quietly guiding the communities of Buddhist monks. Why has it withstood the test of time so well? Why has it been so successful? Perhaps it is because the Lord Buddha understood the basic human condition of every time or place; he knew our predicament and failings, and he could show the way out to those of us who follow so long after him.

The Lord Buddha gave this reflection about why a monk wears a robe:

"Properly considering the robe, I use it: simply to ward off cold, to ward off heat, to ward off the touch of flies, mosquitoes, simply for the purpose of covering the parts of the body which cause shame."

In the Lord Buddha's time, 2,500 years ago, clothing was made without complex machinery. (Although simple 'sewing-frames' are mentioned in the texts which the monks would have used at robe-making *(Kathina)* time.) So the pattern of the robe is very simple and designed so that it can be made up out of patches of cloth, for discarded rags were often used after washing and dyeing. This 'yellow robe' is considered the *banner of the arahant* and emblem of Buddhism. For the ordinary Theravadin *Bhikkhu* it is a privilege to be able to wear this robe, continuing the tradition and practicing to be worthy of it. There are rules as to the robes' size, color, how they are sewn, type of cloth used, etc., and how *Bhikkhus* can acquire them.

The color of the robes depends on the dye used. Until very recently, this would have been natural vegetable dye found in the jungle from roots or trees. (In NE Thailand, for example, we used the heartwood of the jack-fruit tree.) Nowadays chemical dyes are more used and sometimes give that more vivid orange color that one sees in Bangkok.

The color white is used by Buddhist devotees to show their commitment to keeping the Precepts - usually the Eight Precepts - on Observance Days. (White robes are also worn by the *anagarika* or postulant before he becomes a monk.)

The Lord Buddha gave this reflection about finding and eating food:

"Properly considering alms food, I use it: not playfully, nor for intoxication, nor for putting on weight, nor for beautification; but simply for the survival and continuance of this body, for ending its afflictions, for the support of the chaste life, (thinking) I will destroy old feelings (of hunger) and not create new feelings (from overeating). Thus I will maintain myself, be blameless, and live in comfort."

The alms bowl is another practical symbol of Buddhism, and, like the robes, another requisite of the *Bhikkhu*. Although every *Bhikkhu* is given an alms bowl (and a set of robes) when he becomes a monk, not all of them will actually go on an alms round and only a minority - usually they are the forest meditation *Bhikkhus* - will eat from their bowl sitting on the floor. Therefore many monks will eat using plates and dishes, while some will eat sitting on the floor at a small table and others at a normal western-style table. One should not feel shy about asking a monk as to his normal way of eating and then fit in with that.

Those forest *Bhikkhus* who keep the austere practices *(dhuta"nga* or *tudong)* will be stricter about only using one eating vessel. This can simplify life and remind the *Bhikkhu* that although food is necessary for bodily health he does not have to indulge in an obsession with taste. (It also saves washing-up time.)

In India during the Lord Buddha's time much of the land was covered in forests and groves and this was where the wandering mendicants of the different orders would pursue their religious practices. The Lord Buddha spoke of the 'foot of a tree' as the basic shelter for *Bhikkhus,* and this is usually still affirmed to every newly ordained *Bhikkhu*. Later, monasteries were established and well-endowed, and the focus shifted to a more settled life. Mostly only the 'forest monks' now live in the forest where it is quiet and conducive to meditation. Many more monks will live in the village monastery or go to a monastery in the town to study the scriptures.

The Lord Buddha said this about the basics of shelter, whether in the forest or city:

"Properly considering the lodging, I use it: simply to ward off cold, to ward off heat, to ward off the touch of flies, mosquitoes, wind, sun and reptiles; simply for protection from the inclemencies of weather and for the enjoyment of seclusion."

In fact getting the robes and bowl is not so much a problem for once the candidate is accepted by a preceptor, the preceptor will know where suitable requisites may be found. The question should be more about the qualities necessary to become a monk and I have explained some of these in the section on *Becoming a Bhikkhu*. If the candidate's intention is right and he is not disqualified by other factors, he should find a senior monk who can advise him on the places where he might ordain and perhaps recommend him to a preceptor. If the candidate lives in a non-Buddhist country, he can write for details to the country where he is interested in staying. *Bhikkhus* are often traveling and giving Dhamma talks around the world and they would generally be very happy to make suggestions about this.

In certain communities there is a 'postulancy' period when the candidate first wears white robes as an *anagarika* and after a year (or two) may then be given either novice *(samanera)* or full *Bhikkhu* ordination. Once he is accepted for this, all the requisites should be provided. (In some monasteries the candidate is provided with the cloth but has to learn to sew his own robes.) Similarly for the lay person wanting to help supply requisites to the new monk, the best way is to ask details from a senior monk who will explain and help. In some Buddhist countries there are even special shops to supply these requisites but whether this is suitable will depend on the monastery of ordination.

The Theravadin lineage no longer has an 'officially recognized' *Bhikkhuni*-ordination. There are other forms for lay women that still involve 'leaving the home life' and keeping Eight or Ten Precepts as a *dasasila mata* nun. Finding a suitable place is quite difficult but several groups are trying to develop places conducive to Dhamma practice for such nuns.

Some *Bhikkhus* take a daily alms-round as a special practice *(dhutanga* or *tudong)* and will normally always want to go. Many other monks will be happy to receive food brought to them. Please ask or observe how the monk practices. There is no harm in offering to bring the food, for if the monk prefers to walk on an alms-round he can explain about that.

There is a minimum in that the *Bhikkhu* must be properly and modestly dressed, especially in public. During the cold season in India, the Buddha allowed a double-layered outer robe *(Sanghati)* to be used and so - using the Great Standards as a guide - in even colder climates extra layers may be allowable. In countries where hypothermia may be a danger, the use of extra layers seems sensible - especially if this cuts down on heating and medical expenses. (That a *Bhikkhu* lives as frugally as possible is a major aspect of the *Vinaya.)* However, it is generally felt very important that the traditional robes remain the basic dress and 'extra layers' should not obscure this.

There are definite conditions that allow a *Bhikkhu* to ask for help. These would be when he is ill, or in danger, or when he has been formally offered help. Yes, generosity is a virtue highly praised by the Buddha and was often the first virtue he mentioned. It goes against the general modern selfish attitude of 'getting is better than giving' and leads on to contentment and the calm that can lead to deep meditation and wisdom. So, if it makes one happy to make an offering then one can do so without asking first. However, the offering should also be endowed with wisdom so that one gives something that is useful and not beyond one's family's means.

The yellow robe worn by monks is an emblem and reminder of the Triple Gem, as is the Buddha Statue. Therefore one is really bowing to the Buddha, Dhamma and *Sangha*, not to some person or statue. There are two aspects to bowing - the bodily action and the mind. If one bows because it gives one the opportunity to demonstrate one's faith in the Triple Gem, because it seems the right thing to do, and because it leads the mind to calm, then it will be beneficial. If one bows without reason or because one feels that one must do so for appearances sake, then it is a rather empty gesture.

When I bow three times to the Buddha Statue or to senior monks, I mentally recollect *'Buddho,'* then *'Dhammo'* and then *'Sangho'* and also have mindfulness of the bodily posture as it bends forward and the head touches the floor. However, in Western countries this is often misunderstood and can be the source of quite a lot of embarrassment. It is up to the persons themselves to decide what is appropriate under the different circumstances.One should show respect from one's heart in the way that seems best to oneself, recollecting the Triple Gem and doing it mindfully. No good monk (or Buddha statue) is going to take offence if one does not bow.

When the prince who was to become the Buddha left his palace to seek a way beyond aging, sickness and death, it is said that one of the first things that he did was to "shave off his hair and beard and put on the yellow cloth." Buddhist monks always completely shave their head and beard, showing their commitment to the Holy Life *(Brahmacariya)* of one gone forth into the homeless life. (In India some ascetics tear out their hair, while others never touch it so that it becomes a tangled mass.) A rule states that a *Bhikkhu* should not allow his hair to grow beyond a certain length or time, so he will shave usually at least once a fortnight or month, sometimes more frequently. To do this he uses his razor, which is also one of his requisites.

'Hair-of-the-head' *(kesa)* is one of the five parts of the body mentioned in the ordination ceremony and is used to recollect the true nature of the body. The *Bhikkhu* is also not allowed to dye or pluck out any gray hairs, for they are useful reminders of old-age and impermanence. The Vinaya Rule specifies that if a *Bhikkhu* touches or is touched by a woman; it is an offence - a very serious offence - only if the *Bhikkhu* is "overcome by lust, with altered mind." However, the practicing *Bhikkhu* knows that as his mind changes so quickly, he has to be extremely cautious about involving himself in doubtful situations. It is better to be safe than sorry, even if this may seem over-scrupulous. In emergency situations the *Bhikkhu* will have to decide for himself and be sure to take care of his thoughts.

In Thailand it is a tradition (not strictly a rule) that the monk uses a 'receiving cloth' to emphasize that there is no touching. This has become a complex question with various interpretations because of modern conditions. The spirit of the rule is very important - avoiding possibilities of intimacy - while the interpretation will depend on the monk and the circumstances. In countries without proper monasteries there will always have to be something of a compromise.

While it may be a problem or inconvenience, the rules are there to protect and remind the monk about dangerous, unskillful actions. If the monk becomes increasingly involved with money there is a tendency for the whole of his *Bhikkhu*-life to be compromised - and that would be a far greater problem. Soon after the Final Passing Away of the Lord Buddha this sort of question had already become a major controversy and it is now even more complex under modern conditions.

However, modern conditions also have brought their own assistance to keeping these rules. For instance, a *Bhikkhu* can be given an air ticket and travel around the world (if need be) without having any money or attendant. He will need to be met at the airport and helped in the normal way, but that should be natural if he has been invited to come by the lay group. (He should not really be traveling otherwise.) And, of course, a monk can use postage stamps and 'telephone-cards' that add convenience to communicating - when it is appropriate. If he no longer has any interest in the *Bhikkhu*-life, the tendency will be for him to become lax and a bad example for others.

His Dhamma friends therefore will try to re-fire his enthusiasm. However, if that is not possible, becoming a good layman may be better than being a bad monk. (Nevertheless, in some countries there is a cultural expectation of 'ordaining for life' and a corresponding stigma attached to disrobing.) There is a tradition (but not a rule) about a *Bhikkhu* not re-ordaining more than seven times. In most habitable areas of the globe this arc may be low to the horizon but it should still be possible to follow the rule. And if *Bhikkhus* ever reach the Polar Regions they will have the *Great Standards* to guide them.

At the time of the Buddha, some lay people complained that the monks destroyed the 'life' in seeds. Therefore lay people can be asked by the monk if it is allowable for him to eat those fruits. In some monasteries (not all) this is done by the lay people cutting them. It is the Commentary to the Vinaya that mentions about 'great fruits.' This practice, however, is not followed in every monastery. There is an allowance in the Pali texts that 'medicinal-tonics' can be taken in the afternoon while 'lifetime-medicines' may be consumed any time they are needed.

There are different interpretations and practices about how ill a *Bhikkhu* has to be for it to be allowable to take such 'medicines.' Some *Bhikkhus* will not take anything other than pure water, while some will over-stretch the Rule to even drinking 'medicinal' food-drinks (e.g., Ovaltine) in the afternoon. Some *Bhikkhus* will consider tea-leaves allowable (as 'herbs') while some will see it as food or as a 'stimulant' (caffeine) and therefore not appropriate. Also, the ordinary rural villagers of South East Asia (until very recently) would have had no tea or coffee to drink, so such items could be considered quite a luxury. It will depend on local conditions and interpretations, which are allowed for in the Vinaya through the Great Standards.

This is a complicated question. If there is a steward who does the arranging for the *Bhikkhu* in the proper manner then certain things would be allowable. However, there are very strict guidelines about this. Practically speaking, *Bhikkhus* in Thailand are not ordered to renounce all their property, etc., when they receive ordination. (As mentioned elsewhere, the majority of *Bhikkhus* in Thailand will return to lay life within a certain period.) *Bhikkhus* who are serious about dedicating their life to the Holy Life will obviously take the Lord Buddha as their example and like Him renounce all that is worldly.

There are specific rules, not covered in this work, about Community land and property, and the different ways they are managed. The taking of a Teacher *(acariya)* by a *Bhikkhu* and living in dependence *(nissaya)* on him can only be between *Bhikkhus*. And even according to the *Bhikkhuni's* own Rule, in the time of the Lord Buddha, she was not allowed to teach *Bhikkhus*. However, this does not mean that a *Bhikkhu* cannot learn from others. There is a specific rule against *Bhikkhus* owning vehicles.

Obviously, 'motor vehicles' were not available in the Buddha's time and most travel would have been on foot. However, there was the case:

"...when the group-of-six Bhikkhus went in a vehicle yoked with cows and bulls, they were criticized by the lay people. The Buddha then established a fault of Wrong-doing for a Bhikkhu to travel in a vehicle; later illness was exempted from this guideline...

"Traveling in a vehicle in the Buddha's time was an extravagance. A strict application of this training in Thailand is not allowing Bhikkhus to drive or own vehicles, and (officially) not to ride on motorcycles."

Bhikkhus were allowed to use ferry boats, etc. (In Thailand, *Bhikkhus* from riverside monasteries will go on alms round by boat.) In Thailand, one cannot be officially registered as an herbal doctor while still a *Bhikkhu*. While providing medicines for one's fellow monks is very much allowable, it is definitely wrong that a monk dispenses medicine for reward. If a *Bhikkhu* commits a *parajika* offence he is 'defeated' and no longer a *Bhikkhu* even if he is wearing robes. The Community of *Bhikkhus* will have nothing to do with him and will expel him. However, if the accused '*Bhikkhu*' does not admit to the offence and it cannot be proved, the results of kamma must be allowed to run their own course. Buddhism has never engaged in violent witch hunts. And for how lay people dealt with stubborn monks in the Buddha's time.

Generally, the right-practicing *Bhikkhu* will be a person of few wants for he is trying to go to the ending of all desire. However, there may be certain things he may need but may not mention until he is sure that the donors are completely sincere in their invitation. If the donor makes specific suggestions, the *Bhikkhu* may refuse, he may accept, or he may remain silent - and such silence may very well be a positive response (as it was in the Lord Buddha's time). Therefore, as the donor gets to know the *Bhikkhu* he or she will become more sensitive about what is needed and what is appropriate - and be able to interpret any 'silence' in the right way.

PRECEPTS

The awakened mind has gone beyond greed, hatred and delusion. Yet for those of us who are still striving towards this end such unskillful tendencies have to be addressed. We need guidelines to help us become more aware of our actions and speech, so that we do not go off the Buddha's Middle Way. For a start there are the Five Precepts, then the Eight and the

Ten Precepts, and then the 227 *Patimokkha* Rules of the *Bhikkhu*. The Five Precepts are basic human ethical standards - answering the fundamental questions of 'what do I do, what should I say?' These standards are further refined by the Eight Precepts, which allow the lay person to live a life closer to that of the monk - even if temporarily. This may then lead to the Ten Precepts of a novice *(samanera)* or of a *dasasila mata* nun.

The Vinaya and *Patimokkha* rules were set down by the Buddha in response to specific incidents that occurred either within the Community of *Bhikkhus* or through their interaction with the lay community. An explanation of the original circumstances that led to the formulation of a rule is usually included in the scriptural text as an introduction to that rule. The emphasis therefore is always on Dhamma practice with the Precepts or Vinaya as a vital guide and support. When a *Bhikkhu* takes up the training rules, he might find that past habits and tendencies still cause problems - especially in a non-supportive environment. Of course, staying within a suitable environment will simplify this, which is a major reason for some rules. Therefore it is important to remember that the *Bhikkhu* never practices in isolation and always needs the support and understanding of lay Buddhists. There is the need for mutual support and encouragement between the lay and *Bhikkhu* communities. Knowing something of the rules should enable the lay person to appreciate this.

BHIKKHUS

Buddhism has been said to be 'deeply rooted in a country when a local young man can become a *Bhikkhu*, learn and then recite the *Patimokkha* Rule in his own country.' This originally referred to Sri Lanka thousands of years ago but now that Buddhism is moving to the West such conditions are starting to appear there, too. The *Bhikkhu Sangha* or Community of monks is probably the oldest of any of the institutions that have remained faithful to their origins and spread world-wide.

While scholars like to track its historical development from country to country, we could also start with a particular

Bhikkhu and trace the thread back through preceptor after preceptor to the Buddha Himself. Its many remarkable features enable men from different classes, backgrounds and cultures to live together in harmony and fellowship. Most important, it offers ideal conditions for the individual to train and meditate, to awaken to Dhamma, which is the whole point of the Buddha's Teaching.

BECOMING A NOVICE

The first part of the ordination procedure for *Bhikkhus* is known as the Going Forth into Homelessness *(pabbajja).* If it finishes with just that - without going on to the Questioning of the candidate and the acceptance of him by all the gathered *Bhikkhus* into the *Bhikkhu Sangha* - the candidate is known as a *samanera* or novice. This is usually the case when the candidate is less than the twenty years of age necessary to become a *Bhikkhu*. A very young boy is not allowed to become a novice either, but the minimum age will vary according to place.

A *samanera* wears the 'yellow robe' like a full *Bhikkhu* - except he does not have the *Sanghati* (double-thickness robe) - and leads a very similar life. In some places a period as a novice forms part of the preliminary training to become a *Bhikkhu*, while some men decide to remain *samanera* for various reasons. The *samanera* keeps the Ten Precepts and the 75 Training Rules *(sekhiya)* and some other rules of the *Bhikkhu*. Later, when he is ready and if he is old enough, he can ask the *Bhikkhu* community for full ordination *(upasampada).*

BECOMING A BHIKKHU

In the Pali texts, when a man decided to become a *Bhikkhu*, he is often quoted as saying:

"Confined is the household life, a path of dust; the going forth is open and spacious. Not easy is it living in a house to lead the religious life absolutely fulfilled and purified, as polished as mother-of-pearl. Suppose I were to shave off my hair and beard, clothe myself in ochre robes and go forth from homelife into homelessness?"

However, anyone wishing to become a *Bhikkhu* must fulfill certain conditions about which he will be questioned during the actual ordination procedure. The candidate must be male and at least twenty years old. He must never have committed any grievous crimes and, if previously ordained, he must not have been guilty of any Defeater *(Parajika)* offences or have entered some other religion without disrobing first. He should also be of good reputation; fit and healthy enough to carry out the duties of a *Bhikkhu*; not in debt; not subject to government service; and have permission from parents or guardian.

The Ordination ceremony requires a prescribed boundary *(sima)*, a preceptor *(upajjhaya)* and a quorum of *Bhikkhus* to validate the formal *Sangha* Act. In the formal procedure the candidate is examined as to the necessary qualities and, if all the *Bhikkhus* are satisfied, they receive him into the *Sangha*, the Community of *Bhikkhus*. It is in this way that yet another link is added to the *Bhikkhu*-lineage. Henceforth, the new *Bhikkhu* can participate (and make up the necessary quorum) in future assemblies and help receive other new *Bhikkhus* - as *Bhikkhus* have continued to do for two and a half thousand years.

When a candidate requests full admission to the Community (after the *samanera* ordination) he does not make any 'lifetime vows' but offers himself for training and instruction under his Preceptor's guidance. At the end of the ordination ceremony, the Preceptor will immediately instruct the new *Bhikkhu* (or arrange that he is properly taught) about the *Patimokkha* Rule and the other principles that all *Bhikkhus* should follow and observe. For the first five years a *Bhikkhu* is called *navaka* ('new one') and he must live 'dependent' *(nissaya)* on a senior *Bhikkhu* - either his preceptor or teacher *(acariya)* - training in the ways of a *Bhikkhu*.

The preceptor and the new monk should be kind and helpful to each other, in almost a father-and-son relationship. A new *Bhikkhu* who no longer lives under his preceptor must take another senior *Bhikkhu* as his teacher and depend on him instead. For the next five years after his *navaka* period, the *Bhikkhu* is called *majjhima,* ('one in the middle') and he is allowed to live by himself if he is accomplished in certain qualities. When a *Bhikkhu* has completed ten Rains he is called *Thera,* which can be translated as 'an elder who is worthy of respect.' If he is also accomplished in certain extra qualities, he is allowed to give ordination as preceptor, to be a teacher, and have young monks live in dependence on him.

ORDINATION IN SOUTH EAST ASIA

Throughout South East Asia, it is very common for young men to become *Bhikkhus* (or novices) for a short period of their life. Traditionally this occurs during the three months of the Rains Retreat, after which they disrobe and return to lay life, hopefully knowing and appreciating much more about the *Bhikkhu* life - and probably having friends still in the monastery whom they can visit for advice. In Thailand this means that while a small proportion of *Bhikkhus* will spend all their life in the robe, many more Thai men will have tasted the life. Such an ordination is also a rite of passage, for it is a family, even a village event with many people joining in to see the young man off into this new stage of his life.

The new monk will frequently visit his former home on his daily alms round so his ordination has a wider influence, showing the continuing possibility of living the 'Holy Life' started by the Lord Buddha so long ago. It may also be considered a way for the young man to show his gratitude to his parents and grandparents, for they are thought to participate and share in the 'merit' he makes through his ordination. Also, some men might ordain for a time before marriage - one way for the young man to prove his maturity to his fiancée - and then again later in life after retirement.

THE RAINS RETREAT

The *Bhikkhu*'s year is structured around the three months from July to October. In Asia this is the time of the monsoon season - the central period of the agricultural year - when the paddy fields are flooded and the main rice crop is planted. In the Buddha's time (and until modern times), people were less likely to travel around during this period because the roads were bad and there was a danger of crop damage. So the *Bhikkhus* likewise suspended their mendicant wanderings and had to settle in one place. A *Bhikkhu* must make a formal determination to be resident at dawn every day in that place for the whole three month period. (There are exceptional circumstances when he may be allowed to be away, but even then he should return within seven days.)

These three months are often a special time of study or meditation and so are sometimes known as the Rains Retreat or Rains Residence. This is also the normal time when the young men of South East Asia become monks for the traditional three month period. A *Bhikkhu* often measures the length of time he has been a monk according to how many Rains Residences he has undertaken. Therefore instead of saying he has been 'ordained seven years' he might say he has been ordained for 'seven Rains.'

DISROBING

Living the *Bhikkhu*-life properly, following the Buddha's Teaching, requires full commitment and sustained effort. If this is lost and his Dhamma friends cannot rekindle his interest, the *Bhikkhu* is always at liberty to return to lay life. There are no lifetime vows, so perhaps living a good lay life is better than being lax in keeping the *Bhikkhu*'s rules. Nevertheless, in some countries there is a cultural expectation of 'ordaining for life' and a corresponding stigma attached to disrobing.

"A Bhikkhu who is tired of the practice of the Brahma-cariya [Holy Life] and wishes to return to the state of being a lay man may do this by taking leave of the training..."

Disrobing is finalized by the monk clearly proclaiming his change of status before another *Bhikkhu* or lay person. Once the other person understands his statement, he is no longer a *Bhikkhu*. In Thailand there is often a formal ceremony for this that ends with the former monk undertaking the Five Precepts to replace the 227 *Patimokkha* Rule. (This is also considered a step downwards, for the ideal way is certainly to continue with the Holy Life 'for as long as life lasts.') In those countries where temporary ordinations are 'rites of passage,' some men may ordain and disrobe several times in their life - before marriage and after retirement, for example.

However, there seems to be a tradition that *Bhikkhus* do not disrobe and go forth again more than seven times, but this rarely occurs. If a *Bhikkhu* commits a Defeater Offence there is no need for him formally to disrobe because he is automatically expelled by his wrongful action and is no longer a *Bhikkhu* from that moment. He can never reordain during that lifetime.

BUDDHIST NUNS

In the Theravada lineage it seems that the *Bhikkhuni* ordination lineage for women given by the Buddha - equivalent to *Bhikkhu*-ordination for men - was lost in Sri Lanka with the fall of Anuradhapura in Sri Lanka in the eleventh century C.E. and finally with the fall of Pagan in the thirteenth century C.E. *Bhikkhunis* originally observed 311 *Patimokkha* Rules, and there are whole sections of the Pali Vinaya texts devoted to the their rules.

THE VINAYA AND THE PATIMOKKHA

The Buddha laid down that on full and new moon days all the *Bhikkhus* in residence in the same community must come together in a formal meeting. If there is a quorum of at least four *Bhikkhus*, they should listen to the full *Patimokkha* Rule. A competent *Bhikkhu* who has learned this by heart will recite it in the Pali language for the Community so that they can remind themselves of their responsibilities in keeping the major 227 Rules. The complete recitation may take anywhere from thirty-five minutes to an hour, depending on the skill of the reciting *Bhikkhu*.

Before the *Patimokkha* recitation begins, each *Bhikkhu* should admit to any offences that he knows he has committed by formally telling another monk (or monks). Once this is accomplished, the monk is considered 'pure' and can listen to the recitation of the rules. (The recitation includes questions, asking if any *Bhikkhu* present is guilty of the offences.) In many communities it is normal for each *Bhikkhu* to make a 'general confession' of all possible offences to another *Bhikkhu* before listening to the *Patimokkha* recitation.

Different offences are of different seriousness but the most common faults committed by carelessness or mistake can be cleared by 'confession' to another *Bhikkhu*. Admitting to one's mistake and agreeing to do better in the future is the way of growth and progress towards the elimination of all carelessness and absentmindedness.

OFFENCES

When a *Bhikkhu* breaks his precepts or rules it is called an offence *(apatti)*. Such offences are committed by action or word, although intention is (almost always) a decisive factor. Just thinking about doing something wrong is unskillful and may lead to future problems but it is not an offence.

MAJOR RULE GROUPS OF THE PATIMOKKHA

The Four Parajika - The Defeaters

The new *Bhikkhu* is told about the *Parajika* Offences immediately after ordination, so he fully knows that they are the most serious of all the offences and that the consequences of transgressing them causes him to be no longer a *Bhikkhu*. The nature of the act that breaks any of these four *Parajika* rules clearly reveals that the *Bhikkhu* is no longer interested in developing the subtle and refined way of Dhamma. The alternative of voluntarily disrobing is always available if he feels he can no longer keep the Rule and this is considered a much better way to handle this sort of overwhelming desire.

A monk automatically falls from being a *Bhikkhu* by committing any of these four offences of Defeat: sexual-intercourse, murder, major-theft, or falsely claiming supernormal abilities. A *Bhikkhu* who falls into any of these four Defeater offences thereby severs himself irrevocably from the *Bhikkhu* community and is no longer considered a *Bhikkhu*.

The text portrays it with some vivid similes showing their irreparable nature: as 'a man with his head cut off'; as 'a withered leaf fallen from its stem'; as 'a palm tree cut down'; as 'a broken stone.' For while all the other offences can be remedied, these are terminal.

The Thirteen Sanghadisesa - Requiring Formal Meetings of the Community

This is a very serious class of offence. However, any offending *Bhikkhu* can be rehabilitated through confession and supervised probation. Finally, the *Bhikkhu* needs to be reinstated by a specially convened Community (*Sangha*) meeting of at least twenty monks.

The Two Aniyata - Indefinite or Undetermined

The *Bhikkhu* Community (together with the *Bhikkhu* concerned) has to decide which rule, if any, has been infringed.

The 30 Nissaggiya Pacittiya - Confession with Forfeiture

These rules are often concerned with *Bhikkhus* being greedy and excessive in their demand for offerings, or with *Bhikkhus* obtaining requisites through improper means. This oppresses lay donors and, classically, led them to comment: "How can these recluses... not knowing moderation asks for...?" The rules of this category also guide *Bhikkhus* on how they should take care of requisites and restrain the *Bhikkhus* from obtaining items that by their very nature are inappropriate.

This offence can be cleared by forfeiture of the improper item to another *Bhikkhu*(s) and formal confession of the offence. The other classes of offences can usually be resolved by a simple 'confession' to another *Bhikkhu*(s). They are:

The 92 *Pacittiya* - Expiation through Confession

All these offences can be cleared through confession to another *Bhikkhu*.

The 75 Sekhiyavatta - Trainings

These are normally classified as offences of 'wrong-doing' *(dukka.ta)*. There are two aspects to these 'rules of training' which are mainly about etiquette and good manners. First, they are'gauge' for the *Bhikkhu*'s mindfulness so that he becomes aware of his behavior. Second, there is the external perspective of an observer watching the *Bhikkhu*'s activity and noticing the care and refinement with which he moves, eats, etc.

The Seven Adhikaranasamatha - Settlement of Issues

These are general procedures (rather than offences) for dealing with disputes, accusations, offences and duties.

In the full Vinaya texts there is also the class of 'grave' *(thullaccaya)* offence. This is a 'derived offence' from the most serious rules of *Parajika* and *Sanghadisesa* (groups (a) and (b) above) to cover those circumstances when the full offence is not quite carried out but the conduct is still grave enough to be at fault. There is also the *dubbhasita* offence of wrong speech.

COMMITTING OFFENCES

The Lord Buddha would not set down a rule until the situation demanded it, so the Pali often supplies the 'origin story' about how the different rules came about. Certain characters often reappear in the thick of misdeeds and mischief. For instance, one keeps on coming across Venerable Ud*a*yin or the notorious 'group-of-six' monks. Their behavior required attention and rectification from the Buddha, who then made it into a general rule for all the *Bhikkhus*:

"In that case, Bhikkhus, I will formulate a training rule for the Bhikkhus with ten aims in mind: the excellence of the Community, the peace of the Community, the curbing of the shameless, the comfort of the well-behaved Bhikkhus, the restraint of [defilements] related to the present life, the prevention of [defilements] related to the next life, the arousing of faith in the faithless, the increase in the faithful, the establishment of the true Dhamma, and the fostering of discipline."

Later circumstances may have required the Buddha to make amendments or special exceptions and the rule would then have been adjusted accordingly. There are also many other minor offences mentioned in the original Pali texts, which have been further enlarged upon by later Commentaries. So the range of rules has become very extensive, and their observance and interpretation correspondingly wide. Note that it was often lay people's criticism that brought the monk's wrong doings to the attention of the Buddha. (However, also notice how such criticism was often too hasty in blaming all monks rather than just the original delinquent.)

THE GREAT STANDARDS

More than two and a half thousand years have passed since the Vinaya rules were originally set down by the Buddha, and many things have markedly changed since then. Should the rules be modernized and brought up to date? How can this be done? Already during His lifetime, the Buddha made special allowances for different regions (or *desa)* outside the 'Middle Country' of North India - where He lived and taught. These dealt with both the workings of the Community - for example, a smaller quorum for ordination is allowed in distant parts where there are fewer monks - and practical measures, such as special dispensation for footwear and bathing. So there is a precedent for adapting to conditions, but this does not mean the abolishing of any rules.

The Lord Buddha also left us a set of principles that can still be used as a standard to judge new circumstances. These are known as 'The Great Standards.' Properly used they should protect against a wholesale dilution of the Rule. This is how the Great Standards are formulated:

"Bhikkhus, whatever I have not objected to, saying, 'This is not allowable,' if it fits in with what is not allowable, if it goes against what is allowable, that is not allowable for you.

"Whatever I have not objected to, saying, 'This is not allowable,' if it fits in with what is allowable, if it goes against what is not allowable, that is allowable for you.

"And whatever I have not permitted, saying, 'This is allowable,' if it fits in with what is not allowable, if it goes against what is allowable, that is not allowable for you.

"And whatever I have not permitted, saying, 'This is allowable,' if it fits in with what is allowable, if it goes against what is not allowable, that is allowable for you."

Treated with care, these Great Standards should enable *Bhikkhus* to live according to the Vinaya Rule in, for example, isolated communities in non-Buddhist countries with non-tropical climates. They form a touchstone for modern conditions and substances.

STRICTNESS AND BLAMING OTHERS

Among the unenlightened, finding fault with others (rather than dealing with one's own problems) often seems to be one of our most damaging habitual tendencies. We are able to twist whatever we want to this purpose. For *Bhikkhus* there are many cautions:

"... those [monks] who follow the Vinaya blindly... tend to be proud and arrogant, regarding themselves as better behaved and more strict than others, and despising other Bhikkhus as inferior. This in itself is unbecoming and worthy of censure; and when such Bhikkhus have to associate with others whom they feel to be deficient in observing the Vinaya, they do it grudgingly and with a sense of distaste, and thus bring even more trouble on themselves.

"As for the Bhikkhu who behaves in the correct manner, he is bound to feel cheerful because he senses that his behavior is becoming."

"One, who knows the Vinaya well, knows just how far the Vinaya goes. He will thus know what is definite and what is open to interpretation. He will know that a monk who practices contrary to what is clearly stated in the Vinaya... is rightly called alajji [shameless]. But he will remain tolerant and in perfect harmony with those who follow a different practice from his own on matters not clearly covered by the Vinaya..."

Disparate interpretations of the Vinaya rules can lead different communities into claiming that only their understanding is correct and everyone else is wrong. The *Buddhist Monastic Code* has this to say:

"There is, of course, a danger in being too independent in interpreting the tradition, in that strongly held opinions can lead to disharmony in the Community.... At the same time,... there are many areas on which the Vibha"nga [section of the Vinaya] is unclear and lends itself to a variety of equally valid interpretations. For proof of this, we need only look at the various traditions that have developed in the different Theravadin countries, and even within each country. For some reason, although people tend to be very tolerant of different interpretations of the Dhamma, they can be very intolerant of different interpretations of the Vinaya and can get into heated arguments over minor issues having very little to do with the training of the mind."

Venerable Thanissaro continues by emphasizing:

"...that any interpretation based on a sound reading of the [Pali] Canon should be respected: that each Bhikkhu should follow the interpretations of the Community in which he is living, as long as they do not conflict with the Canon, so as to avoid conflict over minor matters in daily life; and that he should also show respect for the differing interpretations of other Communities where they too do not conflict with the Canon, so as to avoid the pitfalls of pride and narrow-mindedness."

In the modern West we find ourselves with the unusual (unique?) situation of having Buddhist monasteries and temples of so many different countries and traditions so close at hand. We should appreciate this abundance and variety, deciding which establishment suits our needs and then not worry about the shortcomings of other places.

3

Schools in Buddhist Mysticism

THE MAHASANGHIKAS

After the 2nd Buddhist council, 100 years after Buddha's *mahaparinibbana,* there was a schism of the *Sangha* into the Theravada and Mahasanghika Schools and 18 Schools subsequently developed from them.

The seeds of sectarianism were inherent in monastic life itself:

1. Its constitution, rules and practices were democratic.
2. The tradition from the beginning had been tolerant of freethinking.
3. Complete absence of authoritarian control in the *Sangha.*
4. No tradition of obedience in matter of faith and belief.
5. The relationship between senior and junior were respect and reverence.

A dispute over a point of dhammavinaya was a 'Vivada' (disagreement in vada or opinion). This could be brought up for settlement before the *Sangha* body. A vote of majority decides the issue. Once accepted by the *Sangha,* the point decided could not be raised again as this would constitute a grave ecclesiastical offence. A schism (*Sangha-bheda*) can be validly initiated by the formation of a party of at least nine qualified members in a *Sangha.* When an original *Sangha* split up into two *Sangha*s, the one with the dissident views would have to leave to a different avasa. Each sect then revised its vinaya rules and the doctrine. They might transpose suttas belonging to one place of collection to another place or omitted others.

Each school also had a version of the Lord's life and it's approved Buddhology. The resident monks of a school would hold periodical rehearsals and recitations of the revised doctrine and vinaya in their own avasas. The new school would have a leader known as Acariya. The schools are called acariyavada, "schools of teachers" and may suggest the rise of prominent teachers who were able to impose their views on certain communities. The names of schools could be from personal names of the acariyas, the name of places or the peculiar doctrine of the school.

Mahasanghika School and its subsidiary schools had common doctrines with minor differences. The Mahasanghika was called such due to its large number of 10,000. Hsuan-Tsang's account of the origin was that the 10,000 comprised of both common folk and Arhants. It was a revolt against the cloistering of the Dhamma, reducing it to a purely monkish religion. They objected to the Theravada monks bounding up the Dhamma and Vinaya, making it a religion for monkhood. Mahasanghika became the symbol of liberalizing movement.

- Introduced the 10 new Vinaya rules

Altered Vinaya Pitaka. Mahadeva's 5 points which lower the status of Arahants. The Mahasanghikas believed that the stage of Arahant is not immune for a fall to a lower stage. Arhants realize only half the truth and are subjected to retrogression:

i. An Arhant may be subjected to temptation.

ii. One may be an Arahant and know it not.

iii. An Arhant may have doubts on matter of doctrine.

iv. One cannot be an Arhant without a teacher.

v. One may attain perfection by meditating with such exclamation as 'How sad, how sad.'

- Concept of Buddha as an omniscient being.

Did not subscribe that Buddha was a human being. Transcendence and Lokuttara Vada held by the Mahasanghikas. They did not like the idea that Buddha was a human being who lived and died. They transcended him to a high divine position even before his enlightenment.

i. Omniscient even before birth. Buddha was in a meditative position in his mother's womb and preached to devas.

ii. He was able to walk immediately after birth.

ii. The marriage of Prince Siddharta was for 'appearance', Yasodhara was not touched and Rahula birth was considered miraculous.

iii. Buddha is of Saha lokadhatu - Buddha can appear everywhere in the world system, Material body (*Rupakaya/ Nirmana kaya*) is unlimited, immeasurable. Created form (*abhinimmito jino*) can be located anywhere to deliver discourses.

iv. Buddha's body is entirely supramundane (*lokuttara*). His material body is entirely pure and indestructible.

v. Buddha's bodily movements are also supramundane. "He cannot have any disease and still he takes medicine to cure himself." It is for following the ways of the world that he shows his iriyapathas (movements of Buddha). *Mahavastu*

vi. The super divine Buddha did not deliver any discourses to his disciples but by the utterance of one word (*sabda*), Buddha expounds all doctrine

vii. Unlimited length of life (*ayu*).

viii. Unlimited divine powers (*prabhava*)

ix. Neither sleeps nor dreams as mind is always in meditation.

x. Buddha can comprehend everything in one moment (*ekaksanika citta*) and his mind is like a mirror.

xi. Buddha is never tired of enlightening sentient beings and awakening the pure faith (*visuddhi saddha*)

A Bodhisattva Ideal:

i. Supramundane. Can take up any form of lower existence for enlightening other forms of beings. Enters his mother's womb and preaches to heavenly beings.
ii. Developed bodhicitta and by fulfilling *paramitas* to become a predestined *Bodhisattva,* then a Buddha. Importance was placed on Bodhicitta than on Brahmacariya and ariyamagga.
iii. Career is marked more by love and compassion for suffering beings than by path culture.
iv. Has no trace of desire, hatred or malice.

Ideals of Mahasanghika:

Ideals of Mahasanghika School were: *Samma Sambodhi, Bodhisattva, Pacceka Bodhi* and then Arahant

Own literature:

The Mahasanghika also had own literature written in Sanskrit.

- Pitaka Vinaya Pitaka
- Agama Sutta
- Sutra Pari*Nibbana* Sutta
- Paramita Perfection
- Avatamsaka Flower Garland. Lotus Sutra.
- Avadana Heroic deeds

Made alterations in the Sutta

Propounded new doctrines contrary to established ones and canonized a number of sutras, which they claimed to be sayings of Buddha. The canon did not include *Parivara, AbhiDhammappakarana, Magga Niddesa* and *Jataka.*

i. Yuan Chwang recorded that Mahasangika had a complete canon of Sutra, Vinaya, Abhidhamma, Dharani and Miscellaneous in 5 parts.

ii. Amaravati Stone Slab referred to 'Pancamatuka' - the 5 texts.

iii. Fa-hien came across the complete transcript of Mahasanghika Vinaya at Pataliputra and translated it 2 years later.

Site - Centre was at Pataliputra mainly Magadha. After leaving Magadha, they settled in North and Northwest India mainly also Lata, Sindhu (Western India). Another group went to south India and settled in Andhra Pradesh around Amaravati, Dhanyakataka, and Nagarjunikonda. Amaravati had been a center of the Mahasanghikas for centuries Inscriptions at Amaravati and Nagajunikonda spoke of the Mahasanghika monks (mahavinayadhara) and nuns (vinayadhara).

THERAVADA

Theravada; literally, "the Teaching of the Elders" or "the Ancient Teaching", is the oldest surviving Buddhist school. It was founded in India. It is relatively conservative, and generally closest to early Buddhism, and for many centuries has been the predominant religion of Sri Lanka (about 70% of the population) and most of continental Southeast Asia (Cambodia, Laos, Burma, Thailand). It is also practiced by minorities in parts of southwest China (by the Shan and Tai ethnic groups), Vietnam (by the Khmer Krom), Bangladesh (by the ethnic groups of Baruas, Chakma, and Magh), Malaysia and Indonesia, whilst recently gaining popularity in Singapore and the Western World. Today Theravada Buddhists number over 100 million worldwide, and in recent decades Theravada has begun to take root in the West and in the Buddhist revival in India.

ORIGIN OF THE SCHOOL

The Theravada school is ultimately derived from the Vibhajjavada (or 'doctrine of analysis') grouping which was a continuation of the older Sthavira (or 'teaching of the Elders') group at the time of the Third Buddhist Council around 250 BCE, during the reign of Emperor Asoka in India. Vibhajjavadins saw themselves as the continuation of orthodox Sthaviras and after the Third Council continued to refer to their school as the Sthaviras/Theras ('The Elders'); their doctrines were probably similar to the older Sthaviras but were not completely identical.

After the Third Council geographical distance led to the Vibhajjavadins gradually evolving into four groups: the Mahîúasaka, Kaúyapîya, Dharmaguptaka and the Tamraparnîya. The Theravada is descended from the Tamraparnîya, which means 'the Sri Lankan lineage'. Some sources claim that only the Theravada actually evolved directly from the Vibhajjavadins. The name of Tamraparniya was given to the Sri Lankan lineage in India but there is no indication that this referred to any change in doctrine or scripture from the Vibhajjavadins, since the name points only to geographical location.

The Theravadin accounts of its own origins mention that it received the teachings that were agreed upon during the Third Buddhist Council, and these teachings were known as the Vibhajjavada. In the 7th century, Chinese pilgrims Xuanzang and Yi Jing refer to the Buddhist school in Sri Lanka as 'Sthavira'. In ancient India, those schools that used Sanskrit as their religious language referred to this school as the 'Sthaviras', but those that use Pali as their religious language referred to this school as the 'Theras'. Both 'Sthaviras' (Sanskrit) and 'Theras' (Pali) both literally mean 'The Elders'. The school has been using the name 'Theravada' for itself in a written forms since at least the fourth century CE when the term appears in the *Dipavamsa*.

There is little information about the later history of Theravada Buddhism in India, and it is not known when it disappeared in its country of origin. The Theravada school had also reached Burma around the time it arrived in Sri Lanka and something of a synergy gradually developed. Around the end of the tenth century C.E, for example, war in Sri Lanka had extinguished Buddhism, and a contingent of Burmese monks had to be imported to rekindle it.

Burmese and Sri Lankan Theravada reinforced each other sufficiently, so that by the time Buddhism died out in India in the eleventh century, it had established a stable home in these countries. Gradually the Theravada form of Buddhism spread to Thailand, Laos, and Cambodia. Royal houses in Sri Lanka and Southeast Asia associated themselves closely with Buddhism. States in those areas strictly enforced orthodoxy, and ensured that Theravada remained traditionalist. This contrasts with the relationship of Buddhism to states throughout most of Buddhism's history in India.

According to Sinhalese tradition, Buddhism was first brought to Sri Lanka by Mahinda, who is believed to have been the son of the Mauryan emperor Asoka, in the third century BCE, as a part of the missionary activities of the Asokan era. In Sri Lanka, Mahinda established the Mahavihara Monastery of Anuradhapura. Later it became divided into three subgroups, known after their monastic centers as the Mahavihara, the Abhayagirivihara, and the Jetavanavihara. In 1164, with the guidance of two monks from a forest branch of the Mahavihara, Sri Lanka King reunited all *Bhikkhus* in Sri Lanka into the orthodox Mahavihara School.

A few years after the arrival of Sthavira Mahinda, Sanghamitta, who is also believed to be the daughter of Emperor Asoka, came to Sri Lanka. She started the first nun order in Sri Lanka, but the nun order died out in Sri Lanka in the 11th century and in Burma in the 13th. In 429 CE, by request of China's emperor, nuns from Anuradhapura were sent to China to establish the Nun Order. The order was then spread to Korea. In 1996, 11 selected Sri Lankan nuns were ordained fully as *Bhikkhunis* by a team of Theravada monks in concert with a team of Korean Nuns in India. There is disagreement among Theravada vinaya authorities as to whether such ordinations are valid.

In the last few years the head of the Dambulla chapter of the Siyam Nikaya in Sri Lanka has carried out ordination ceremonies for hundreds of nuns. This has been criticized by some other leading figures in the Siyam Nikaya and

Amarapura Nikaya, and the governing council of Burmese Buddhism has declared that there can be no valid ordination of nuns in modern times, though some Burmese monks disagree with this. According to Mahavamsa the Sri Lanka chronical, after the conclusion of the Third Buddhist Council, a missionary was also sent to Suvannabhumi where two monks Sona and Uttara, are said to have proceeded.

Scholar opinions differ as to where exactly this land of Suvannabhumi is located, but Suvannabhumi is believed to be located somewhere in the area which now includes lower Burma, Thailand, Malay Peninsula and Sumatra Island. The Mon and Pyu were one of the earliest people to inhabit Burma. Recent archaeological findings at Pyu settlement at Samon Valley (around 100km south-east of Bagan) have shown that they have trade links with India at around 500 BC-400 BC and with China at around 200 BC. Chinese sources which have been dated to around 240 A.D. have mentioned a Buddhist kingdom by the name of Lin-Yang, which some scholars have identified it as the ancient Pyu kingdom of Beikthano which is 300km north of Yangon.

The Burmese slowly become Theravadin when they come into contact with the Pyu and Mon civilization. The Mon was also one of the earliest people to inhabit Thailand. The Thai slowly become Theravadin when they come into contact with the Mon civilization. Despite its success in Southeast Asia, Theravada Buddhism in China has generally been limited to areas bordering Theravada countries. In Chinese historiography, it is normally referred to as Hinayana, a term used in Mahayana texts to denigrate Buddhists who did not accept the Mahayana sutras; this usage is increasingly regarded as derogatory within the Buddhist community.

MODERN DEVELOPMENTS

The following modern trends or movements have been identified.

- Modernism: attempts to adapt to the modern world and adopt some of its ideas; includes among other things

  - green movement
  - syncretism with other Buddhist traditions
  - women's rights
- Reformism: attempts to restore a supposed earlier, ideal state of Buddhism; includes in particular the adoption of Western scholars' theories of original Buddhism (in recent times the "Western scholarly interpretation of Buddhism" is the official Buddhism prevailing in Sri Lanka and Thailand.)
- Ultimatism: tendency to concentrate on advanced teachings such as the Four Noble Truths at the expense of more elementary ones
- Neotraditionalism; includes among other things
  - revival of ritualism
  - remythologization
- Insight meditation
- Social action
- Devotional religiosity
- Reaction to Buddhist nationalism
- Renewal of forest monks
- Revival of samatha meditation

Buddhist revivalism has also reacted against changes in Buddhism affected by colonialist regimes. Western colonialists and Christian missionaries deliberately imposed a particular type of Christian monasticism on Buddhist clergy in Sri Lanka and colonies in Southeast Asia, restricting monks' activities to individual purification and temple ministries. Prior to British colonial control, monks in both Sri Lanka and Burma had been responsible for the education of the children of lay people, and had produced large bodies of literature. After the British takeover, Buddhist temples were strictly administered, and only permitted to use their funds on strictly religious activities.

Christian ministers were given control of the education system and their pay became state funding for missions.

Foreign, especially British rule had an enervating effect on the *Sangha*. According to Walpola Rahula, Christian missionaries displaced and appropriated the educational, social, and welfare activities of the monks, and inculcated a permanent shift in views regarding the proper position of monks in society through their institutional influence upon the elite. Many monks in post-colonial times have been dedicated to undoing this paradigm shift. Movements intending to restore Buddhism's place in society have developed in both Sri Lanka and Burma.

Theravada promotes the concept of Vibhajjavada (Pali), literally "Teaching of Analysis." This doctrine says that insight must come from the aspirant's experience, critical investigation, and reasoning instead of by blind faith; however, the scriptures of the Theravadin tradition also emphasize heeding the advice of the wise, considering such advice and evaluation of one's own experiences to be the two tests by which practices should be judged. In Theravada, the cause of human existence and suffering (*Dukkha*) is identified as craving (*tanha*), which carries with it the defilements (*kilesas*). The level of defilement can be coarse, medium, and subtle.

It is a phenomenon that frequently arises, remains temporarily and then vanishes. Theravadins believe defilements are not only harmful to one, but also harmful to others. They are the driving force behind all inhumanities a human being can commit. Theravadins believe these defilements are the habits born of ignorance (*avijja*) which afflict the minds of all unenlightened beings. It is believed that unenlightened beings are under the influence of the defilements, unenlightened beings cling to them through ignorance of the truth. But in reality, those mental defilements are nothing more than taints that have afflicted the mind and create suffering and stress.

It is also believed that unenlightened beings cling to the body, assuming it as their own "Self", but in reality the body is an impermanent phenomenon formed from the four basic elements (often characterized by Earth, Water, Fire and Air) and after death the body will decompose and disperse. The mental defilements' frequent instigation and manipulation of the mind is believed to have prevented the mind from seeing the true nature of reality. Unskillful behavior in turn can strengthen the defilements, but following the Noble Eightfold Path can weaken or eradicate them. It is also believed that unenlightened beings experience the world through their imperfect six sense doors (eye, ear, nose, tongue, tactile sense, and mind) and then use the mind clouded by defilements to form their own interpretation, perception and conclusion. In such a condition the perception or conclusion made will be based on that being's own illusion of reality.

In the state of *jhana*, the five physical sense doors will fade, the mental defilements will be suppressed, and wholesome mental traits will become strengthened. The mind can then be used to investigate and gain insight into the true nature of reality. There are three stages of defilements. During the stage of passivity the defilements lies dormant at the base of the mental continuum as latent tendencies (*anusaya*), but through the impact of sensory stimulus it will manifest (*pariyutthana*) itself to the surface of consciousness in the form of unwholesome thoughts, emotions, and volitions. If they gather additional strength, the defilement will reach the dangerous stage of transgression (*vitikkama*), which will then involve physical or vocal actions.

It is believed that in order to be free from suffering and stress these defilements need to be permanently uprooted. Initially the defilements are restrained through mindfulness to prevent them from taking over the mind and bodily action. They are then uprooted through internal investigation, analyzing, experiencing and understanding the true nature of those defilements by using *jhana*. This process needs to be repeated for each and every defilement. The practice will then lead the meditator to realize the Four Noble Truths, Enlightenment and *Nibbana*. *Nibbana* (the Pali form of the Sanskrit *Nirvana*) is the ultimate goal of Theravadins. *Nibbana* is said to be the perfect bliss and the person is liberated from the repeated cycle of birth, illness, aging and death.

Theravadins believe that every individual is personally responsible for their own self-awakening and liberation, as they are the ones that were responsible for their own actions and consequences (Pali, *kamma*; Sanskrit, *karma*). Simply learning or believing in the true nature of reality as expounded by the Buddha is not enough, the awakening can only be achieved if the individual personally knows it by direct experience and realizes it for themselves. They will have to follow and practice the Noble Eightfold Path as taught by the Buddha to discover the reality for them. In Theravada belief, Buddhas, gods or deities are incapable of giving a human being the awakening or lifting them from the state of repeated cycle of birth, illness, aging and death (*samsara*).

For Theravadins, Buddha is only a Teacher of the Noble Eightfold Path, while gods or deities are still subject to anger, jealousy, hatred, vengeance, craving, greed, delusion, and death. It is believed that some people who practice with earnestness and zeal can attain *Nibbana* within a single lifetime, as did many of the first few generations of Buddha's disciples. For others, the process may take multiple lifetimes, with the individual reaching higher and higher states of realization. One who has attained *Nibbana* is called an *arahant*.

It is believed that the *Nibbana* is most quickly attained as a disciple of Buddha, since Lord Buddha is believed to have possessed the ultimate knowledge on how to guide a person through the process of enlightenment. According to the early scriptures, the *Nibbana* attained by Arahants is identical to that attained by the Buddha himself, as there is only one type of *Nibbana*. Buddha was superior to Arahants because the Buddha had discovered the path all by himself, and has taught it to others (ie; metaphorically turning the wheel of Dhamma). Arahants, on the other hand, attained *Nibbana* due in part to the Buddha's teachings.

Theravadins revere the Buddha as a single supremely gifted person but do recognize the existence of other such Buddhas in the distant past and future. Maitreya (Pali: *Metteyya*), for example, is mentioned very briefly in the Pali

Canon as a Buddha who will come in the distant future. Traditionally Theravadins can either have the conviction (or "faith") in the Buddha's teaching or practice the minor precepts in the hope of gaining some minor benefits or they can investigate and verify by direct experience the truth of the Buddha's teaching by practicing the *jhana* which is part of the Noble Eightfold Path for their own Enlightenment.

FUNDAMENTALS OF THERAVADA

One thing that should be mentioned first and foremost is that the Theravada philosophy is a continuous analytical process of life, not a mere set of ethics and rituals. The ultimate theory of Theravada uses the Four Noble Truths, also known as the Four Sublime Truths. In the simplest form these can be described as the problem, the cause, the solution and the pathway to solution (implementation).

THE FOUR NOBLE TRUTHS

A formal description of the Four Noble Truths follows:

1. *Dukkha* (suffering) - This can be somewhat broadly classified into three categories. Inherent suffering or the suffering one undergoes in all the worldly activities, what one suffers in day-to-day life: birth, aging, diseases, death, sadness, etc. In short, that entire one feels from separating from 'loving' attachments and/or associating with 'hating' attachments is encompassed into the term. The second class of suffering, called suffering due to Change, implies that things suffer due to attaching themselves to a momentary state which is held to be 'good'; when that state is changed, things are subjected to suffering. The third, termed 'Sankhara *Dukkha*', is the most subtle. Beings suffer simply by not realizing that they are mere aggregates with no definite, unchanging identity.
2. *Dukkha Samudaya* (cause of suffering) - Craving, which leads to Attachment and Bondage, is the cause of suffering. Formally, this is termed 'Tanha'. It can be classified into three instinctive drives. 'Kama Tanha' is

the Craving for any pleasurable sense object (which involves sight, sound, touch, taste, smell and mental perceptives). 'Bhava Tanha' is the Craving for attachment to an ongoing process, which appears in various forms, including the longing for existence. 'Vibhava Tanha' is the Craving for detachment from a process, which includes non-existence and causes the longing for self-annihilation.

3. *Dukkha Nirodha* (cessation of suffering) - One cannot possibly adjust the whole world to one's taste in order to eliminate suffering and hope that it will remain so forever. This would violate the chief principle of Change. Instead, one adjusts one's own mind through detachment so that the Change, of whatever nature, has no effect on one's peace of mind. Briefly stated, the third Noble Truth implies that elimination of the cause (craving) eliminates the result (suffering). This is inferred in the scriptural quote by Lord Buddha, 'Whatever may result from a cause, shall be eliminated by the elimination of the cause'.
4. *Dukkha Nirodha Gamini Patipada* (pathway to freedom from suffering) - This is the Noble Eightfold Pathway towards freedom or *Nibbana*. The path can roughly be rendered into English as right view, right intention, right speech, right actions, right livelihood, right effort, right mindfulness and right concentration.

THE THREE CHARACTERISTICS

These are the three characteristics of all conditioned phenomena in Theravada thought.

1. *Anicca* (impermanence): Change is. All conditioned phenomena are subject to Change, including physical characteristics, qualities, assumptions, theories, knowledge, etc. Nothing is permanent, because, for something to be permanent there has to be an unchanging cause behind it. Since all causes are recursively bound together, there can be no ultimate unchanging cause.
2. *Dukkha* (suffering) - Craving causes suffering, since what

is craved is transitory, changing, and perishing. It is the impermanence of the object of craving that causes disappointment and sorrow. There is a tendency to label practically everything in the world, as either 'good', 'comfortable' or 'satisfying', as opposed to 'bad', 'uncomfortable', and 'unsatisfying'. It is we that label things in the world in the term of 'liking' or 'dislike', so we are the ones who create suffering in the first place. If one succeeds in giving up the tendency to label things and free him from the instincts that drive him towards attaining what he himself labels collectively as 'liking', he attains the ultimate freedom. The problem, the cause, the solution and the implementation, all of these are within oneself, not outside.

3. *Anatta* (not-self) - The concept '*Anatta*' can be rendered as lack of fixed, unchanging identity; no phenomenon constitutes an individual's permanent, essential Self. A living being is a composite of the five aggregates (*khandhas*), which is the physical forms (*rupa*), feelings or sensations (*vedana*), perception (*sanna*), mental formations (*sankhara*), and consciousness (*vinnana*), none of which can be identified as One's Self. From the moment of conception, all entities (including all living beings) are subject to a process of continuous change.

A practitioner should, on the other hand, develop and refine his or her mind to a state so as to see through this phenomenon. Direct realization of these three characteristics leads to freedom from worldly bonds and attachments, thus leading to the state where one is completely, ultimately free, the state which is termed '*Nibbana*', which literally means 'Freedom'.

THE THREE NOBLE DISCIPLINES

The pathway towards '*Nibbana*' or the Noble Eightfold Pathway is sometimes stated in a more concise manner, known as the Three Noble Disciplines. These are known as discipline (*sîla*), training of mind (*Samadhi*) and wisdom (*pañña*).

MEDITATION

Meditation (Pali: *Bhavana*) means the positive reinforcement of one's mind. Broadly categorized into Samatha and Vipassana, Meditation is the key tool implemented in attaining *jhana*. Samatha literally means "to make skillful", and has other renderings also, among which are "tranquilizing, calming", "visualizing", and "achieving". Vipassana means "insight", or "abstract understanding". In this context, Samatha Meditation makes a person skillful in concentration of mind. Once the mind is sufficiently concentrated, Vipassana allows one to see through the veil of ignorance (of the Four Noble Truths).

In the Pali Canon discourses, the Buddha frequently instructs his disciples to practice *Samadhi* (concentration) in order to establish and develop *jhana* (full concentration). *Jhana* is the instrument used by the Buddha himself to penetrate the true nature of phenomena (through investigation and direct experience) and to reach Enlightenment. Right Concentration (*samma-Samadhi*) is one of the elements in the Noble Eightfold Path. *Samadhi* can be developed from mindfulness with breathing (*anapanasati*), from visual objects (*kasina*), and repetition of phrases.

The traditional list contains 40 objects of meditation (*kammatthana*) to be used for Samatha Meditation. Every object has a specific goal; for example, meditation on the parts of the body (*kayanupassana* or *kayagathasathi*) will result in a lessening of attachment to our own bodies and those of others, resulting in a reduction of sensual desires. *Metta* (loving kindness) generates the feelings of goodwill and happiness toward us and other beings; *Metta* practice serves as an antidote to ill-will, wrath and fear.

Levels of attainment

Through practice, (Theravadin) practitioners can achieve four stages of enlightenment:

1. Stream-Enterers - Those who have destroyed the first three fetters (false view of self, doubt, and clinging to rites and

rituals), will be safe from falling into the states of misery (they will not be born as an animal, *peta* (ghost), or hell being). At most they will have to be reborn only seven more times before attaining *Nibbana*.

2. Once-Returners - Those who have destroyed the three fetters (false view of *self*, doubt, and clinging to rites and rituals), and the lessening of lust and hatred. They will attain *Nibbana* after being born once more in the world.
3. Non-Returners - Those who have destroyed the five lower fetters (that bind beings to the world of the senses). They will never again return to the human world and after they die, they will be born in the high heavenly worlds, there to attain *Nibbana*. Attaining the state of non-returner is portrayed in the early texts as the ideal goal for laity.
4. Arahants - Those who have reached Enlightenment, realized *Nibbana*, and have reached the quality of deathlessness, free from all the fermentations of defilement; whose ignorance, craving and attachments have ended. Attaining the state of arahant is portrayed in the early texts as the ideal goal for monastics.

SCRIPTURES

The Theravada school upholds the Pali Canon or Tipitaka as the most authoritative collection of texts on the teachings of Gautama Buddha. The Sutta and Vinaya portion of the Tipitaka shows considerable overlap in content to the Agamas, the parallel collections used by non-Theravada schools in India which are preserved in Chinese and partially in Sanskrit, Prakrit, and Tibetan, and the various non-Theravada Vinayas. On this basis, both these sets of texts are generally believed to be the oldest and most authoritative texts on Buddhism by scholars. It is also believed that much of the Pali Canon, which is still used by Theravada communities, was transmitted to Sri Lanka during the reign of Asoka.

After being orally transmitted (as was the custom in those days for religious texts) for some centuries, were finally committed to writing in the last century BCE, at what the

Theravada usually reckons as the fourth council, in Sri Lanka. Theravada is one of the first Buddhist schools to commit the whole complete set of its Buddhist canon into writing. Much of the material in the Canon is not specifically "Theravadin", but is instead the collection of teachings that this school preserved from the early, non-sectarian body of teachings. According to Peter Harvey, it contains material which is at odds with later Theravadin orthodoxy. He states:

The Theravadins, then, may have added texts to the Canon for some time, but they do not appear to have tampered with what they already had from an earlier period.

The Pali Tipitaka consists of three parts: the Vinaya Pitaka, Sutta Pitaka and Abhidhamma Pitaka. Of these, the Abhidhamma Pitaka is believed to be a later addition to the first two pitakas, which, in the opinion of many scholars, were the only two pitakas at the time of the First Buddhist Council. The Pali Abhidhamma was not recognized outside the Theravada school. In the 4th or 5th century CE Buddhaghosa Thera wrote the first Pali commentaries to much of the Tipitaka (which were based on much older manuscripts, mostly in old Sinhalese), and after him many other monks wrote various commentaries, which have become part of the Theravada heritage.

These texts, however, do not enjoy the same authority as the Tipitaka does. The Tipitaka is composed of 45 volumes in the Thai edition, 40 in the Burmese and 58 in the Sinhalese, and a full set of the Tipitaka is usually kept in its own (medium-sized) cupboard.

The commentaries, together with the Abhidhamma, define the specific Theravada heritage. Related versions of the Sutta Pitaka and Vinaya Pitaka were common to all the early Buddhist schools, and therefore do not define only Theravada, but also the other early Buddhist schools, and perhaps the teaching of Gautama Buddha himself. Theravada Buddhists consider much of what is found in the Chinese and Tibetan scriptural collections to be apocryphal, meaning that they are not authentic words of the Buddha.

LAY AND MONASTIC LIFE

Traditionally, Theravada Buddhism has observed a distinction between the practices suitable for a lay person and the practices undertaken by ordained monks (and, in ancient times, nuns). While the possibility of significant attainment by laymen is not entirely disregarded by the Theravada, it occupies a position of significantly less prominence than in the Mahayana and Vajrayana traditions. This distinction - as well as the distinction between those practices advocated by the Pali Canon, and the folk religious elements embraced by many monks - has motivated some scholars to consider Theravada Buddhism to be composed of multiple separate traditions, overlapping though still distinct.

Most prominently, the anthropologist Melford Spiro in his work *Buddhism and Society* separated Burmese Theravada into three groups: *Apotropaic Buddhism* (concerned with providing protection from evil spirits), *Kammatic Buddhism* (concerned with making merit for a future birth), and *Nibbanic Buddhism* (concerned with attaining the liberation of *Nibbana*, as described in the Tipitaka). He stresses that all three are firmly rooted in the Pali Canon. These categories are not accepted by all scholars, and are usually considered non-exclusive by those who employ them. The role of lay people has traditionally been primarily occupied with activities that are commonly termed 'merit making' (falling under Spiro's category of kammatic Buddhism).

Merit making activities include offering food and other basic necessities to monks, making donations to temples and monasteries, burning incense or lighting candles before images of the Buddha, and chanting protective or merit-making verses from the Pali Canon. Some lay practitioners have always chosen to take a more active role in religious affairs, while still maintaining their lay status. Dedicated lay men and women sometimes act as trustees or custodians for their temples, taking part in the financial planning and management of the temple.

Others may volunteer significant time in tending to the mundane needs of local monks (by cooking, cleaning, maintaining temple facilities, etc.). Lay activities have traditionally not extended to study of the Pali scriptures, or the practice of meditation, though in the 20th Century these areas have become more accessible to the lay community, especially in Thailand.

A number of senior monastics in the Thai Forest Tradition, including Ajahn Buddhadasa, Luang Ta Maha Bua, Ajahn Plien Panyapatipo, Ajahn Pasanno, and Ajahn Jayasaro, have begun teaching meditation retreats outside of the monastery for lay disciples.

In the UK, Ajahn Chah a disciple of Ajahn Mun, set up a monastic lineage at Chithurst in West Sussex, "Cittaviveka", with his disciple Ajahn Sumedho, and then "Amaravati" in Hertfordshire was founded which has a retreat center for lay retreats. Ajahn Sumedho extended this to Harnham in Northumberland as Aruna Ratanagiri under the present guidance of Ajahn Munindo, another disciple of Ajahn Chah. *Nibbana,* the highest goal of Theravada Buddhism, is attained through study and the practice of morality, meditation and wisdom (*sila, Samadhi, panna*). The goal of *Nibbana* (and its associated techniques) has traditionally been seen as the domain of the fully ordained monastic, whereas many of the same techniques can be used by laypeople to generate happiness in their lives, without focusing on *Nibbana.*

Monastic roles in the Theravada can be broadly described as being split between the role of the (often urban) scholar monk and the (often rural or forest) meditation monk. Both types of monks serve their communities as religious teachers and officiants by presiding over religious ceremonies and providing instruction in basic Buddhist morality and teachings. Scholar monks undertake the path of studying and preserving the Pali literature of the Theravada. They may devote little time to the practice of meditation, but may attain great respect and renown by becoming masters of a particular section of the Pali Canon or its commentaries. Masters of the Abhidhamma, called Abhidhammika, are particularly respected in the scholastic tradition.

Meditation monks, often called forest monks because of their association with certain wilderness-dwelling traditions, are considered to be specialists in meditation. While some forest monks may undertake significant study of the Pali Canon, in general meditation monks are expected to learn primarily from their meditation experiences and personal teachers, and may not know more of the Tipitaka than is necessary to participate in liturgical life and to provide a foundation for fundamental Buddhist teachings. More so than the scholastic tradition, the meditation tradition is associated with the attainment of certain supernatural powers described in both Pali sources and folk tradition.

These powers include the attainment of *Nibbana*, mind-reading, supernatural power over material objects and their own material bodies, seeing and conversing with gods and beings living in hell, and remembering their past lives. These powers are called *abhiñña*. Sometimes the remains of the cremated bone fragment of an accomplished forest monk are believed able to transfom itself into crystal-like relics (*sãrira-dhãtu*).

ORDINATION

The minimum age for ordaining as a Buddhist monk is 20 years, reckoned from conception. However, boys under that age are allowed to ordain as novices (*Samanera*), performing a ceremony such as *Shinbyu* in Burma. Novices shave their heads, wear the yellow robes, and observe ten basic precepts. Although no specific minimum age for novices is mentioned in the scriptures, traditionally boys as young as seven are accepted. This tradition follows the story of the Lord Buddha's son, Rahula, who was allowed to become a novice at the age of seven. Monks follow 227 rules of discipline, while nuns follow 311 rules.

In most Theravada countries, it is a common practice for young men to ordain as monks for a fixed period of time. In Thailand and Burma, young men typically ordain for the 3 month Rain Retreat (*vassa*), though shorter or longer periods of ordination are not rare. Traditionally, temporary ordination was even more flexible among Laotians. Once they had undergone their initial ordination as young men, Laotian men were permitted to temporarily ordain again at any time, though married men were expected to seek their wife's permission. Throughout Southeast Asia, there is little stigma attached to leaving the monastic life. Monks regularly leave the robes after acquiring an education, or when compelled by family obligations or ill-health.

Ordaining as a monk, even for a short period, is seen as having many virtues. In many Southeast Asian cultures, it is seen as a means for a young man to 'repay' his parents for their work and effort in raising him, because the merit from his ordination accrues to them as well. Thai men who have ordained as a monk may be seen as more fit husbands by Thai women, who refer to men who have served as monks with a colloquial term meaning 'cooked' to indicate that they are more mature and ready for marriage. Particularly in rural areas, temporary ordination of boys and young men traditionally gave peasant boys an opportunity to gain an education in temple schools without committing to a permanent monastic life.

In Sri Lanka, temporary ordination is not practiced, and a monk leaving the order is frowned upon. The continuing influence of the caste system in Sri Lanka may play a role in the taboo against temporary ordination and leaving the monkhood. Though Sri Lankan monastic nikayas are often organized along caste lines, men who ordain as monks temporarily pass outside of the conventional caste system, and as such during their time as monks may act (or be treated) in a way that would not be in line with the expected duties and privileges of their caste.

Some well-known Theravadin monks are: Ajahn Mun Bhuridatta, Ajahn Chah, Ledi Sayadaw, Ajahn Plien Panyapatipo, Ajahn Sumedho, Ajahn Brahm, Bhikkhu Bodhi, Buddhadasa, Mahasi Sayadaw, Nyanaponika Thera, Preah Maha Ghosananda, Sayadaw U Pandita, Ajahn Amaro, Thanissaro Bhikkhu and Walpola Rahula.

MONASTIC PRACTICES

The practices usually vary in different sub-schools and monasteries within Theravada. But in the most orthodox forest monastery, the monk usually models his practice and lifestyle on that of the Buddha and his first generation of disciples by living close to nature in forest, mountains and caves. Forest monasteries still keep alive the ancient traditions through following the Buddhist monastic code of discipline in all its detail and developing meditation in secluded forests.

In a typical daily routine at the monastery during the 3 month vassa period, the monk will wake up before dawn and will begin the day with group chanting and meditation. At dawn the monks will go out to surrounding villages bare-footed on alms-round and will have the only meal of the day before noon by eating from the bowl by hand. Most of the time is spent on Dhamma study and meditation. Sometimes the abbot or a senior monk will give a Dhamma talk to the visitors. Laity who stays at the monastery will have to abide by the traditional eight Buddhist precepts.

After the end of the Vassa period, many of the monks will go out far away from the monastery to find a remote place (usually in the forest) where they can hang their umbrella tents and where it is suitable for the work of self-development. When they go wandering, they walk barefoot, and go wherever they feel inclined, and those requisites which are necessary will be carried along. These generally consist of the bowl, the three robes, a bathing cloth, an umbrella tent, a mosquito net, a kettle of water, a water filter, razor, sandals, some small candles, and a candle lantern.

The monks do not fix their times for walking and sitting meditation, for as soon as they are free they just start doing it; nor do they determine for how long they will go on to meditate. Some of them sometimes walk from dusk to dawn whereas at other times they may walk from between two to seven hours. Some may decide to fast for days or stay at dangerous places where ferocious animals live in order to aid their meditation. Those monks who have been able to achieve a high level of attainment will be able to guide the junior monks and lay Buddhists toward the four degrees of spiritual attainment.

LAY DEVOTEE

In Pali the word for a male lay devotee is *Upasaka*. *Upasika* is its female equivalent. One of the duties of the lay followers, as taught by the Buddha, is to look after the needs of the monk/nuns. They are to see that the monk/nuns do not suffer from lack of the four requisites: food, clothing, shelter and medicine. As neither monks nor nuns are allowed to have an occupation, they depend entirely on the laity for their sustenance. In return for this charity, they are expected to lead exemplary lives. In Burma and Thailand, the monastery was and is still regarded as a seat of learning. In fact today about half of the primary schools in Thailand are located in monasteries.

Religious rituals and ceremonies held in a monastery are always accompanied by social activities. In times of crisis, it is to the monks that people bring their problems for counsel. Traditionally, a ranking monk will deliver a sermon four times a month: when the moon waxes and wanes and the day before the new and full moons. The laity also has a chance to learn meditation from the monks during these times. It is also possible for a lay disciple to become enlightened. As Bhikkhu Bodhi notes, "The Suttas and commentaries do record a few cases of lay disciples attaining the final goal of *Nibbana*. However, such disciples either attain Arahantship on the brink of death or enter the monastic order soon after their attainment. They do not continue to dwell at home as Arahant householders, for dwelling at home is incompatible with the state of one who has severed all craving."

MONASTIC ORDERS WITHIN THERAVADA

Theravada monks typically belong to a particular nikaya, variously referred to as monastic orders or fraternities. These different orders do not typically develop separate doctrines, but may differ in the manner in which they observe monastic rules. These monastic orders represent lineages of ordination, typically tracing their origin to a particular group of monks that established a new ordination tradition within a particular country or geographic area. In Sri Lanka caste plays a major role in the division into nikayas.

Some Theravada Buddhist countries appoint or elect a *Sangharaja*, or Supreme Patriarch of the *Sangha*, as the highest ranking or seniormost monk in a particular area, or from a particular nikaya. The demise of monarchies has resulted in the suspension of these posts in some countries, but patriarchs have continued to be appointed in Thailand. Burma and Cambodia ended the practice of appointing a *Sangharaja* for some time, but the position was later restored, though in Cambodia it lapsed again.

- *Bangladesh*:
    - Sangharaj Nikaya
    - Mahasthabir Nikaya
- *Burma* (Myanmar):
    - Thudhamma Nikaya
    - Shwekyin Nikaya
    - Dvara Nikaya
- *Sri Lanka*:
    - Siam Nikaya
        - Malwaththa
        - Asgiriya
        - Waturawila (or Mahavihara Vamshika ShyamoPali Vanavasa Nikaya)
    - Amarapura NikayaMany Sub orders including
        - Dharmarakshitha
        - Kanduboda (or Swejin Nikaya)
        - Tapovana (or Kalyanavamsa)
    - Ramañña Nikaya
        - Galduwa (or Kalyana Yogashramaya Samsthava)
        - Delduwa

- *Thailand and Cambodia*
  - Maha Nikaya
  - Dhammayuttika Nikaya

Festivals and Customs

Theravada Religious festivals:

- Magha Puja
- Vesakha Puja
- Asalha Puja
- Uposatha
- Vassa (Rain Retreat)

THE THERAPEUTAE OF EGYPT

The "Therapeutae" (male, pl.) and "Therapeutrides" (female, pl.), according to the account in *De vita contemplativa* by the Jewish philosopher Philo of Alexandria (c. 20 BCE - 50 CE) who appears to have been personally acquainted with them, were "philosophers" (cf. I.2) that lived on a low hill by the Lake Mareotis close to Alexandria in circumstances resembling lavrite life (cf. *Π*.22), and were "the best" of a kind given to "perfect goodness" that "exists in many places in the inhabited world" (cf. *Π*.21).

At the time various explanations of the name were given. Philo derives the name Therapeutae/Therapeutides from Greek èåñáðåýù in the sense of "cure" or "worship" (cf. I.2), whilst Pseudo-Dionysius favours the meaning "servants". Both were, of course, unfamiliar with Buddhism. However, according to the linguist Zacharias P. Thundy, "Therapeutae", the name of this coenobitic order, might have been a Hellenization of "Theravada".

The similarities between the Therapeutae and Buddhist monasticism, combined with Indian evidence of Buddhist missionary activity to the Mediterranean around 250 BC (the Edicts of Asoka), have been pointed out. The Therapeutae would have been the descendants of Asoka's emissaries to the West, and would have influenced the early formation of

Christianity. It must be noted, however, the Macmillan *Encyclopedia of Buddhism* states that theories of influences of Buddhism on early Christianity are without historical foundation.

SARVASTIVADA

Sarvastivada is an early school of Buddhism that held to 'the existence of all dharmas in the past, present and future, the 'three times'. The Abhidharma Kosa-bhasya, a later text, states:

"25c-d. He who affirms the existence of the dharmas of the three time periods [past, present and future] is held to be a Sarvastivadin."

Sarvastivada is a Sanskrit term that holds the semantic field: "the theory of all exists". The Pali equivalent is Sabbatthivada. Although there is some dispute over how the word "sarvastivada" is to be analyzed, the general consensus is that it is to be parsed into three parts: *sarva* "all" or "every" + *asti* "exist" + *vada* "speak", "say" or "theory". This equates perfectly with the Chinese term, shuôyîqièyÒu bù, which is literally "the sect that speaks of the existence of everything", as used by Hsuan Tsang and other translators.

PHILOSOPHY

Though the sarvastivadins would themselves claim that their teaching of 'all exists' (sarvasti) is a direct teaching of the Buddha himself, as shown by their attributing the earliest abhidharma texts to direct disciples of the Buddha, notably to Sariputra and constant reference to the sutras throughout, the school in its entirety is more rightly to be considered as part of the age of scholastic Buddhism. It was the most influential school in the northwestern part of India. In a Chinese context, the word abhidharma refers to the sarvastivada abhidharma, although Dharmaguptaka, Pudgalavada and Theravada also had an abhidharma.

During the first century BC, in the Gandharan cultural area (consisting of Oddiyana, Gandhara and Bactria,

Tokharistan, across the Khyber Pass), the sthaviriyas used Gandhari to write their literature in Kharosthî. During this time, the sarvastivada abhidharma primarily consisted of the *Abhidharmahrdaya* authored by Dharmashresthin, a native from Tokharistan, and the *Ashtagrantha* authored/compiled by Katyayaniputra. Both texts were translated by Samghadeva in 391 A.D. and in 183 A.D. respectively, but they were not completed until 390 in Southern China.

Although the sarvastitva was the central thesis, there were different theories on how 'sarvam' and even 'asti' were actually to be explained and understood among the Gandharan diverse sarvastivadins. Vasubandhu's *Koshabhasya*, an elaborate yoga manual based on the Hrdaya, describes four main theses on sarvasti: 'There are four types of sarvastivadins accordingly as they teach a difference in existence (*bhavanyathatva*), a difference in characteristic (*laksananyathatva*), a difference in condition (*avasthanyathatva*), and mutual difference (*anyonyathatva*).

Later sarvastivada takes a combination of the first and third theses as its model. It was on this basis that the school's doctrines were defended in the face of growing external, and sometimes even internal, criticism. The doctrines of sarvastivada were not confined to 'all exists', but also include the theory of momentariness (*ksanika*), conjoining (*samprayukta*) and simultaneity (*sahabhu*), conditionality (*hetu* and *pratyaya*), the culmination of the spiritual path (*marga*), and others. These doctrines are all inter-connected and it is the principle of 'all exists' that is the axial doctrine holding the larger movement together when the precise details of other doctrines are at stake.

The sarvastivada was also known by other names, particularly *hetuvada* and *yuktivada*. Hetuvada comes from hetu – 'cause', which indicates their emphasis on causation and conditionality. Yuktivada comes from yukti – 'reason' or even 'logic', which shows their use of rational argument and syllogism. When the sarvastivada school held a synod in Kashmira during the reign of Kanishka I (ca. 158-176), the Gandharan most important text, the Astagrantha of

Katyayaniputra was rewritten in Sanskrit making necessary revisions. This revised text was now known as Jbanaprasthana, Course of Knowledge. Though the Gandharan Astagrantha had many vibhasas, the new Kashmira Astagrantha i.e. the Jnanaprasthana had a Sanskrit Mahavibhasa, compiled by the Kashmira sarvastivada synod.

The Jnanaprasthana and its Mahavibhasa, which took more than a generation to complete, were then declared the Vaibhasika orthodoxy, said to be 'Buddha's word', Buddhabhasita. This new Vaibhasika orthodoxy, however, was not readily accepted by the Gandharan sarvastivadins, though gradually they adapted their views to the new Kawmira orthodoxy. The Gandharan sarvastivadins used the same Vinaya from Mathura. As a matter of fact, their abhidharma was meant for meditational practices. They made use of the Hrdaya which is a manual for attaining arhat. However, the long Gandharan Vinaya was abridged to a Sanskrit Dashabhanavara in the Kashmira synod by removing the avadanas and jatakas, stories and illustrations.

After the declaration of the Vaibhasika orthodoxy, the Gandharan non-vaibhasika sarvastivadins, the majority, were called 'sautrantikas' (those who uphold the sutras). Interestingly, the Kawmira orthodoxy, the Vaibhasikas disappeared in the later part of the 7th century. Subsequently, the old Gandharan sarvastivadins, the non-vaibhasika sautrantikas, were named 'mulasarvastivadins', who then at a later went to Tibet. It has been suggested that the minority Vaibhasikas were absorbed into the majority sautrantika sarvastivadins as a possible result of the latter's adaptations.

Moreover, Mishrakabhidharmahrdaya, a title which means that 'sautrantika views were mixed with vaibhasika views' was composed by Dharmatrata in the 4th century in Gandharan area. Vasubandhu (ca.350-430), a native from Purusapura in Gandhara, composed his Kowa based on this text and the Astagrantha. While in Kawmira, he wrote his karikas which were well received there but he faced intense opposition, notably from Samghabhadra, a leading sarvastivada pundit, when he composed his bhasya. By his bhasya, Vasubandhu made it clear to the Vaibhasikas that he was a sautrantika, which is why he was fiercely opposed by the sarvastivada vaibhasikas in Kawmira.

In reply to Vasubhandhu's bhasya, Samghabhadra wrote a text, the Nyananusara 'according to reason'. This work is presently only extant in Chinese (from Xuanzang's translation and little is known of it in English).

4

Mahayana Buddhism

MAHAYANA VINAYA

The Vinaya Pitaka is a Buddhist scripture, one of the three parts that make up the Tripitaka. Its primary subject matter is the monastic rules for monks and nuns. The name Vinaya Pitaka (*vinayapitaka*) is the same in Pali, Sanskrit and other dialects used by early Buddhists in India, and means basket of discipline. Each school traditionally claimed that its own version was compiled at the First Council shortly after the Buddha's death, and recited by UPali, with little later addition. As the versions are different, scholars do not take this literally. However, as the different versions are fairly similar, most scholars consider most of the Vinaya to be fairly early, that is, dating from before the separation of schools. However, Dr Gregory Schopen, Professor of Sanskrit, Tibetan, and Buddhist Studies in the University of Texas at Austin, argues against this assumption on various grounds.

He suggests that similarities may be due to later standardization. He also points out that many inscriptions from early times on show that monks owned property, contrary to the Vinaya. He argues that there is no evidence that this represents a decline from an early period of observance, and suggests that the Vinaya may be an attempt by self-appointed elite to impose their standards on everyone else.

The Pali version of the *Patimokkha*, the code of conduct that applies to Buddhist monastics, contains 227 major rules for *Bhikkhus* and 311 major rules for *Bhikkhunis*. The Vibhanga section(s) of Vinaya Pitaka constitute(s) a commentary on these rules, giving detailed explanations of them along with the origin stories for each rule. The *Khandhaka/Skandhaka* sections give numerous supplementary rules grouped by subject, again with origin stories.

The Buddha called his teaching the "Dhamma-Vinaya", emphasizing both the philosophical teachings of Buddhism as well as the training in virtue that embodies that philosophy. In the collected Chinese editions of the Scriptures the Vinaya pitaka has a broader sense, including all four Chinese vinayas listed above, parts of others, non-canonical vinaya literature, lay vinaya and Bodhisattva vinaya.

PLACE IN THE TRADITION

According to the scriptures, in the first years of the Buddha's teaching the *Sangha* lived together in harmony with no vinaya, as there was no need, because all of the Buddha's early disciples were highly realized if not fully enlightened. As the *Sangha* expanded situations arose which the Buddha and the lay community felt were inappropriate for samanas. According to tradition, the first rule to be established was the prohibition against sexual acts. The origin story tells of an earnest monk whose family was distraught that there was no male heir and so persuaded the monk to impregnate his wife. According to tradition, all three, the monk, his wife and son who both later ordained, eventually became fully enlightened arahants.

The vinaya is very important to Buddhists -"Whatever Dhamma and Vinaya I have pointed out and formulated for you, that will be your Teacher when I am gone."

BODHICHITTA

In Buddhism, bodhicitta is the wish to attain complete enlightenment (that is, Buddhahood) in order to be of benefit to all sentient beings trapped in cyclic existence (*samsara*) who has not yet reached Buddhahood. One who has bodhicitta as the primary motivation for all of his or her activities is called a *Bodhisattva*? Etymologically, the word is a combination of the Sanskrit words bodhi and citta. *Bodhi* means "awakening" or "enlightenment". *Citta* is derived from the Sanskrit root *cit,* and denotes "that which is conscious" – mind or consciousness. *Bodhicitta* may be translated as "awakening mind" or "thought of enlightenment".

Bodhicitta may also be defined as the union of compassion and wisdom. This is a development of the concept of luminous mind in the Pali Canon. While the compassion and wisdom aspects of *bodhicitta* are actually highly dependent on each other, in the Mahayana tradition (the school of Buddhism within which the relevant terminology is most fully developed) they are often referred to as:

- Relative bodhicitta, in which the practitioner works for the good of all beings as if it were his own.
- Absolute, or ultimate, bodhicitta, which refers to the wisdom of *sunyata* (*œunyata*, a Sanskrit term often translated as "emptiness", though the alternatives "openness" or "spaciousness" probably convey the idea better to Westerners). The concept of *œunyata* in Buddhist thought does not refer simply to nothingness, but to freedom from attachments (particularly attachment to the idea of a static or essential self) and from fixed ideas about the world and how it should be. The classic text on *œunyata* is the *Prajñaparamita Hrdaya Sûtra,* a discourse of the Buddha commonly referred to as the "Heart Sûtra."

So, the term bodhicitta in its most complete sense would combine both:

- The arising of spontaneous and limitless compassion for all sentient beings, and
- The falling away of the attachment to the illusion of an inherently existent self.

Some bodhicitta practices emphasize the absolute (e.g. vipaœyana); others emphasize the relative (e.g. *Metta*), but both aspects are seen in all Mahayana practice as essential to enlightenment, especially in the Tibetan practices of tonglen and lojong. Without the absolute, the relative can degenerate into pity and sentimentality, whereas the absolute without the relative can lead to nihilism and lack of desire to engage other sentient beings for their benefit. *Bodhicitta* may be viewed as having different levels: one useful classification is that given by Patrul Rinpoche in his *Words of My Perfect Teacher*. He states that the lowest level is the way of the King, who primarily seeks his own benefit but who recognizes that his benefit depends crucially on that of his kingdom and his subjects.

The middle level is the path of the boatman, who ferries his passengers across the river and simultaneously, of course, ferries himself as well. The highest level is that of the shepherd, who makes sure that all his sheep arrive safely ahead of him and places their welfare above his own. Among the most important source texts on bodhichitta, within the Mahayana tradition in which the teaching arose, are Œantideva's *A Guide to the Bodhisattva's Way Of Life* (c. 700 CE), Thogme Zangpo's *Thirty-Seven Practices of a Bodhisattva* (12th century CE), Langri Tangpa's *Eight Verses for Training the Mind* (c. 1100 CE), and the lojong (mind training) proverbs authored by Geshe Chekhawa in the 12th century CE.

LUMINOUS MIND IN THE NIKAYAS

Luminous mind (also, "brightly shining mind," "brightly shining citta") is a term used by the Buddha in the Pali Canon. It is described as the most fundamental aspect of the mind, and is said to be "brightly shining" whether or not this is realized. It is given no direct doctrinal interpretation in the Pali discourses; one way the Mahayana interprets it is as bodhicitta. The Astasahasrika Perfection of Wisdom Sutra describes bodhicitta thus: "That citta is no citta since it is by nature brightly shining."

This is in accord with Anguttara Nikaya I, 10 which goes from a reference to brightly shining citta to saying that even the slightest development of loving-kindness is of great benefit. This implies that loving-kindness - and the related state of compassion - is inherent within the luminous mind as a basis for its further development. The observation that the ground state of consciousness is of the nature of loving-kindness implies that empathy is innate to consciousness and exists prior to the emergence of all active mental processes.

SIGNIFICANCE

That bodhicitta is the primary positive factor to be cultivated is particularly emphasized by the Mahayana and Vajrayana (or tantric) schools of Buddhism. In Mahayana and Vajrayana Buddhism, the goal of Buddhist practice is primarily for an individual to escape from *samsara* with the aspiration to be reborn infinite numbers of times to liberate all those other beings still trapped in *samsara*. While the teaching and terminology of bodhichitta is most developed in Mahayana Buddhism, its practice and realization are independent of sectarian considerations since they are fundamentally a part of the human experience. There are, of course, *Bodhisattvas* recognized not only in the Theravada school of Buddhism, but in all other religious traditions and among those of no formal religious tradition.

The present fourteenth Dalai Lama, for instance, regarded Mother Teresa as one of the greatest modern *Bodhisattvas*. Buddhism has no monopoly either on compassion or on the realization of the fundamentally illusory nature of our view of "self" and the world. Buddhism teaches that many *Bodhisattvas* neither teach nor announce themselves in any way at all, but live apparently ordinary lives and help other sentient beings by stealth. It is regarded as a very healthy contemplation to hold the view that *all* other beings may actually be hidden *Bodhisattvas*, including those we do not like.

Followers of the Mahayana, in particular, believe that the attainment of Buddhahood is not only possible by all sentient beings, but inevitable. Since all beings karmically connected ("all in the same boat", as it were), either we will all attain liberation or we will all drown in the ocean of *samsara*. Mahayana teaches that even those who have initially chosen personal liberation from *samsara* will be awakened eventually by Buddhas and entreated to develop bodhicitta and become fully enlightened in order to help liberate all sentient beings.

Mahayana Buddhism teaches that the broader motivation of achieving one's own enlightenment in order to help all sentient beings, bodhicitta, is the best possible motivation one can have for any action, whether it be working in one's vocation, teaching others, or even making an incense offering. The Six Perfections (*Paramitas*) of Buddhism only become true "perfections" when they are done with the motivation of *bodhicitta*. Thus, the action of giving (Skt. *dana*) can be done in a mundane sense, or it can be a *paramita* if it is conjoined with bodhicitta.

CULTIVATION

The seeds of both Absolute and Relative bodhicitta often arise spontaneously – for example, when seeing someone close to us who is suffering, or in the face of a major unexpected event that upsets our world view. Unfortunately they can also vanish again just as quickly, which is why many Buddhist traditions, and in particular the Mahayana, provide specific methods for the intentional cultivation of both absolute and relative bodhicitta. This cultivation is considered to be one of the most difficult aspects of the path to complete enlightenment.

Any teaching or activity cannot be held to be a genuine Mahayana activity unless it is conjoined with at least a contrived bodhicitta. Practitioners of the Mahayana make it their primary goal to go beyond contrived forms of bodhicitta and to develop a genuine, uncontrived *bodhicitta* which remains within their mindstreams continuously without having to rely on conscious effort.

Among the many methods for developing uncontrived Bodhicitta given in Mahayana teachings are:

- The awareness that all sentient beings have been your mother in infinite previous lives
- Contemplation of the Four Immeasurables (*Brahmaviharas*) - Immeasurable Loving-Kindness (*Maitri*), Immeasurable

Compassion (*Karuna*), Immeasurable Joy in the Good Fortune of Others (*Mudita*), and Immeasurable Equanimity (*Upeksa*)

- The practice of the *paramitas* (Generosity, Patience, Virtue, Effort, Meditation, and Insight).
- The Taking and Sending (tonglen) practice, in which one takes in the pain and suffering of others on the inbreath and sends them love, joy, and healing on the outbreath., and the Lojong ('Mind Training') practices of which tonglen forms a part.

Classical Tibetan Mahayana teachings hold that there are two distinct lineages by which one may cultivate uncontrived bodhicitta: (1) through the Seven Fold Cause-and-Effect method and (2) by Exchanging Self with Others (which uses the aforementioned *tonglen* practice). These two methods are explained in detail (along with a method for combining them) in Pabongka Rinpoche's seminal work *Liberation in the Palm of Your Hand.*

PARAMITAS

The term *paramita* or Paramî (Sanskrit and Pali respectively) means "Perfect" or "Perfection". In Buddhism, the *paramitas* refer to the perfection or culmination of certain virtues. In Buddhism, these virtues are cultivated as a way of purification, purifying karma and helping the aspirant to live an unobstructed life, while reaching the goal of Enlightenment.

THERAVADA BUDDHISM

Theravada Buddhism's teachings on the *paramitas* can be found in late canonical books and post-canonical commentaries.

CANONICAL SOURCES

In the Pali Canon's Buddhavamsa the Ten Perfections (*dasa paramiyo*) are (original terms in Pali):

1. *Dana parami*: generosity, giving of oneself
2. *Sîla parami*: virtue, morality, proper conduct

3. *Nekkhamma parami*: renunciation
4. *Pañña parami*: transcendental wisdom, insight
5. *Viriya (also spelt vîriya) parami*: energy, diligence, vigour, effort
6. *Khanti parami*: patience, tolerance, forbearance, acceptance, endurance
7. *Sacca parami*: truthfulness, honesty
8. *Adhitthana (adhitthana) parami*: determination, resolution
9. *Metta parami*: loving-kindness
10. *Upekkha (also spelt upekha) parami*: equanimity, serenity

Two of the above virtues, *Metta* and *Upekkha*, also comprise two of the Four Immeasurables (Brahmavihara).

Historicity

The Theravadin teachings on *paramitas* can be found in canonical books (*Jataka, Apadana, Buddhavamsa, and Cariyapitaka*) and post-canonical commentaries which were added to the Pali Canon at a later time, and thus they are not an original part of the Theravadin teachings. The oldest parts of the Sutta Pitaka (for example, *Majjhima Nikaya, Digha Nikaya, Samyutta Nikaya and* the *Anguttara Nikaya*) do not have any mention of the *Paramitas*. Some scholars even refer to the teachings of the *paramitas* as a semi-Mahayana teaching which was added to the scriptures at a later time, in order to appeal to the interests and needs of the lay community, and to popularize their religion.

TRADITIONAL PRACTICE

Bodhi (2005) maintains that, in the earliest Buddhist texts (which he identifies as the first four nikayas), those seeking suffering's extinction (*Nibbana*) pursued the Noble Eightfold Path. As time went on, a backstory was provided for the multi-life development of the Buddha; as a result, the ten perfections were identified as part of the path for the Buddha-to-be (Pali: *bodhisatta*; Sanskrit: *Bodhisattva*). Over subsequent centuries, the paramis were seen as being significant to both aspirants of Buddhahood and of arahantship. Thus, Bodhi (2005) summarizes:

"It should be noted that in established Theravada tradition the paramîs are not regarded as a discipline peculiar to candidates for Buddhahood alone but as practices which must be fulfilled by all aspirants to enlightenment and deliverance, whether as Buddhas, *paccekabuddhas*, or disciples. What distinguish the supreme *Bodhisattva* from aspirants in the other two vehicles are the degree to which the paramîs must be cultivated and the length of time they must be pursued. But the qualities themselves are universal requisites for deliverance, which all must fulfill to at least a minimal degree to merit the fruits of the liberating path."

MAHAYANA BUDDHISM

In Mahayana Buddhism, the Lotus Sutra (*Saddharmapundarika*) lists the Six Perfections as (original terms in Sanskrit):

1. *Dana paramita* : generosity, giving of oneself
2. *Śîla paramita* : virtue, morality, discipline, proper conduct
3. *Ksanti (kshanti) paramita* : patience, tolerance, forbearance, acceptance, endurance
4. *Vîrya paramita* : energy, diligence, vigor, effort
5. *Dhyana paramita* : one-pointed concentration, contemplation
6. *Prajña paramita* : wisdom, insight

Note that this list is also mentioned by the Theravada commentator Dhammapala, who says it is equivalent to the above list of ten. In the Ten Stages (*Dasabhumika*) Sutra, four more *paramitas* are listed:

1. *Upaya paramita*: skillful means
2. *Pranidhana (pranidhana) paramita*: vow, resolution, aspiration, determination
3. *Bala paramita*: spiritual power
4. *Jñana paramita*: knowledge

VAJRAYANA BUDDHISM

According to the perspective of Vajrayana Buddhism, Mahayana practitioners have the choice of two practice paths: the path of perfection (Sanskrit: *paramitayana*) or the path of tantra (Sanskrit: tantrayana), which is the Vajrayana. Traleg Kyabgon Rinpoche renders "paramita" into English as "transcendent action" and then frames and qualifies it:

When we say that *paramita* means "transcendent action," we mean it in the sense that actions or attitude are performed in a non-egocentric manner. "Transcendental" does not refer to some external reality, but rather to the way in which we conduct our lives and perceive the world - either in an egocentric or a non-egocentric way. The six *paramitas* are concerned with the effort to step out of the egocentric mentality. Keown, *et al.* (2003) hold that the Six Perfections comprise the *Gyulü*.

SILAPARAMITA

This *paramita* is the enlightened quality of virtuous and ethical behavior, morality, self-discipline, impeccability, personal integrity, honor, and harmlessness. The essence of this *paramita* is that through our love and compassion we do not harm others; we are virtuous and harmless in our thoughts, speech, and actions. This practice of ethical conduct is the very foundation for progressing in any practice of meditation and for attaining all higher realizations on the path. Our practice of generosity must always be supported by our practice of ethics; this ensures the lasting results of our generosity. We should perfect our conduct by eliminating harmful behavior and following the *Bodhisattva* precepts.

We abstain from killing, stealing, sexual misconduct, lying, divisive speech, harsh speech, gossip, greed, malice, and wrong views. Following these precepts or guidelines is not meant to be a burden or a restriction of our freedom. We follow these precepts so we can enjoy greater freedom, happiness, and security in our lives, because through our virtuous behavior we are no longer creating suffering for ourselves and others. We must realize that unethical behavior is always the cause of suffering and unhappiness.

If we give even the slightest consideration to the advantages of cultivating ethical behavior and the disadvantages of unethical behavior, we will certainly develop great enthusiasm for this practice of ethics. Practicing the perfection of ethics, we are free of negativity, we cause no harm to others by our actions, our speech is kind and compassionate, and our thoughts are free of anger, malice, and wrong views. When our commitment is strong in the practice of ethics we are at ease, naturally confident, without stress, and happy because we are not carrying any underlying sense of guilt or remorse for our actions; we have nothing to hide. Maintaining our personal honor and integrity, our moral impeccability, this is the cause of all goodness, happiness, and even the attainment of enlightenment.

KSHANTI-PARAMITA

This *paramita* is the enlightened quality of patience, tolerance, forbearance, and acceptance. The essence of this *paramita* of patience is the strength of mind and heart that enables us to face the challenges and difficulties of life without losing our composure and inner tranquility. We embrace and forbear adversity, insult, distress, and the wrongs of others with patience and tolerance, free of resentment, irritation, emotional reactivity, or retaliation. We cultivate the ability to be loving and compassionate in the face of criticism, misunderstanding, or aggression. With this enlightened quality of patience, we are neither elated by praise, prosperity, or agreeable circumstances, nor are we angry, unhappy or depressed when faced with insult, challenge, hardship, or poverty.

This enlightened attribute of patience, acceptance, and tolerance is not a forced suppression or denial of our thoughts and feelings. Rather, it is a quality of being which comes from having our heart open and our mind deeply concentrated upon the Dharma. In this way, we have a clear and correct understanding of impermanence, of cause and effect (karma), and with strong determination and patience we remain in harmony with this understanding for the benefit of all beings. The ability to endure, to have forbearance, is integral to our Dharma practice. Without this kind of patience we cannot accomplish anything.

A true *Bodhisattva* practices patience in such a way that even when we are hurt physically, emotionally, or mentally by others, we are not irritated or resentful. We always make an effort to see the goodness and beauty in others. In practicing this perfection of patience and forbearance, we never give up on or abandon others-we help them cross over the sea of suffering. We maintain our inner peace, calmness, and equanimity under all circumstances, having enduring patience and tolerance for ourselves and others. With the strength of patience, we maintain our effort and enthusiasm in our Dharma practice. Therefore, our practice of patience assists us in developing the next *paramita* of joyous effort and enthusiastic perseverance.

VIRYA-PARAMITA

This *paramita* is the enlightened quality of energy, vigor, vitality, endurance, diligence, enthusiasm, continuous and persistent effort. In order to practice the first three *paramitas* of generosity, virtuous conduct, and patience in the face of difficulties, we need this *paramita* of joyous effort and perseverance. Joyous effort makes the previous *paramitas* increase and become even more powerful influences in our life. The essence of this *paramita* of joyous effort is the courage, energy, and endurance to continuously practice the Dharma and pursue the supreme goal of enlightenment for the highest good of all beings.

From a feeling of deep compassion for the suffering of all sentient beings, we are urged to unfailing, persistent, and joyous effort. We use our body, speech, and mind to work ceaselessly and untiringly for the benefit of others, with no expectations for personal recognition or reward. We are always ready to serve others to the best of our ability. With joyous effort, devoted energy, and the power of sustained application, we practice the Dharma without getting sidetracked by anything or falling under the influence of laziness. Without developing *Virya Paramita*, we can become easily disillusioned and drop our practice when we meet with adverse conditions.

The word virya means persistence and perseverance in the face of disillusionment, energetically striving to attain the supreme goal of enlightenment. When we cultivate this type of diligence and perseverance we have a strong and healthy mind. We practice with persistent effort and enthusiasm because we realize the tremendous value and benefit of our Dharma practice. Firmly establishing ourselves in this paramita, we also develop self-reliance, and this becomes one of our most prominent characteristics. With joyous effort and enthusiastic perseverance, we regard failure as simply another step toward success, danger as an inspiration for courage, and affliction as another opportunity to practice wisdom and compassion. To develop strength of character, self-reliance, and the next *paramita* of concentration, is not an easy achievement, thus we need enthusiastic perseverance on the path.

DHYANA-PARAMITA

This *paramita* is the enlightened quality of concentration, meditation, contemplation, *Samadhi*, mindfulness, mental stability. Our minds have the tendency to be very distracted and restless, always moving from one thought or feeling to another. Because of this, our awareness stays fixated in the ego, in the surface layers of the mind and emotions, and we just keep engaging in the same habitual patterns of behavior. The perfection of concentration means training our mind so that it does what we want it to do.

We stabilize our mind and emotions by practicing meditation, by being mindful and aware in everything we do. When we train the mind in this way, physical, emotional, and mental vacillations and restlessness are eliminated. We achieve focus, composure, and tranquility. This ability to concentrate and focus the mind brings clarity, equanimity, illumination. Concentration allows the deep insight needed to transform the habitual misperceptions and attachments that cause confusion and suffering. As we eliminate these misperceptions and attachments, we can directly experience the joy, compassion, and wisdom of our true nature.

There is no attainment of wisdom and enlightenment without developing the mind through concentration and meditation. This development of concentration and one-pointedness requires perseverance. Thus the previous *paramita* of joyous effort and perseverance brings us to this *paramita* of concentration. In addition, when there is no practice of meditation and concentration, we cannot achieve the other *Paramitas*, because their essence, which is the inner awareness that comes from meditation, is lacking. To attain wisdom, compassion, and enlightenment, it is essential that we develop the mind through concentration, meditation, and mindfulness.

PRAJNA-PARAMITA

This *paramita* is the enlightened quality of transcendental wisdom, insight, and the perfection of understanding. The essence of this *paramita* is the supreme wisdom, the highest understanding that living beings can attain-beyond words and completely free from the limitation of mere ideas, concepts, or intellectual knowledge. Beyond the limited confines of intellectual and conceptual states of mind, we experience the awakened heart-mind of wisdom and compassion-*Prajna paramita. Prajna paramita* is the supreme wisdom (*Prajna*) that knows emptiness and the interconnectedness of all things. This flawless wisdom eliminates all false and distorted views of the absolute.

We see the essential nature of reality with utmost clarity; our perception goes beyond the illusive and deceptive veils of material existence. With the perfection of wisdom, we develop the ability to recognize the truth behind the temporary display of all appearances. *Prajna paramita* is a result of contemplation, meditation, and rightly understanding the nature of reality. Ultimately, the full realization of *Prajna paramita* is that we are not simply a separate self trying to do good. Rather, virtuously serving the welfare of all beings is simply a natural expression of the awakened heart. We realize that the one serving, the one being served, and the compassionate action of service, are all the same totality-there is no separate ego or self to be found in any of these.

With this supreme wisdom, we go beyond acceptance and rejection, hope and fear, dualistic thoughts, and ego-clinging. We completely dissolve all these notions, realizing everything as a transparent display of the primordial truth. If our ego is attached even to the disciplines of these *Paramitas,* this is incorrect perception and we are merely going from one extreme to another. In order to free ourselves from these extremes, we must release our ego attachment and dissolve all dualistic concepts with the insight of supreme wisdom. This wisdom transforms the other five *paramitas* into their transcendental state as well. Only the illumination of supreme wisdom makes this possible.

5

Karma and Rebirth in Early Buddhism

Rebirth in Buddhism is the doctrine that the consciousness of a person, upon the death or dissolution of the aggregates (*skandhas*), becomes one of the contributing causes for the arising of a new group of *skandhas*. The consciousness arising in the new person is neither identical to, nor entirely different from, the old consciousness, but forms part of a causal continuum or stream with it.

The basic cause for this persistent re-arising of personality is the abiding of consciousness in avijja (ignorance); when ignorance is uprooted, rebirth ceases. Within one life and across multiple lives, the empirical, changing self not only objectively affects its surrounding external world, but also generates (consciously and unconsciously) its own subjective image of this world, which it then lives in as 'reality'. It lives in a world of its own making in various ways.

It "tunes in" to a particular level of consciousness (by meditation or the rebirth it attains through its karma) which has a particular range of objects - a world - available to it. It furthermore selectively notices from among such objects, and then processes what has been sensed to form a distorted interpretive model of reality: a model in which the 'I am' conceit is a crucial reference point. When *Nibbana* is experienced, though, all such models are transcended: the world stops 'in this fathom-long carcase'.

In traditional Buddhist cosmology, these lives can be in any of a large number of states of being, including those of humans, any kind of animal, and several types of supernatural being. The type of rebirth that arises at the end of one life is conditioned by the karmas (actions of body, speech and mind) of previous lives; good karmas will yield a happier rebirth, bad karmas will produce one which is unhappy. In the traditional Buddhist languages of Pali and Sanskrit, there is no word corresponding exactly to the English "rebirth".

A rebirth, that is, the state one is born into, is referred to as jati, i.e. simply "birth", also referring to the process of being born or coming into the world in any way. The entire process of change from one life to the next is called punarbhava (Sanskrit) or punabbhava (Pali), literally "becoming again"; it is also known simply as bhava, i.e. "becoming". The process seen from a universal perspective, encompassing all living beings, is called *samsara*. The story of the Buddha's life presented in the early texts does not allude to the idea of rebirth prior to his enlightenment, leading some to suggest that he discovered it for himself.

REBIRTH AS CYCLE OF CONSCIOUSNESS

Another view of rebirth describes the cycle of death and rebirth in the context of consciousness rather than the birth and death of the body. In this view, remaining impure aggregates, *skandhas*, reform consciousness into a new form. Buddhist meditation teachers suggest that through careful observation of the mind, it is possible to see consciousness as being a sequence of conscious moments rather than a continuum of awareness.

Each moment is an experience of an individual mind-state: a thought, a memory, a feeling, a perception. A mind-state arises, exists and, being impermanent, ceases following which the next mind-state arises. Thus the consciousness of a sentient being can be seen as a continuous series of birth and death of these mind-states. In this context rebirth is simply the persistence of this process.

Clearly this explanation of rebirth is wholly divorced from rebirth which may follow bodily death. The explanation of rebirth as a cycle of consciousness is consistent with other core Buddhist beliefs, such as *anicca* (impermanence), *Dukkha* (unsatisfactoriness) and anatta (non-self). Furthermore, it is possible to observe a karmic link between these mind-states. In the practice of Vipassana meditation, the meditator uses "bare attention" to observe the endless round of mind-states. This observation derives insight and understanding from seeing this cycle of birth; death and rebirth without interfering, owning or judging the individual states of mind that arise and pass away.

This understanding enables them to limit the power of desire, which according to the second noble truth of Buddhism is the cause of *Dukkha* (suffering, unsatisfactoriness) thus making possible the realisation of *Nibbana*. So it can be concluded that the understanding of rebirth in the context of the cycle of consciousness is an invaluable and practical component of the fundamental aim of Buddhism.

REBIRTH AS BUDDHIST REINCARNATION

Within Buddhism, the term rebirth or re-becoming (Sanskrit: *punarbhava*; Pali: *punabbhava*) is preferred to "reincarnation", as the latter is taken to imply there is a fixed entity that is reborn. However, this still leaves the question as to what exactly the process of rebirth entails. The lack of a fixed self does not mean lack of continuity. One of the metaphors used to illustrate this is that of fire. For example, a flame is transferred from one candle to another, or a fire spreads from one field to another. In the same way that it depends on the original fire, there is a conditioned relationship between one life and the next; they are not identical but neither are they completely distinct. The early Buddhist texts make it clear that there is no permanent consciousness that moves from life to life.

According to the early texts, rebirth should be understood in terms of a 'stream of consciousness', or an 'evolving consciousness', whose quality is conditioned by karma. The medieval Pali scholar Buddhaghosa labeled the consciousness described in the early texts as constituting a condition for a new birth as 'rebirth-linking consciousness' (*patisandhi*), which connected the arising of a new life with the moment of death.

Some schools were led to the conclusion that karma continued to exist in some sense and adhere to a particular person until it had worked out its consequences. Another school, the Sautrantika, made use of a more poetic model to account for the process of karmic continuity. For them, each act 'perfumed' the individual and led to the planting of a 'seed' that would later germinate as a good or bad karmic result. While all Buddhist traditions seem to accept some notion of rebirth, there is no unified view about precisely how events unfold after the moment of death. Theravada Buddhism generally asserts that rebirth is immediate.

The Tibetan schools, on the other hand, hold to the notion of a bardo (intermediate state) which can last up to forty-nine days, and this has led to the development of a unique 'science' of death and rebirth, a good deal of which is set down in what is popularly known as *The Tibetan Book of the Dead*. While Theravada Buddhism generally denies there is an intermediate state, some early Buddhist texts seem to support it. One school that adopted this view was the Sarvastivada, who believed that between death and rebirth there is a sort of limbo in which beings do not yet reap the consequences of their previous actions but in which they may still influence their rebirth.

The death process and this intermediate state were believed to offer a uniquely favourable opportunity for spiritual awakening. There are many references to rebirth in the early Buddhist scriptures. These are some of the more important: Mahakammavibhanga Sutta (*Majjhima Nikaya* 136); Upali Sutta (*Majjhima Nikaya* 56); Kukkuravatika Sutta (*Majjhima Nikaya* 57); Moliyasivaka Sutta (*Samyutta Nikaya 36.21*); Sankha Sutta (*Samyutta Nikaya* 42.8).

REBIRTH IN HISTORICAL CONTEXT

The Buddha lived at a time of great philosophical creativity in India, and many different concepts of the nature of life and death were proposed at that time. Some thinkers were materialists, believing that there was no existent consequent upon the end of a life, and that there was an *atman* (self) which was annihilated upon death. Others believed in a form of cyclic existence, where a being is born, lives, dies and then is re-born, but in the context of a type of determinism or fatalism, in which karma played no role.

Others were "eternalists", postulating an eternally existent *atman,* comparable to the Western concept of the soul: when a being (or his body) dies, the *atman* survives death and is re-embodied (reincarnates) as another living being, based on its karmic inheritance. This last belief is the one that has come to be dominant (with certain modifications) in modern Hinduism. The Buddha is said to have taught a concept of rebirth that was distinct from that of any Indian teacher contemporary with him.

This concept was consistent with the common notion of a sequence of related lives stretching over a very long time, but was constrained by two core Buddhist concepts: anatt*a*, that there is no irreducible *atman* or "self" tying these lives together; and anicca, that all compounded things are subject to dissolution, including all the components of the human person and personality. The Buddha's detailed conception of the connections between action (karma), rebirth, and their ultimate causes is set out in the twelve links of dependent origination.

DHAMMA WITHOUT REBIRTH

In line with the present-day stress on the need for religious teachings to be personally relevant and directly verifiable, in certain Dhamma circles the time-honored Buddhist doctrine of rebirth has come up for severe re-examination. Although only a few contemporary Buddhist thinkers still go so far as to suggest that this doctrine be scrapped as "unscientific," another opinion has been gaining ground to the effect that whether or not rebirth itself be a fact, the doctrine of rebirth has no essential bearings on the practice of Dhamma and thence no claim to an assured place in the Buddhist teachings.

The Dhamma, it is said, is concerned solely with the here and now, with helping us to resolve our personal hangups through increased self-awareness and inner honesty. All the rest of Buddhism we can now let go as the religious trappings of an ancient culture utterly inappropriate for the Dhamma of our technological age. If we suspend our own predilections for the moment and instead go directly to our sources, we come upon the indisputable fact that the Buddha himself taught rebirth and taught it as a basic tenet of his teaching. Viewed in their totality, the Buddha's discourses show us that far from being a mere concession to the outlook prevalent in his time or an Asiatic cultural contrivance, the doctrine of rebirth has tremendous implications for the entire course of Dhamma practice, affecting both the aim with which the practice is taken up and the motivation with which it is followed through to completion.

The aim of the Buddhist path is liberation from suffering, and the Buddha makes it abundantly clear that the suffering from which liberation is needed is the suffering of bondage to *samsara*, the round of repeated birth and death. To be sure, the Dhamma does have an aspect which is directly visible and personally verifiable. By direct inspection of our own experience we can see that sorrow, tension, fear and grief always arise from our greed, aversion and ignorance, and thus can be eliminated with the removal of those defilements. The importance of this directly visible side of Dhamma practice cannot be underestimated, as it serves to confirm our confidence in the liberating efficacy of the Buddhist path.

However, to downplay the doctrine of rebirth and explain the entire import of the Dhamma as the amelioration of mental suffering through enhanced self-awareness is to deprive the Dhamma of those wider perspectives from which it derives its full breadth and profundity. By doing so, one seriously risks reducing it in the end to little more than a sophisticated ancient system of humanistic psychotherapy. The Buddha himself has clearly indicated that the root problem of human existence is not simply the fact that we are vulnerable to sorrow, grief and fear, but that we tie ourselves through our egoistic clinging to a constantly self-regenerating pattern of birth, aging, sickness and death within which we undergo the more specific forms of mental affliction.

He has also shown that the primary danger in the defilements is their causal role in sustaining the round of rebirths. As long as they remain unabandoned in the deep strata of the mind, they drag us through the round of becoming in which we shed a flood of tears "greater than the waters of the ocean." When these points are carefully considered, we then see that the practice of Dhamma does not aim at providing us with a comfortable reconciliation with our present personalities and our situation in the world, but at initiating a far-reaching inner transformation which will issue in our deliverance from the cycle of worldly existence in its entirety.

Admittedly, for most of us the primary motivation for entering upon the path of Dhamma has been a gnawing sense of dissatisfaction with the routine course of our unenlightened lives rather than a keen perception of the dangers in the round of rebirths. However, if we are going to follow the Dhamma through to its end and tap its full potential for conferring peace and higher wisdom, it is necessary for the motivation of our practice to mature beyond that which originally induced us to enter the path. Our underlying motivation must grow toward those essential truths disclosed to us by the Buddha and, encompassing those truths, must use them to nourish its own capacity to lead us toward the realization of the goal.

Our motivation acquires the requisite maturity by the cultivation of right view, the first factor of the Noble Eightfold Path, which as explained by the Buddha includes an understanding of the principles of kamma and rebirth as fundamental to the structure of our existence. Though contemplating the moment is the key to the development of insight meditation, it would be an erroneous extreme to hold that the practice of Dhamma consists wholly in maintaining mindfulness of the present.

The Buddhist path stresses the role of wisdom as the instrument of deliverance, and wisdom must comprise not only a penetration of the moment in its vertical depths, but a comprehension of the past and future horizons within which our present existence unfolds. To take full cognizance of the principle of rebirth will give us that panoramic perspective from which we can survey our lives in their broader context and total network of relationships. This will spur us on in our own pursuit of the path and will reveal the profound significance of the goal toward which our practice points, the end of the cycle of rebirths as mind's final liberation from suffering.

KARMIC REBIRTH IN PALI BUDDHISM

In traditional Pali Canon/Theravada Buddhism karma (*kamma*) plays out its decisive role on the field of the double-eternity of every existent being, and even of the universe itself. That is, both the past and future of every existent being, human or other, are endless. Every presently existing being is but one link in a chain of continuing existences in various forms from a beginningless eternity in the past on into an endless future eternity, unless an existential breakthrough (enlightenment) can be achieved. There is a second notable feature about any existence: the seeming arbitrariness of its form and fortunes. On the human level some are born healthy, handsome, into wealthy families and experience good fortune all their lives.

Others are born ugly and diseased and into poverty and distress. But who on any level knows when illness, disaster, or death may strike? Existence, at least in the human form, seems to be totally arbitrary in its allocation of goods and ills. Why should this be so? This is the major problem that all religions have sought to solve. For Theravada Buddhism the answer is clear. Our lives are governed by karma. Wrote the late Venerable Nyanatiloka in his Buddhist Dictionary:

> Karma (Skt.), Pali: *kamma* "Action," correctly speaking denotes the wholesome and unwholesome volitions...and their concomitant mental factors, causing rebirth and shaping the destiny of beings.

And again, quoting from the Pali Canon:

There is Karma (action), O monks, that ripens in hell...Karma that ripens in the animal world...Karma that ripens in the heavenly world...threefold...is the fruit of karma: ripening during the [human] lifetime…ripening in the next birth…ripening in later births.

And what is the power of karma? It is but the continuing power of the deeds done by sentient beings when in their human form. The possible forms of rebirth from the human state include eons-long hells (purgatories), unhappy spirit-forms, animal existences, and ages-long celestial existences. One can readily understand the attractiveness of this version of existence. It rationalizes and moralizes what seem to be the thrustings of a blind, random fate or a capricious deity. One no longer can reasonably feel aggrieved and wronged by one's present evil fortunes; they are the merited result of wrong dispositions and actions in some former human existence. And good fortune is the fruit of past ethically good deeds.

So too it teaches the human being to cherish his or her present human status as a priceless opportunity to create "good" karma, i.e. that leading to fortunate rebirths and offering a basis for eventual release from the rebirth cycle (*samsara*). For all other than human states are but the reward or punishment-or better, the inevitable karmic ripening of deeds done as a human being. They are but the spending of one's good or bad karmic capital, so to speak. There is an important corollary to this version of the dynamics of reality: each chain of individualized existence is an almost single-line affair. Each individual's karma, in its creation and working out, remains almost entirely a single-channel, closed-circuit course.

No one else can increase, or decrease, my individual stock of merit or demerit. Yes, there was (is) a tradition of sharing merit but it seems to apply to a kind of general fund of merit, not to other individual accounts. This has somewhat characteristically led to a blunting of charitable and socially reformative activity in Theravadin societies, for each individual is now in the state to which his/her past deeds have led. That is, each one gets what one deserves. And charity tends to be almost exclusively directed toward the *Sangha,* where it produces superior merit-dividends compared to that directed toward lay persons or general community needs.

Yes, there are the higher sublime states of spirit which are praised in the Pali scriptures as the summit-attainments of the good life: loving kindness, compassion, sympathetic joy in the joy of others, and equanimity, a state of unruffled benevolence toward all beings. But on the whole, rather than ameliorative or redemptive activity, these seem to be the marks of superior spiritual achievement on the part of those of great spiritual maturity, or occasionally by those of lesser attainments.

In the main it is the merit-for-human-rebirth concern that wins out, given this context. This basic belief in the perpetual rebirth of the individual as determined by past karmic merit/demerit, until and unless nirvanic salvation is achieved, seems to have remained firmly in place in most of Asian Buddhism, Theravada or Mahayana. A few random examples scattered over the centuries of the existence of Buddhism will make this evident; it seems that one finds this belief wherever one touches down in Asian Buddhism. For example, we may note the general ambience of the *Lotus Sûtra,* so influential in Asia.

The *Lotus Sûtra* exudes the philosophy of karmic rebirth on almost every page; karmic-determined birth is taken for granted throughout: *arhats* are promised Buddhahood in some far-off but certain blessed future existence; many of the great saints of the past appear on stage.

Indeed the whole *sûtra* is a spectacle of glorious spiritual destinies being played out in future eons in a multitude of universes. Then there are the Pure Land *Sûtras.* Therein we read of Amitabha Buddha who has become a Buddha by virtue of countless eons of virtuous deeds and can now offer sinful human beings, with much past "karmic indebtedness," the destruction of their past moral-spiritual liabilities out of his infinite store of merit.

Saint Hoonen, founder of Japanese Pure Land Buddhism in the 12th-13th centuries gives expression to this prevailing sense of karma-bound rebirth as the lot of all men:

For the sin or merit of a former life, men may be born to good or evil in this fleeting world.

Suzuki Shoosan, 16th-17th century samurai turned Zen master in mid-life, speaks of "the six forms of transmigration and the four types of birth," and sees himself striving for enlightenment "birth after birth."

To come down to the present: The late Yasutani Roshi, using modern terms, spoke as follows:

Now in our subconscious are to be found the residual impressions of our life experiences including those of previous existences, going back to time immemorial.

And in the present-present Abe Masao, likewise from a Zen perspective, speaks of acting in "wisdom and compassion...operating to emancipate innumerable sentient beings from transmigration."

This is not the total account of the matter however. The development of Mahayana life and doctrine resulted in important modifications of the rebirth-karma complex of ideas and practice. Central to the change of their significance was the development of the bodhisattvic theme and ideal. Nagarjuna's (circa 150-250) philosophy of emptiness (*sûnyata*) contributed importantly to that development. He took as his Buddhist philosophic mission the destruction of the rigid fixities of Buddhist scholasticism. He maintained that rigidly held intellectual concepts are convenient linguistic devices but do not represent reality. Most opposites or contrasts, for example, are mutually interdependent. This is true even of those ultimate Buddhist opposites, *samsara* and *nirvana*. Thus as Frederick Streng has written:

The spiritual ideal is [for Nagarjuna] not release (*nirvana*) from conditioned existence by an individual person, because that effort implies an essential distinction between *nirvana* and conditioned existence (*samsara*). Rather the idea is of a

Bodhisattva ("enlightenment being") whose awareness of the nonsubstantiality.... of Bodhisattvahood is expressed in a kind of wisdom that seeks the release of all beings.

Thus Nagarjuna moved Buddhist thought to a new fluidity of the concept of karmic destiny: no longer could, should, one look upon one's spiritual destiny as hermetically sealed off from another's. Indeed they intertwine; one cannot be rescued from one's own spiritual predicament without his/her fellow-creatures' rescue. This of course is the bodhisattvic ideal, now being broadened from the pre-enlightenment career of Gotama Buddha to apply to everyman!

Obviously this was a tremendously significant step for Buddhist ethics. Fully developed it linked all creatures indissolubly to each other for good or ill. In his pre-enlightenment career the Buddha-to-be (*Bodhisattva*) lived countless lives (as animal, spirit, human being) always in selfless service and even life-sacrifice for others. Now this quality of life is to be that of everyone. In the *Vimalakîrti Sûtra* the bodhisattvic quality of life is extended to, preeminently embodied in, the life of the layman Vimalakîrti, who, though a full-fledged active layman, has a more penetrating understanding of Buddhist truths than the great saints of early Buddhism!

This new *Bodhisattva* ideal was given eloquent expression by "Santideva (7th-8th centuries) in his *Path of Light* in these words. By constant use the idea of "I" attaches itself to foreign drops of seed and blood, although the thing exists not [as a genuine entity]. Then why should I not conceive my fellow's body as my own self?...I will cease to live as self and will take as myself my fellow creatures... why should not he [man] not conceive his self to lie in his fellows also?..take thine own self lose its pleasures and bear the sorrow of thy fellows. Cast upon its [one's own] head the guilt even of others' works.

Such a man would "be a protector of the unprotected, a guide to wayfarers, a ship, a dyke, and a bridge for them who seek the further Shore, a lamp for them who need a lamp, a bed for them who need a bed, a slave for them who need a slave." This new bodhisattvic Buddhist then vows that even when on the verge of final nirvanic enlightenment (release from samsaric rebirth) he/she will not enter into final release from the cycles of rebirth until all other beings have attained their release. There is one further development to be noted before turning to the nature of Western Buddhism. Hua-yen Buddhism, developed in 7th century China, provided a cosmic philosophical model of organic interrelatedness that universalized and undergirded the bodhisattvic ideology. Its basic typology is contained in the concept of an organically integrated universe, using the model of Indra's Net.

Writes Robert Gimello:

> This inspired trope [the net of Indra] pictures a universe in which each constituent of reality is like a multifaceted jewel placed at one of the knots of a vast net. There is such a jewel at each knot, and each jewel reflects not only the rest of the jeweled net in its entirety but also each and every other jewel in its individuality. Thus, each particular reflects the totality, the totality so reflected is both a unity and a multiplicity...All things and beings, Hua-yen teaches, are like this net.

Obviously the Hua-yen philosophy fits hand in glove with the bodhisattvic ideal of human life. No one can gain spiritual freedom independently of others. The organically interconnected texture of the universe makes this impossible. Thus Hua-yen universalizes and firmly establishes the bodhisattvic vision of the truly good life.

KARMIC REBIRTH AND BUDDHIST ETHICS IN THE WEST

As Buddhism in its various forms has made its way into the Western world all of its doctrines, traditions, and practices have faced a challenging new cultural and social situation. The main Buddhist concern has been to maintain the basic Buddhist perspective on human life and conduct in a new and different context. Of course Buddhism in its two and one half millenium-long history in Asia has successfully established itself in several differing cultures due to its tremendous flexibility. But perhaps the West poses a greater challenge to it than any of the Asian traditionalist cultures it infiltrated. The Western civilizational emphasis is upon frenetic activity. Here history is not viewed as cyclically repetitive as in so many Asian cultures, but as a kind of ongoing torrent of change, which lurches, plunges, progresses forward to some new and unpredictable new state.

These changes are perceived as due in great part to human intentions and actions; humans create history. And of special relevance to our immediate topic, in the West each human birth is an absolutely *de novo* affair, a totally new beginning without karmic past. Its individual qualities are explained in terms of physical, psychical inheritance through its parents; and its social environment will further shape its nature and career. Many in the West believe in a future eternity of existence for each of these new human beings (an immortal soul), its nature determined by the quality of life lived in this one-and-only human life, one-life karma so to speak. Others believe that this life is the totality of one's existence, and should be lived to its hedonic full.

The prevailing quality of Western life and culture, with its attendant idolization of "success," "achievement," "prosperity," and historical-social "progress" and "improvement" is perceived by Western Buddhists to be profoundly un- or even anti-Buddhist in spirit. Ken Jones, for example, in his The Social Face of Buddhism, terms Western culture "egoic"; it magnifies and idealizes the very qualities of greed, violence (expressed hatred) and self-esteem (first-personalized delusion) that Buddhism considers its basic enemy. How then can Buddhism, marching to a totally different drumbeat of ideas and goals in life, create meaningful Western forms? And in terms of our special interest, how does the Buddhist ethic of karmic rebirth fit in here, if at all?

We may note two general types of Buddhist reaction to this cultural situation. The first is what may be termed the "suppression" of the karmic-rebirth theme in the presentation of the Buddhist message. Karmically qualified rebirth may be the taken-for-granted belief in such meditation-centered groups as Insight Meditation and the U Ba Khin (Burmese) oriented movements, but such a belief is not urged upon beginners nor does it appear in their publications to any observable degree. At the very least it is not a talking-point. The same can be said of the other end of the Buddhist spectrum, the Zen Buddhist publications and centers. No doubt enlightenment through *zazen* always has karmic and rebirth connotations, but they are made little of upon the American scene at least.

In all of these the emphasis is upon what one might call the rebirth-karma of personal transformation. The important "karma-force" and karmic-determination are that of the "karmic" influence of thoughts, aspirations, and emotions upon the character, attitudes, and consequent actions of Cedilla; a person. Here an emotion or thought is "reborn" as an attitude or character trait which irrevocably finds expression in one's actions. This might be called thought-character-action karma, or psychic karma. There are those Western-born Buddhists-and their numbers and influence in the shaping of Western Buddhism will only increase through the years-who find some of the Asian Buddhist emphasis upon karmic rebirth unnecessary. As an example of this tendency, we may take the before-mentioned Ken Jones as the spokesman of a Westernized Buddhism.

On the cover of his book we read that he "has been a social activist of one kind or another, for much of his life and a Buddhist trainee for the last eight years" [in 1989]. His book therefore is a good example of what a Western-born person, reared and educated in a Christian-humanist-scientific and socially activist culture, finds of value in the Asian Buddhist tradition, how he interprets it, and what he considers authentically Buddhist attitudes and actions in a Western society. With respect to the Asian Buddhist doctrine of rebirth he writes:

None of the arguments advanced in this book require either rejection or acceptance of the notion of rebirth.

What then of the doctrine of karma which historically has been so tightly tied to that of rebirth? He finds it in need of reinterpretation:

[T]he better known Sanskrit karma has acquired Hindu meanings of "fate" and "justice" which have nothing to do with [true] Buddhism.

In place of "karma" he would use the Pali form "*kamma*" and would interpret it thus:

Kamma, however, seems to me to be both a logical element in fundamental Buddhist teaching and an interestingly suggestive idea in the discussion of Buddhist social theory.

Thus with one fell stroke the strong Asian Buddhist concern about gaining merit for a "good" future rebirth by "good" actions is swept away. In fact Jones finds some of the motivations in the developed Theravada tradition that speak of the "good" next life to be gained by "good" actions, to be totally anti-Buddhists because they pander to greed and pride. Thus to take as an example the following kind of statement by a prominent Buddhist layman in Burma:

A person who steadfastly and continuously observes the Five Precepts can gain the following beneficial results: (1) he can gain great wealth and possessions; (2) he can gain great fame and reputation; (3) he can appear with confidence and courage in the midst of a public assembly; (4)..he can die with calmness and equanimity; (5) after his death he will be born into the world of Devas.

In Jones' view all of the above fruits and rewards of living according to Buddhist ethical principles would represent the glorification of the very greed and delusion that Buddhists seek to escape! The first three rewards represent the essence of the "egoic" Western culture which Jones believes to be the spiritual antithesis of Buddhism and which Buddhist social action would seek to modify and transform. His purified (truly Buddhist) version of *kamma* is stated thus:

The theory of karma is the theory of cause and effect, of action and reaction. Every volitional action produces its effects or results. If a good action produces good effects and bad action bad effects, it is not justice or reward...but this in virtue of its own nature, its own law. To this revision of the traditionally accepted version of *kamma* (karma), freed from its fateful connotations, Jones would add a significant new meaning, that of "social kamma." He complains that much of traditional [Eastern] Buddhism has assumed that "Society is...*no* more than the aggregate of individuals composing it," hence the mere sum of individual karmic strands.

To put his statement into figurative language: A society in traditional Buddhist thought is a collection of parallel and intertwined channels of separate karmic destinies. But Jones rejects this version of social "structure" for one of societal *kamma*. Society as a super-individual entity has a moral-immoral character that affects all of its members for better or worse. It too must be modified Buddhistically for individuals to achieve their full spiritual destiny. Therefore, writes Jones: "A socially engaged Buddhism needs no other rationale than that of being an amplification of traditional Buddhist morality [five precepts], a social ethic brought forth by the needs and potentialities of present-day society."

Significantly for the future of Western Buddhism, and interestingly in terms of its historic past, two of the ideational patterns noted in the development of Mahayana Buddhism have been picked up as especially useful and ethically-socially significant: the bodhisattvic motif and the Hua-yen vision of an organically interconnected world.

Writes Jones in defense of a socially activist Buddhism:

The great *Bodhisattva* vow to "liberate all beings" now also implies a concern for changing the social conditions which in every way discomfit us. These are surely among the conditions which the Buddha declared "lead to passion, not release therefrom, to bondage, not release therefrom; and to the piling up of rebirths; these to wanting much, not wanting little; to discontent, not to contentment; these to sociability, not to solitude; these to indolence, not to exertion; these to luxury, not to frugality."

It might be noted in passing that some of the items, e.g. those calling for solitude and frugality, speak more of monastic than ordinary living. However the main point is clear; Buddhists must work for a society that does not idolize individual acquisitiveness and purely personal satisfactions to the detriment of others.

The other integrative and social-action motif strongly supporting the bodhisattvic theme which Jones finds useful is that of Indra's net. To redescribe it in Jones' words:

At each intersection in Indra's net is a light reflecting jewel (that is, a phenomenon, entity, thing [person]) and each jewel contains another Net *ad infinitum*. The jewel at each intersection exists only as a reflection of all the others and hence has no [independent] self nature. Yet it also exists as a separate entity to sustain the others.

This is to say, in the strengthening of the bodhisattvic motif that no one being, or small cluster of beings, actually exists independently, or even semi-independently, of the others. Here is an organic vision of the universe that ties all mankind, all living creatures, and the very physical world together in one organic wholeness. No one can pursue private goals and goods without affecting others. Such a view of the world makes every action a "social action."

This viewpoint leads Jones to make a number of specific recommendations. He believes along with E. F. Schumacher that "small is beautiful" economically; that the ruling economic gigantism works against the true welfare of men, stimulates the fires of greed, and leads to the deprivation and oppression of the many. He would favor small businesses and speaks of the formation of "free autonomous cooperatives," as well as "right livelihood cooperatives." He lauds the "creative non-violence" of Gandhi and Martin Luther King as "a natural and direct expression of Buddhadharma." Environmentalist values are likewise to be promoted. He also favors "democratic and egalitarian values." To sum it up Jones suggests that the proper mix of Buddhist values in the modern world can be summarized thus:

> The psycho-social transformation suggested here is a continuously sustained metamorphosis, in which a significant number of people change the whole social climate by actualizing these [Buddhist humanist] social values in their social values in their own experience...and [do] the work needed to make them the norms of public behaviour.

Not all Western Buddhists would agree with Jones in his delineation of a socially active Buddhism as its proper role. Many look upon Buddhism as a refuge from the wear and tear of daily life and from the frenetic pace of life in the West, not as a bugle call to action. What is more promising to the activity driven Westerner than the Buddhist emphasis upon inward purity of spirit and its cherishing in the meditative life in quiet retreats and peaceful isolation?

Many perceive this as the main mission of Buddhism in the West: To offer centers where there are solitude and spiritual leaders and healers. To them it seems that social-reformism overlooks the basic problem of mankind, that it is ruled by greed, hatred, and delusions about life and self- the basic three evils as seen by Buddhism. As Kenneth Kraft, editor of Inner Peace, World Peace puts the view of many Buddhists about social reformism: "A reform that is pursued only from a socio-political standpoint they assert will at best provide [only] temporary solutions, and at the worst it will perpetuate the very ills it aims to cure." Only the purifying of individual hearts and lives will effect genuine social change.

This of course is a very old and fundamental Buddhist view: The world will only be changed for the better by individuals who have been changed for the better through spiritual discipline. The fully stated form of this is that only when one is oneself fully enlightened can one "save" others. The 11th-12th century Tibetan monk Milarepa put it thus:

> One should not be over-anxious and hasty in setting out to serve others before one has one realized Truth in its fullness; to do so, would be like the blind leading the blind.

He goes on to say that since there will "be no end of sentient beings for one to serve," a *Bodhisattva* need be in no hurry to help them. Obviously Milarepa is more concerned for the would-be *Bodhisattva's* spiritual progress than the alleviation of suffering or righting of wrongs in contemporary society. But most in the West, even Buddhists, do not have Milarepa's robust confidence in the perpetual rebirth of all beings or his almost callous unconcern for present sufferers.

To this approach Robert Aitken responds thus:

There is no end to the process of perfection, and so the perfectionist cannot begin *Bodhisattva* work. [But] compassion and peace are a practice on cushions in the meditation hall, and also within the family, on the job, and at political forums. Do your best with what you have and you will mature in the process?

Perhaps the right Buddhist attitude for modern Buddhists in the West is, as many Western-born Buddhists would see it, that of a watchful awareness of one's own inwardness, nourished by meditation, and appropriate outward activity according to Buddhist principles. These must be pursued jointly, not set against each other, in a pattern of social inaction.

Now we may return in the end to the initial question: Can there be a viable and authentic Buddhist ethic without a belief in perpetual rebirth governed by the karma of an infinite number of past existences? The answer, explicit or implicit, of many contemporary Buddhists in the West, and perhaps some in Asia, is a resounding yes! Even without those beliefs the central Buddhist ethical values can and, in the interest of all living creatures, should be vigorously followed. Indeed it is perhaps possible to say that both Buddhism and Buddhist ethics may be better off without the karmic-rebirth factor to deal with.

6

Eckhart and Buddhism

The attempt is only a tentative and sketchy one, far from being systematic and exhaustive. But I hope the reader will find something in it which evokes his curiosity enough to undertake further studies of this fascinating topic. When I first read-which was more than a half century ago-a little book containing a few of Meister Eckhart's sermons, they impressed me profoundly, for I never expected that any Christian thinker ancient or modern could or would cherish such daring thoughts as expressed in those sermons. While I do not remember which sermons made up the contents of the little book, the ideas expounded there closely approached Buddhist thoughts, so closely indeed, that one could stamp them almost definitely as coming out of Buddhist speculations.

As far as I can judge, Eckhart seems to be an extraordinary "Christian." While refraining from going into details we can say at least this: Eckhart's Christianity is unique and has many points which make us hesitate to classify him as belonging to the type we generally associate with rationalized modernism or with conservative traditionalism. He stands on his own experiences which emerged from a rich, deep, religious personality. He attempts to reconcile them with the historical type of Christianity modeled after legends and mythology. He tries to give an "esoteric" or inner meaning to them, and by so doing he enters fields which were not touched by most of his historical predecessors.

First, let me give you the views Eckhart has on time and creation. These are treated in his sermon delivered on the commemoration day for St. Germaine. He quotes a sentence from Ecclesiasticus: "In his days he pleased God and was found just." Taking up first the phrase "In his days," he interprets it according to his own understanding:

> ... there are more days than one. There is the soul's day and God's day. A day, whether six or seven ago, or more than six thousand years ago, is just as near to the present as yesterday. Why? Because all time is contained in the present Now-moment. Time comes of the revolution of the heavens and day began with the first revolution. The soul's day falls within this time and consist of the natural light in which things are seen. God's day, however, is the complete day, comprising both day and night. It is the real Now-moment, which for the soul is eternity's day, on which the Father begets his only begotten Son and the soul is reborn in God.
>
> The soul's day and God's day are different. In her natural day the soul knows all things above time and place; nothing is far or near. And that is why I say, this day all things are of equal rank. To talk about the world as being made by God tomorrow, yesterday, would be talking nonsense. God makes the world and all things in this present now. Time gone a thousand years ago is now as present and as near to God as this very instant. The soul who is in this present now, in her the Father bears his one-begotten Son and in that same birth the soul is born back into God. It is one birth; as fast as she is reborn into God the Father is begetting his only Son in her.
>
> God the Father and the Son have nothing to do with time. Generation is not in time, but at the end and limit of time. In the past and future movements of things, your heart flits about; it is in vain that you attempt to know eternal things; in divine things, you should be occupied intellectually....
>
> Again, God loves for his own sake, acts for his own sake: that means that he loves for the sake of love and acts for the sake of action. It cannot be doubted that God would never have begot his Son in eternity if [his idea of] creation were other

than [his act of] creation. Thus God created the world so that he might keep on creating. The past and future are both far from God and alien to his way.

From these passages we see that the Biblical story of Creation is thoroughly contradicted; it has not even a symbolic meaning in Eckhart, and, further, his God is not at all like the God conceived by most Christians. God is not in time mathematically enumerable. His creativity is not historical, not accidental, and not at all measurable. It goes on continuously without cessation with any beginning, with no end.

It is not an event of yesterday or today or tomorrow, it comes out of timelessness, of nothingness, of Absolute Void. God's work is always done in an absolute present, in a timeless "now which is time and place in itself." God's work is sheer love, utterly free from all forms of chronology and teleology. The idea of God creating the world out of nothing, in an absolute present, and therefore altogether beyond the control of a serial time conception will not sound strange to Buddhist cars. Perhaps they may find it acceptable as reflecting their doctrine of Emptiness (*śûnyata*).

Below are further quotations from Eckhart giving his views on "being," "life," "work," etc.:

Being is God.... God and being are the same-or God has being from another and thus himself is not God.... Everything that is has the fact of its being through being and from being. Therefore, if being is something different from God, a thing has its being from something other than God. Besides, there is nothing prior to being because that which confers being creates and is a creator. To create is to give being out of nothing.

Eckhart is quite frequently metaphysical and makes one wonder how his audience took to his sermons-an audience which is supposed to have been very unscholarly, being ignorant of Latin and all the theologies written in it. This problem of being and God's creating the world out of nothing must have puzzled them very much indeed. Even the scholars might have found Eckhart beyond their understanding, especially when we know that they were not richly equipped with the experiences which Eckhart had.

Mere thinking or logical reasoning will never succeed in clearing up problems of deep religious significance. Eckhart's experiences are deeply, basically, abundantly rooted in God as being which is at once being and not-being: he sees in the "meanest" thing among God's creatures all the glories of his is-ness (*isticheit*). The Buddhist enlightenment is nothing more than this experience of is-ness or suchness (*tathata*), which in itself has all the possible values (*guna*) we humans can conceive.

God's characteristic is being. The philosopher says one creature is able to give another life. For in being, mere being, and lies all that is at all. Being is the first name. Defect means lack of being. Our whole life ought to be being. So far as our life is being so far it is in God. So far as our life is feeble but taking it as being, it excels anything life can ever boast. I have no doubt of this, that if the soul had the remotest notion of what being means she would never waver from it for an instant. The most trivial thing perceived in God, a flower for example as espied in God, would be a thing more perfect than the universe. The vilest thing present in God as being is better than angelic knowledge.

This passage may sound too abstract to most readers. The sermon is said to have been given on the commemoration day of the "blessed martyrs who were slain with the swords." Eckhart begins with his ideas about death and suffering which come to an end like everything else that belongs to this world. He then proceeds to tell us that "it behooves us to emulate the dead in dispassion (*niht betrüeben*) towards good and ill and pain of every kind," and he quotes St. Gregory: "No one gets so much of God as the man who is thoroughly dead," because "death gives them [martyrs] being,-they lost their life and found their being." Eckhart's allusion to the flower as espied in God reminds us of Nansen's interview with Rikko in which the Zen master also brings out a flower in the monastery courtyard.

It is when I encounter such statements as these that I grow firmly convinced that the Christian experiences are not after all different from those of the Buddhist. Terminology is all that divides us and stirs us up to a wasteful dissipation of energy. We must however weigh the matter carefully and see whether there is really anything that alienates us from one another and whether there is any basis for our spiritual edification and for the advancement of a world culture.

When God made man, he put into the soul his equal, his active, everlasting masterpiece. It was so great a work that it could not be otherwise than the soul and the soul could not be otherwise than the work of God. God's nature, his being, and the Godhead all depend on his work in the soul. Blessed, blessed be God that he does work in the soul and that he loves his work! That work is love and love is God. God loves himself and his own nature, being and Godhead, and in the love he has for himself he loves all creatures, not as creatures but as God. The love God bears himself contains his love for the whole world.

Eckhart's statement regarding God's self-love which "contains his love for the whole world" corresponds in a way to the Buddhist idea of universal enlightenment. When Buddha attained the enlightenment, it is recorded; he perceived that all beings non-sentient as well as sentient were already in the enlightenment itself. The idea of enlightenment may make Buddhists appear in some respects more impersonal and metaphysical than Christians. Buddhism thus may be considered more scientific and rational than Christianity which is heavily laden with all sorts of mythological paraphernalia. The movement is now therefore going on among Christians to denude the religion of this unnecessary historical appendix.

While it is difficult to predict how far it will succeed, there are in every religion some elements which may be called irrational. They are generally connected with the human craving for love. The Buddhist doctrine of enlightenment is not after all such a cold system of metaphysics as it appears to some people. Love enters also into the enlightenment experience as one of its constituents, for otherwise it could not embrace the totality of existence. The enlightenment does not mean to run away from the world, and to sit cross-legged at the peak of the mountain, to look down calmly upon a bomb-struck mass of humanity. It has more tears than we imagine.

Thou shalt know him [God] without image, without semblance and without means.-"But for me to know God thus, with nothing between, I must be all but he, he all but me."-I say, God must be very I, I very God, so consummately one that this he and this I are one "is," in this is-ness working one work eternally; but so long as this he and this I, to wit, God and the soul, are not one single here, one single now, the I cannot work with nor be one with that he. What is life? God's being is my life, but if it is so, then what is God's must be mine and what is mine God's. God's is-ness is my is-ness, and neither more nor less. The just live eternally with God on a par with God neither deeper nor higher. All their work is done by God and God's by them.

Going over these quotations, we feel that it was natural that orthodox Christians of his day accused Eckhart as a "heretic" and that he defended himself. Perhaps it is due to our psychological peculiarities that there are always two opposing tendencies in the human way of thinking and feeling; extrovert and introvert, outer and inner, objective and subjective, exoteric and esoteric, traditional and mystical. The opposition between these two tendencies or temperaments is often too deep and strong for any form of reconciliation. This is what makes Eckhart complain about his opponents not being able to grasp his point. He would remonstrate: "Could you see with my heart you would understand my words, but, it is true, for the truth itself has said it." Augustine is however tougher than Eckhart: "What is it to me though any comprehend not this!"

One of Eckhart's heresies was his pantheistic tendency. He seemed to put man and God on an equal footing: "The Father begets his Son in me and I am there in the same Son and not another." While it is dangerous to criticize Eckhart summarily as a pantheist by picking one or two passages at random from his sermons, there is no doubt that his sermons contain many thoughts approaching pantheism. But unless the critics are a set of ignorant misinterpreters with perhaps an evil intention to condemn him in every way as a heretic, a fair-minded judge will notice that Eckhart everywhere in his sermons is quite careful to emphasize the distinction between the creature and the creator as in the following:

"Between the only begotten Son and the soul there is no distinction." This is true. For how could anything white be distinct from or divided from whiteness? Again, matter and form are one in being; living and working. Yet matter is not, on this account, form, or conversely. So in the proposition. A holy soul is one with God, according to John 17:21. That they all may be one in us, even as we are one. Still the creature is not the creator, nor is the just man God.

God and Godhead are as different as earth is from heaven. Moreover I declare: the outward and the inward man are as different, too, as earth and heaven. God is higher, many thousand miles. Yet God comes and goes. But to resume my argument: God enjoys himself in all things. The sun sheds his light upon all creatures, and anything he sheds his beams upon absorbs them, yet he loses nothing of his brightness. "

From this we can see most decidedly that Eckhart was far from being a pantheist. In this respect Mahayana Buddhism is also frequently and erroneously stamped as pantheistic, ignoring altogether a world of particulars. Some critics seem to be ready and simple-minded enough to imagine that all doctrines that are not transcendentally or exclusively monotheistic are pantheistic and that they are for this reason perilous to the advancement of spiritual culture. It is true that Eckhart insists on finding something of a Godlike nature in each one of us, otherwise the birth of God's only Son in the soul would be impossible and his creatures would forever be something utterly alienated from him.

As long as God is love, as creator, he can never be outside the creatures. But this cannot be understood as meaning the oneness of one with the other in every possible sense. Eckhart distinguishes between the inner man and the outer man and what one sees and hears is not the same as the other. In a sense therefore we can say that we are not living in an identical world and that the God one conceives for oneself is not at all to be subsumed under the same category as the God for another. Eckhart's God is neither transcendental nor pantheistic. God goes and comes, he works, he is active, he becomes all the time, but Godhead remains immovable, imperturbable, and inaccessible.

The difference between God and Godhead is that between heaven and earth and yet Godhead cannot be himself without going out of himself, that is, he is he because he is not he. This "contradiction" is comprehended only by the inner man, and not by the outer man, because the latter sees the world through the senses and intellect and consequently fails to experience the profound depths of Godhead. Whatever influence Eckhart might have received from the Jewish (Maimonides), Arabic (Avicenna), and Neoplatonic sources, there is no doubt that he had his original views based on his own experiences, theological and otherwise, and that they were singularly Mahayanistic. Coomaraswamy is quite right when he says:

> Eckhart presents an astonishingly close parallel to Indian modes of thought; some whole passages and many single sentences read like a direct translation from Sanskrit.... It is not of course suggested that any Indian elements whatever are actually present in Eckhart's writing, though there are some Oriental factors in the European tradition, derived from neo-Platonic and Arabic sources. But what is proved by analogies is not the influence of one system of thought upon another, but the coherence of the metaphysical tradition in the world and at all times.

It is now necessary to examine Eckhart's close kinship with Mahayana Buddhism and especially with Zen Buddhism in regard to the doctrine of Emptiness. The Buddhist doctrine of Emptiness is unhappily greatly misunderstood in the West. The word "emptiness" or "void" seems to frighten people away, whereas when they use it among themselves, they do not seem to object to it.

While some Indian thought is described as nihilistic, Eckhart has never been accused of this, though he is not sparing in the use of words with negative implications, such as "desert," "stillness," "silence," "nothingness." Perhaps when these terms are used among Western thinkers, they are understood in connection with their historical background. But as soon as these thinkers are made to plunge into a strange, unfamiliar system or atmosphere, they lose their balance and condemn it as negativistic or anarchistic or upholding escapist egoism.

According to Eckhart,

I have read many writings both of heathen philosophers and sages, of the Old and the New Testaments, and I have earnestly and with all diligence sought the best and the highest virtue whereby man may come most closely to God and wherein he may once more become like the original image as he was in God when there was yet no distinction between God and himself before God produced creatures. And having dived into the basis of things to the best of my ability I find that it is no other than absolute detachment (*abegescheidenheit*) from everything that is created. It was in this sense when our Lord said to Martha: "One thing is needed," which is to say: He who would be untouched and pure needs just one thing, detachment.

What then is the content of absolute detachment? It cannot be designated "as this or that," as Eckhart says. It is pure nothing (*bloss niht*); it is the highest point at which God can work in us as he pleases.

Perfect detachment is without regard, without either lowliness or loftiness to creatures; it has no mind to be below nor yet to be above; it is minded to be master of itself, loving none and hating none, having neither likeness nor unlikeness, neither this nor that, to any creature; the only thing it desires to be is to be one and the same. For to be either this or that is to want something. He who is this or that is somebody; but detachment wants altogether nothing. It leaves all things unmolested.

While Buddhist emphasis is on the emptiness of all "composite things" (*skandha*) and is therefore metaphysical, Eckhart here insists on the psychological significance of "pure nothingness" so that God can take hold of the soul without any resistance on the part of the individual. But from the practical point of view the emptying of the soul making it selfless can never be thoroughly realized unless we have an ontological understanding of the nature of things, that is, the nothingness of creaturely objects. For the created have no reality; all creatures are pure nothing, for "all things were made by him [God] and without him was not anything made" (John, 1:3).

Further, "If without God a creature has any being however small, then God is not the cause of all things. Besides, a creature will not be created, for creation is the receiving of being from nothing." What could this mean? How could any being come from nothing or non-being? Psychology herein inevitably turns to metaphysics. We here encounter the problem of Godhead.

This problem was evidently not touched upon frequently by Eckhart, for he warns his readers repeatedly, saying: "Now listen: I am going to say something I have never said before." Then he proceeds: "When God created the heavens, the earth, and creatures, he did no work; he had nothing to do; he made no effort." He then proceeds to say something about Godhead, but he does not forget to state: "For yet again I say a thing I never said before: God and Godhead are different as earth is from heaven."

Though he often fails to make a clear distinction between the two and would use "God" where really "Godhead" is meant, his attempt to make a distinction is noteworthy. With him God is still a something as long as there is any trace of movement or work or of doing something. When we come to the Godhead, we for the first time find that it is the unmoved, a nothing where there is no path (*apada*) to reach. It is absolute nothingness; therefore it is the ground of being from where all beings come.

While I subsisted in the ground, in the bottom, in the river and fount of Godhead, no one asked me where I was going or what I was doing: there was no one to ask me. When I was flowing all creatures spake God. If I am asked, Brother Eckhart, when went ye out of your house? Then I must have been in. Even so do all creatures speak God? And why do they not speak the Godhead? Everything in the Godhead is one, and of that there is nothing to be said. God works, the Godhead does no work, there is nothing to do; in it is no activity. It never envisaged any work. God and Godhead are as different as active and inactive. On my return to God, where I am formless, my breaking through will be far nobler than my emanation. I alone take all creatures out of their sense into my mind and make them one in me. When I go back into the ground, into the depths, into the well-spring of the Godhead, no one will ask me whence I came or whither I went. No one missed me: God passes away.

What would Christians think of "the divine core of pure (or absolute) stillness," or of "the simple core which is the still desert onto which no distinctions ever creep"? Eckhart is in perfect accord with the Buddhist doctrine of *úûnyata*, when he advances the notion of Godhead as "pure nothingness" (*ein bloss niht*). The notion of Godhead transcends psychology.

Eckhart tells us that he has made frequent references in his sermons to "a light in the soul that is uncreated" and that "this light is not satisfied by the simple still, motionless essence of the divine being that neither gives nor takes. It is more interested in knowing where this essence came from." This "where" is where "the Father, the Son, and the Holy Ghost" have not yet made their distinctions? To come in touch with this source and to know what it is, that is to say, "to see my own face even before I was born" I must plunge into "the vast emptiness of the Absolute Tao."

"To see one's face which one has even prior to his birth" is ascribed to Hui-nêng (Yeno, died 713), the sixth patriarch of Zen Buddhism in China. This corresponds to Eckhart's statement which he quotes as by "an authority": "Blessed are the pure in heart that leave everything to God now as they did before ever they existed." Those who have not tasted wine in the cellar may put in a question here: "How could we talk about a man's purity of heart prior to his existence? How could we also talk about seeing our own face before we were born?"

Eckhart quotes St. Augustine: "There is a heavenly door for the soul into the divine nature-where somethings are reduced to nothing." Evidently we have to wait for the heavenly door to open by our repeated or ceaseless knocking at it when I am "ignorant with knowing, loveless with loving, dark with light." "Everything comes out of this basic experience and it is only when this is comprehended that we really enter into the realm of emptiness where the Godhead keeps our discriminatory mind altogether "emptied out to nothingness."

What is the Absolute Tao? Before we go on to the Zen conception of the "Absolute Tao" or Godhead who sets itself up on "pure nothingness," it may be appropriate to comment on the Taoist conception of it as expounded by Lao-tzu. He was one of the early thinkers of China on philosophical subjects and the theme of the *Tao Tê Ching* ascribed to him is *Tao*. Tao literally means "way" or "road" or "passage," and in more than one sense corresponds to the Sanskrit Dharma. It is one of the key terms in the history of Chinese thought. While Taoism derives its name from this term, Confucius also uses it extensively. With the latter however it has a more moralistic than metaphysical connotation.

It is Taoists who use it in the sense of "truth," "ultimate reality," "logos," etc. Lao-tzu defines it in his *Tao Tê Ching* as follows:

> The Way is like an empty vessel
> That yet may be drawn from
> Without ever needing to be filled.
> It is bottomless: the very progenitor of
> all things in the world....
> It is like a deep pool that never dries
> I do not know whose child it could be.

It looks as if it were prior to God.

There is another and more detailed characterization of Tao in Chapter XIV:

When you look at it you cannot see it;
It is called formless.
When you listen to it you cannot hear it;
It is called soundless.
When you try to seize it you cannot hold it;
It is called subtle.
No one can measure these three to their ultimate ends,
Therefore they are fused to one.
It is up, but it is not brightened;
It is down, but it is not obscured.
It stretches endlessly,
And no name is to be given.
It returns to nothingness.
It is called formless form, shapeless shape.
It is called the intangible.
You face it but you cannot see its front.
You follow it but you cannot see its back.
Holding on to the Ancient Way (*Tao*)
You control beings of today.
Thus you know the beginning of things,
Which is the essence of the Way (*Tao-chi*).

When these quotations are compared with Eckhart's, we see points common to both. Lao-tzu is expressing in his classical Chinese way what the medieval Dominican preacher would talk about in his German vernacular. Lao-tzu is poetical and concrete, full of imageries, whereas Eckhart the theologian is more conceptual. He would say:

"God has no before or after."

"God is neither this nor that."

"God is perfect simplicity."

"Prior to creatures, in the eternal now, I have played before the Father in his eternal stillness."

For comparison I will give another definition for Tao from *Tao Tê Ching*, Chapter XXV:

There is something in a state of fusion,
It is born prior to heaven and earth.
How still! How lonely!
It stands by itself unchanging,
It moves about everywhere unfailingly.
Let us have it as mother [of all things] under the heavens.
I do not know its name,
But if needed call it Great.
The Great walks on,
Walks on to the farthest end,
And then returns.
Therefore the Tao is great,
Heaven is great,
Earth is great,
The ruler is great.
Within the realm there are four greats
And the ruler is one of them.
Man is earth when conforming to earth,
He is heaven when conforming to heaven,
He is Tao when conforming to Tao.
Let him thus conform himself to the suchness (*tzu jan*) of things.

R. B. Blakney remarks in his preface to the *Tao Tê Ching* translation that Lao-tzu's book fascinated him for many years and that he finally could not help producing his own translation in spite of the fact that there are already a large number of such translations available. He suspects that every foreigner who at all knows the Chinese language and can read Lao-tzu in the original would feel the same as this new translator did. This remark or confession on the part of the translator is highly significant. In my view the fascination he feels about Lao-tzu is not just due to the Old Philosopher's contribution to "the literature of mysticism," but partly to the language in which it is expressed.

It may be better to say that the charm one feels about Chinese literature comes quite frequently from visually going over those unwieldy ideogrammatic characters with which thoughts or feelings are made communicative. The Chinese books are best perused in large type printed from the wooden blocks. Besides this visual appeal of the ideograms there is an element in the Chinese language which, while rare in others, especially in Indo-European languages, expresses more directly and concretely what our ordinary conceptualized words fail to communicate.

For instance, read the *Tao Tê Ching*, Chapter XX, in the original and compare it with any of the translations you have at hand and see that the translations invariably lack that rich, graphic, emotional flavor which we after more than two thousand five hundred years can appreciate with deep satisfaction. Arthur Waley is a great Chinese scholar and one of the best interpreters of Chinese life. His English translation of Lao-tzu is a fine piece of work in many senses, but he cannot go beyond the limitations of the language to which he is born. The following story may not have historicity but it is widely circulated among Zen followers who are occasionally quite disrespectful of facts.

It is worth our consideration as illustrating the way in which the Zen teachers handle the problem of "Emptiness" or "absolute nothingness" or the "still desert" lying beyond "this and that" and prior to "before and after." The story and comments are taken from a Chinese Zen textbook of the Sung dynasty of the eleventh century. The text is studied very much in Japan and some of the stories are used as *kô-an* (problems given to Zen students for solution). Bodhidharma, who is the first Zen patriarch in China, came from India in the sixth century. The Emperor Wu of the Liang dynasty invited him to his court. The Emperor Wu, a good pious Buddhist studying the various Mahayana *Sûtras* and practicing the Buddhist virtues of charity and humility, asked the teacher from India: "The *Sûtras* refer so much to the highest and holiest truth, but what is it, my Reverend Master?"

Bodhidharma answered, "A vast emptiness and no holiness in it." The Emperor: "Who are you then who stand before me if there is nothing holy, nothing high in the vast emptiness of ultimate truth?" Bodhidharma: "I do not know, your Majesty." The Emperor failed to understand the meaning of this answer and Bodhidharma left him to find a retreat in the North. When Bodhidharma's express purpose of coming to China was to elucidate the teaching of "vast emptiness" (*úûnyata*), why did he answer "I do not know" to the Emperor's all-important and to-the-very-point question? It is evident; however, that Bodhidharma's answer could not have been one of an agnostic who believes in the unknowability of ultimate truth.

Bodhidharma's unknowability must be altogether of a different sort. It is really what Eckhart would like to see us all have-"transformed knowledge, not ignorance which comes from lack of knowing; it is by knowing that we get to this unknowing. Then we know by divine knowing, and then our ignorance is ennobled and adorned with supernatural knowledge." It was this kind of unknowing which is transcendental, divine, and supernatural that he wished his imperial friend to realize. From our ordinary relative point of view Bodhidharma may seem too abrupt and unacceptable. But the fact is that the knowledge or "I do not know" which is gained only by "sinking into oblivion and ignorance" is something quite abrupt or discrete or discontinuous in the human system of knowability, for we can get it only by leaping or plunging into the silent valley of Absolute Emptiness.

There is no continuity between this and the knowledge we highly value in the realm of relativity where our senses and intellect move. The Zen teachers are all unknowing knowers or knowing unknowers. Therefore their "I do not know" does not really mean our "I do not know." We must not take their answers in the way we generally do at the level of relative knowledge. Therefore, their comments which are quoted below do not follow the line we ordinarily do. They have this unique way. Yengo, (1063-1135) gives his evaluation of the *mondo* ("question and answer") which took place between Bodhidharma and the Emperor Wu of the Liang dynasty in the following words:

Bodhidharma came to this country, via the southern route, seeing that there was something in Chinese mentality which responds readily to the teaching of Mahayana Buddhism. He was full of expectations; he wanted to lead our countrymen to the doctrine of "Mind-alone" which cannot be transmitted by letters or by means of word of mouth. The Mind could only be immediately taken hold of whereby we attain to the perception of the Buddha-nature, that is, to the realization of Buddhahood. When the Nature is attained, we shall be absolutely free from all bondage and will not be led astray because of linguistic complications. For here Reality itself is revealed in its nakedness with no kinds of veil on it. In this frame of mind Bodhidharma approached the Emperor. He also thus instructed his disciples. We see that Bodhidharma's [emptied mind] had no premeditated measures, no calculating plans. He just acted in the freest manner possible; cutting everything asunder that would obstruct his seeing directly into the Nature in its entire nakedness. Here was neither good nor evil, neither right nor wrong, neither gain nor loss....

The Emperor Wu was a good student of Buddhist philosophy and wished to have the first principle elucidated by the great teacher from India. The first principle consists in the identity of being and non-being beyond which the philosophers fail to go. The Emperor wondered if this blockage could somehow be broken down by Bodhidharma. Hence his question. Bodhidharma knew that whatever answers he might give would be frustrating.

"What is Reality? What is Godhead?"

"Vast emptiness and no distinctions whatever [neither Father nor Son nor Holy Ghost]."

No philosopher however well trained in his profession could ever be expected to jump out of this trap, except Bodhidharma himself who knew perfectly well how to cut all limitations down by one blow of a sword. Most people nowadays fail to get into the ultimate signification of Bodhidharma's pronouncement and would simply cry out, "vast emptiness" as if they really experienced it. But all to no purpose! As my old master remarks, "When a man truly understands Bodhidharma, he for the first time finds himself at home quietly sitting by the fireside," Unfortunately, the Emperor Wu happened to be one of those who could not rise above the limitations of linguistics. His views failed to penetrate the screen of *meum* and *tuum* (you and me). Hence his second question: "Who are you who face me?" Bodhidharma's blunt retort, "I do not know," only helped make the august inquirer blankly stare.

Later, when he learned more about Bodhidharma and realized how stupid he was to have missed the rare opportunity of going deeper into the mystery of Reality, he was greatly upset. Hearing of Bodhidharma's death after some years he erected a memorial stele for him and inscribed on it: "Alas! I saw him, I met him, I interviewed him, and failed to recognize him. How sad! It is all past now. Alas, history is irrevocable!" He concluded his eulogy thus:

"As long as the mind tarries on the plane of relativity,

It forever remains in the dark.

But the moment it loses itself in the Emptiness,

It ascends the throne of Enlightenment."

After finishing the story of the Emperor Wu, Yengo the commentator puts this remark: "Tell me by the way where Bodhidharma could be located." This is expressly addressed to the readers and the commentator expects us to give him an answer. Shall we take up his challenge? There is another commentator on this episode, who lived some years prior to the one already referred to. This one, called Seccho (980-1052), was a great literary talent and his comments are put in a versified form full of poetic fantasies. Alluding to the Emperor Wu's attempt to send a special envoy for Bodhidharma, who after the interview crossed the Yangtzu Chiang and found a retreat somewhere in the North, the commentator goes on:

"You [the Emperor Wu] may order all your subjects to fetch him [Bodhidharma],

But he will never show himself up again!

We are left alone for ages to come

Vainly thinking of the irrevocable past.

But stop! Let us not think of the past!

The cool refreshing breeze sweeps all over the earth,

Never knowing when to suspend its work."

Seccho (the master commentator) now turns around and surveying the entire congregation (as he was reciting his versified comments), asks: "O Brethren, is not our Patriarch to be discovered among us at this very moment?" After this interruption, Seccho continues, "Yes, yes, be is here! Let him come up and wash the feet for me!" It would have been quite an exciting event if Eckhart appeared to be present at this session which took place in the Flowery Kingdom in the first half of the eleventh century! But who can tell if Eckhart is not watching me writing this in the most modern and most mechanized city of New York?

A few more remarks about "Emptiness."

Relativity is an aspect of Reality and not Reality itself. Relativity is possible somewhere between two or more things, for this is the way that makes one get related to another. A similar argument applies to movement. Movement is possible in time; without the concept of time there cannot be a movement of any sort. For a movement means an object going out of itself and becoming something else which is not itself. Without the background of time this becoming is unthinkable.

Therefore, Buddhist philosophy states that all these concepts, movement and relativity, must have their field of operation, and this field is designated by Buddhist philosophers as Emptiness (*úûnyata*). When Buddha talks about all things being transient, impermanent, and constantly changing, and therefore teaches that there is nothing in this world which is absolutely dependable and worth clinging to as the ultimate seat of security, he means that we must look somewhere else for things permanent (*jô*), bliss-imparting (*raku*), autonomous (*ga*), and absolutely free from defilements (*jô*).

According to the *Nirvana Sûtra* (of the Mahayana school), these four (*jô-raku-ga-jô*) are the qualities of *Nirvana*, and *Nirvana* is attained when we have knowledge, when the mind is freed from thirst (*tanha*), cravings (*asava*), and conditionality (*sankhara*). While *Nirvana* is often thought to be a negativistic idea the Mahayana followers have quite a different interpretation. For they include autonomy (*ga, atman)* as one of its qualities (*guna*), and autonomy is free will, something dynamic. *Nirvana* is another name for the Emptiness. The term "emptiness" is apt to be misunderstood for various reasons. The hare or rabbit has no horns; the turtle has no hair growing on its back. This is one form of emptiness. The Buddhist *úûnyata* does not mean absence.

A fire has been burning until now and there is no more of it. This is another kind of emptiness. Buddhist *úûnyata* does not mean extinction. The wall screens the room: on this side there is a table, and on the other side there is nothing, space is unoccupied. Buddhist *úûnyata* does not mean vacancy. Absence, extinction, and unoccupancy-these are not the Buddhist conception of emptiness. Buddhists' Emptiness is not on the plane of relativity. It is Absolute Emptiness transcending all forms of mutual relationship, of subject and object, birth and death, God and the world, something and nothing, yes and no, affirmation and negation.

In Buddhist Emptiness there is no time, no space, no becoming, no-thing-ness; it is what makes all these things possible; it is a zero full of infinite possibilities; it is a void of inexhaustible contents. Pure experience is the mind seeing itself as reflected in it; it is an act of self-identification, a state of suchness. This is possible only when the mind is *śûnyata* itself, that is, when the mind is devoid of all its possible contents except itself. But to say "except itself" is apt to be misunderstood again. For it may be questioned, what is this "itself"? We may have to answer in the same way as St. Augustine did: "When you ask, I do not know; but when you do not, I know."

The following dialogue w hich took place between two Zen masters of the T'ang dynasty will help show us what methodology was adopted by Zen for communicating the idea of "itself." One master called Isan (771-853) was working with his disciples in the garden, picking tea leaves. He said to one of the disciples in the garden called Kyôzan, who also was a master: "We have been picking the tea leaves all day; I hear your voice only and do not see your form. Show me your primeval form." Kyôzan shook the tea bushes. Isan said, "You just got the action, but not the body." Kyôzan then said, "What would be your answer?" Isan remained quiet for a while. Thereupon Kyôzan said, "You have got the body, but not the action." Isan's conclusion was, "I save you from twenty blows of my stick."

As far as Zen philosophy is concerned this may be all right, as these two masters know what each is seeking to reveal. But the business of philosophers of our modern epoch is to recognize or to probe the background of experience on which these Zen masters stand and try to elucidate it to the best of their capacity. The masters are not simply engaged in mystifying the bystanders. To say "empty" is already denying itself. But you cannot remain silent. How to communicate the silence without going out of it is the crux. It is for this reason that Zen avoids as much as possible resorting to linguistics and strives to make us go underneath words, as it were to dig out what is there.

Eckhart is doing this all the time in his sermons. He picks out some innocent words from the Bible and lets them disclose an "inner act" which he experiences in his unconscious consciousness. His thought is not at all in the words. He turns them into instruments for his own purposes. In a similar way the Zen master makes use of anything about himself including his own person, trees, stones, sticks, etc. He may then shout, beat, or kick. The main thing is to discover what is behind all these actions. In order to demonstrate that Reality is "Emptiness," the Zen master may stand still with his hands folded over his chest. When he is asked a further question, he may shake the tea plant or walk away without a word, or give you a blow of a stick.

Sometimes the master is more poetic and compares the mind of "emptiness" to the moon, calling it the mind-moon or the moon of suchness. An ancient master of Zen philosophy sings of this moon:

The mind-moon is solitary and perfect:

The light swallows the ten-thousand things.

It is not that the light illuminates objects,

Nor are objects in existence.

Both light and objects are gone,

And what is it that remains?

The master leaves the question unanswered. When it is answered the moon will no longer be there. Reality is differentiated and Emptiness vanishes into emptiness. We ought not to lose sight of the original moon, primeval mind-moon, and the master wants us to go back to this, for it is where we have started first. Emptiness is not a vacancy, it holds in it infinite rays of light and swallows all the multiplicities there are in this world. Buddhist philosophy is the philosophy of "Emptiness," it is the philosophy of self-identity.

Self-identity is to be distinguished from mere identity. In an identity we have two objects for identification; in self-identity there is just one object or subject, one only, and this one identifies itself by going out of itself. Self-identity thus involves a movement. And we see that self-identity is the mind going out of itself in order to see itself reflected in itself. Self-identity is the logic of pure experience or of "Emptiness." In self-identity there are no contradictions whatever. Buddhists call this suchness. I once talked with a group of lovers of the arts on the Buddhist teaching of "Emptiness" and Suchness, trying to show how the teaching is related to the arts.

The following is part of my talk. To speak the truth, I am not qualified to say anything at all about the arts, because I have no artistic instincts, no artistic education, and have not had many opportunities to appreciate good works of art. All that I can say is more or less conceptual. Take the case of painting. I often hear Chinese or Japanese art critics declare that Oriental art consists in depicting spirit and not form. For they say that when the spirit is understood the form creates itself; the main thing is to get into the spirit of an object which the painter chooses for his subject. The West, on the other hand, emphasizes form, endeavors to reach the spirit by means of form.

The East is just the opposite: the spirit is all in all. And it thinks that when the artist grasps the spirit, his work reveals something more than colors and lines can convey. A real artist is a creator and not a copyist. He has visited God's workshop and has learned the secrets of creation-creating something out of nothing. With such a painter every stroke of his brush is the work of creation, and it cannot be retraced because it never permits a repetition. God cannot cancel his fiat; it is final, irrevocable, it is an ultimatum. The painter cannot reproduce his own work. When even a single stroke of his brush is absolute, how can the whole structure or composition be reproduced, since this is the synthesis of all his strokes, every one of which has been directed toward the whole?

In the same way every minute of human life as long as it is an expression of its inner self is original, divine, creative, and cannot be retrieved. Each individual life thus is a great work of art. Whether or not one makes it a fine inimitable masterpiece depends upon one's consciousness of the working of *śûnyata* within oneself.

How does the painter get into the spirit of the plant, for instance, if he wants to paint a hibiscus as Mokkei (Mu-chi) of the thirteenth century did in his famous picture, which is now preserved as a national treasure at Daitokuji temple in Kyoto? The secret is to become the plant itself. But now can a human being turn himself into a plant? Inasmuch as he aspires to paint a plant or an animal, there must be in him something which corresponds to it in one way or another. If so, he ought to be able to become the object he desires to paint.

The discipline consists in studying the plant inwardly with his mind thoroughly purified of its subjective, self-centered contents. This means to keep the mind in unison with the "Emptiness" or Suchness, whereby one who stands against the object ceases to be the one outside that object but transforms him into the object itself.

This identification enables the painter to feel the pulsation of one and the same life animating both him and the object. This is what is meant when it is said that the subject is lost in the object, and that when the painter begins his work it is not he but the object itself that is working and it is then that his brush, as well as his arm and his fingers, become obedient servants to the spirit of the object. The object makes its own picture. The spirit sees itself as reflected in itself. This is also a case of self-identity.

It is said that Henri Matisse looked at an object which he intended to paint for weeks, even for months, until its spirit began to move him, to urge him, even to threaten him, to give it an expression. A writer on modern art, I am told, says that the artist's idea of a straight line is different from that of the mathematician, for the former conceives a straight line as fusing with a curve.

I do not know whether this quotation is quite correct, but the remark is most illuminating. For a straight line that remains always straight is a dead line and the curve that cannot be anything else is another dead line.

If they are at all living lines, and this ought to be the case with every artistic production, a straight line is curved and a curve is straight; besides there ought to be what is known as "dimensional tension" in every line. Every living line is not just on one plane, it is suffused with blood, and it is tridimensional.

Color with the artist is not just red or blue, it is more than perceptual, it is charged with emotion. This means that color is a living thing with the artist. When he sees red it works out its own world; the artist bestows a heart on the color. The red does not stop just at being one of the seven colors as decomposed through the prism. As a living thing it calls out all other colors and combines them in accordance with its inner promptings. Red with the artist is not a mere physical or psychological event; it is endowed with a spirit.

These views are remarkably Oriental. There is another striking statement made by a Western artist. According to him, when he is thoroughly absorbed in a visual perception of any kind, he feels within himself certain possibilities out of the visual representation which urge him to give them an expression.

The artist's life is that of the creator. God did not make the world just for the sake of making something. He had a certain inner urge, he wanted to see himself reflected in his creation. That is what is meant when the Bible speaks about God's making man after his own likeness. It is not man alone that is God's image, the whole world is his image, and even the meanest flea as Eckhart would say shares God's is-ness in its is-ness. And because of this is-ness the whole world moves on.

So with the artist. It is due to his is-ness being imbued into his works that they are alive with his spirit, The artist himself may not be conscious of all this proceeding, but Zen knows and is also prepared to impart the knowledge to those who would approach it in the proper spirit. The is-ness of a thing is not just being so, but it contains in it infinite possibilities which Buddhists call *tê* in Chinese, *toku* in Japanese, and guna in Sanskrit. This is where lies "the mystery of being," which is "the inexhaustibility of the Emptiness."

The following story of Rakan Osho (Lohan Hoshang), of Shôshu, China, who lived in the ninth century, is given here to illustrate how Zen transforms one's view of life and makes one truly see into the is-ness of things. The verse relates his experience. It was in the seventh year of Hsien-tung [867 A.D.] that I for the first time took up the study of the Tao [that is, Zen].

Wherever I went I met words and did not understand them.

A lump of doubt inside the mind was like a willow-basket.

For three years, residing in the woods by the stream, I was altogether unhappy.

When unexpectedly I happened to meet the Dharmaraja [Zen master] sitting on the rug,

I advanced towards him earnestly asking him to dissolve my doubt.

The master rose from the rug on which he sat deeply absorbed in meditation;

He then baring his arm gave me a blow with his fist on my chest.

This all of a sudden exploded my lump of doubt completely to pieces. p. 35

Raising my head I for the first time perceived that the sun was circular.

Since then I have been the happiest man in the world, with no fears, no worries;

Day in day out, I pass my time in a most lively way.

Only I notice my inside filled with a sense of fullness and satisfaction;

I do not go out any longer, hither and thither, with my begging bowl for food.

What is of the most significant interest in his verse-story of Rakan Osho's experience is that "he for the first time perceived that the sun was round." Everybody knows and sees the sun and the Osho also must have seen it all his life.

Why then does he specifically refer to it as circular as if he saw it really for the first time? We all think we are living, we really eat, sleep, walk, talk. But are we really? If we were, we would never be talking about "dread," "insecurity," "fear," "frustration," "courage to be," "looking into the vacant," "facing death."

7

Basis of Buddhist Philosophy

In both schools of Buddhism, the most important philosophical bases are the Four Noble Truths and Noble Eightfold Path. The Buddha encapsulated the nature and cause of human suffering in the Four Noble Truths, and the steps to eliminate suffering he formulated into the Noble Eightfold Path. All major schools of Buddhism accept these two essential teachings as the fundamental principles of Buddhism. The Four Noble Truths are as follows:

The first Noble Truth is 'Dukka'. The Buddha taught that everyone has suffering and unsatisfactoriness in their lives. This is inescapable, begins at birth, continues through ageing, and ends at death. Buddha deduced that most people would like to reduce the amount of suffering in their lives. In defining suffering, Buddha included birth, ageing, death, sickness, association with unpleasant people and conditions, wanting things that are not possessed, not wanting things that are possessed, separation from loved ones, grief, pain, distress and suffering from change when something an individual likes stops. He taught that before people can reduce and then eliminate suffering, they first need to understand how suffering begins, and this is described in the second Noble Truth.

The second Noble Truth is 'The Origin of Dukka'. Dukka originates from a "thirst" which can be seen as a combination of desire, craving and greed. In defining thirst, Buddha included many things, including a thirst for sense pleasures, that is, things that people enjoy consuming. A thirst for becoming something that the individual is not or for not being what they are. It is a desire for wealth and power for material things as well as for non-material things such as ideas, ideals, habits, opinions, beliefs and concepts. All of these things, Buddha taught, produce suffering in peoples lives. The more people are attached to these things, the more they suffer when they do not have them.

The third Noble Truth is 'The Cessation of Dukka'. To eliminate Dukka completely, Buddha taught that people have to eliminate the main root cause of Dukka, which is craving and attachment. The third Noble Truth is that well-being and the end of suffering is possible and obtainable. The fourth Noble Truth is 'The Path Leading to the Realization of *Nirvana*'. Buddha taught that there is a path that will lead to the end of suffering. It is called 'The Noble Eightfold Path', and it is based on ethical conduct, mental discipline and wisdom. The Noble Eightfold Path consists of cultivating ethical conduct, mental discipline and wisdom. It includes right speech, action, livelihood, effort, mindfulness, concentration, thought and understanding.

Ethical conduct is built on the concept of universal love for all living beings. For someone to practice ethical conduct, two qualities that should be developed equally are compassion and wisdom. Compassion represents love, charity, kindness and tolerance on an emotional level. Wisdom represents the same qualities on an intellectual level. Ethical conduct consists of practicing right speech, right action and right livelihood, and practicing them with compassion and wisdom. Right speech includes more than simply abstaining from lying. It also includes saying no words that will bring about enmity, no harsh, rude, malicious or abusive language, and no gossip.

Right Action includes moral, peaceful and honorable conduct. This includes abstaining from destroying life, from stealing, from dishonest dealings or actions that will harm another person and Right Livelihood concerns abstaining from making a living through a profession that brings harm to others. This would include trading in or manufacturing weapons and poisons, killing animals, and work that involves cheating or tricking other people. Mental discipline is the section of the Noble Eightfold Path concerning meditation. Meditation aims to cleanse the mind of hatred, worries, restlessness, attachment to sense pleasures and ideas, of greed, craving and desire. It aims at producing a peaceful mind based in equilibrium and tranquility. Meditation achieves this by keeping the mind in the present moment as opposed to worrying about or speculating about past memories or regrets, or daydreaming about desires in the future.

Meditation can be practiced at all times by being aware of thoughts and actions. Mental discipline consists of practicing right effort, right mindfulness and right concentration. Right Effort is the will to prevent unwholesome states of mind from arising, and getting rid of unwholesome states of mind that have already arisen. Furthermore, to produce wholesome states of mind not yet arisen, and to perfect wholesome states of mind that already exist.

Right Mindfulness is to be aware of all activities that involve the body, feelings, sensations, thoughts, ideas, and conceptualizations and to be aware of all of these whether they are pleasant, unpleasant or neutral. Right Concentration is the determination not to become absorbed in or think about anger, hatred, laziness, worry or lustful desires.

The remaining factors, right thought and right understanding constitute wisdom. Right thought includes selfless renunciation, and thoughts of love and non-violence. Therefore, lack of wisdom is selfishness, ill will, hatred and violence. Right Understanding implies understanding the true nature of things without name or label. This is only possible when the mind is free from desire, attachment and greed. According to the Buddha, by following these precepts, an individual can at least reduce the amount of suffering that they encounter in their lives, and at best, attain enlightenment. Enlightenment is the realization of the true nature of the world.

'Buddhist' peculiar to or originated from the Teaching of the Buddha, in the manifold forms it assumes, all however relating back to the same fundaments. It will be more difficult to give a definition or even a description of the term 'Philosophy'. It is however very clear that 'philosophy' in its Western (viz. Greco-Christian) context shows a different 'content' than that in the East (predominantly Indian and/or Chinese). From almost every definition of philosophy it goes to show that Western philosophy centers on the question of 'being', the 'first (or last) cause' and the 'absolute'. It tries to find an explanation, analyzes the experiential data and attempts to develop dialectic around it.

Western philosophy then will be mainly concerned with metaphysics, and especially with ontological questions. Another facet of Western philosophy (and mysticism) is that it places itself outside the realm of religion, even in those cases where its use lies in giving a coherent structure to religion (viz. Scholasticism). In the East, philosophy endeavors towards a coherent scheme around which multiple soteriological practices can be weighed, evaluated and structured. The search here is not the search for an explanation (the why-question) but for efficiency (the how-question). It is not so much the 'absolute truth' that counts, but the effectiveness of a given system or practice.

It is therefore not the question of 'being' but the question of 'knowledge and knowing' (epistemology versus ontology) (viz. Wisdom) that will be the center of philosophical thought in the East. There is the search for understanding the connections and inter-relationships between phenomena and the ability to express them.

It is an attempt to translate the non-conceptual (meditative or mystical) into concepts and words, with the clear purpose of describing the salvific process or way to liberation (Enlightenment or *Nirvana*...), without however confusing the 'description' with the 'described'. Emphasis therefore is put on psychology and epistemology as the basis for the development of a soteriology.

Thus, there is no search for the 'absolute' as there is in the West, but an uninterrupted input of relativism and self-critique. It is therefore the religious aspect that is dominant, integrating both philosophy and mysticism. A non-religious philosophy, while characteristic for the West, is conceived as impossibility in the Eastern context. Even Confucianism, with its initial rejection of all things supernatural takes into account the concept of Heaven (T'ien) and its Virtue (working or effectiveness).A Buddhist 'philosophy' will make no exception to this rule.

FUNDAMENTS OF BUDDHISM

The basic principles of the Teaching of the Buddha are found within the Four Noble Truths:

- The Universality of Suffering
- The Cause of Suffering
- The Cessation of Suffering
- The Way that leads to the Cessation of Suffering

(1) and (2) are situated mainly on the psychological level of the world of experience. Both the 'inner' and 'outer' world is seen as nothing more than a representation of the mind. Our knowledge originates in the subject. Not the world is illusory, but the glasses through which I see the world makes that the world as it appears to me is an ego-illusion. If one looks at the meaning of these Four Noble Truths, one comes to the conclusion that the first three Noble Truths point to a theoretical model in which (1) can be taken as consensual, generally acceptable and not necessarily Buddhist; while (2) and (3) are causal: (2) as the cause of suffering, and (3) as the cause of the cessation of suffering. Truth (4) on the contrary is typically Buddhist in its referral to praxis.

The concept 'suffering' is usually misinterpreted, due to a Christian or materialistic point of view. The term 'duhkha', although mostly translated as 'suffering' reaches much further than our ordinary conception of the term suffering: it implies not just our bodily or social torments or vexations, but also -

and primarily so - our mental torments. Therefore duhkha would be better described as 'universal unsatisfactoriness' or 'dissatisfaction with the existing situation'. In a certain sense we can also consult philosophers from the West for possible 'better' translations of duhkha. John Locke 1 (1632-1704) speaks of 'uneasiness', thereby remarking that this is the basic feeling, the drive behind every thought or action of humanity. Also found are terms such as 'Unerfülltheit' etc. It is through the use of these, that the term 'suffering' can be taken out of its physical-material context.

In a certain sense we could look upon the Buddhist concept of 'suffering' as being the interval, the distance between the existentially experienced and our expectations, on the one hand 'desire' and 'attachment', on the other hand fear:

Suffering here, does not belong to the sphere of salvation or enlightenment - as is often the case in other religions but is a characteristic of the existential world in which existence unfolds. This 'suffering' stands loose from the sphere of *nirvana*: this becomes clear although paradoxically expressed in the *'Heart-Sutra'* ("Here, there is no suffering, no cause of suffering, no cessation of suffering, no path that leads to the cessation of suffering.").

Duhkha indeed is one of the universal characteristics of that which exists, viz. the 'experienced'. As the locus typicus goes:

- All forms of existence are characterized by suffering;
- All forms of existence are characterized by impermanence;
- All elements of existence are characterized by non-self.

The distinction between 'forms of existence' and 'elements of existence' is of the utmost importance. All 'things' or 'beings' are compound: these are the 'forms' that existence takes on. (*Samskara* = compound).This 'compound' is characterized by its composing elements or components (dharma = principle, basic principle, characteristic...). If one would use the example of computer science as a metaphor, one could picture a dharma as corresponding to a unit of communication (bit) or a unit of transmission (baud). *Samskara* than would correspond with a 'message' or 'data'.

Both samskara and dharma have in fact a multitude of meanings that are not always clearly distinguishable. The Monier-Monier Williams Sanskrit-English Dictionary for example gives the following lemma for 'samskara': "...the faculty of memory, mental impression or recollection, impression on the mind of acts done in a former state of existence. Buddh: mental conformation or creation of the mind (such as that of the external world, regarded by it as real though actually non-existent...". In the Pali Text Society Dictionary on the other hand we read for the same lemma:

- Aggregate of the conditions or essential properties of a given process or result e.g. the essentials or 'elements' of anything; - essential conditions, antecedents or synergy (co-ordinated activity), mental coefficients, requisite for act, speech, thought.
- One of the five khandhas, or constitutional elements of physical life..."

'Suffering' is unavoidable since all 'things' are impermanent (not-remaining = Skt. *anitya*). This impermanence has given rise to a lot of esthetical expressions such as the inevitable withering of a flower, or morning dew, etc. Often this theme of impermanence is emotionally interpreted as the 'transitory nature of all things' through which a sense of doom is evoked, e.g. in poetry. Yet anitya should be understood as objectively neutral: if things where 'doomed' to perish or to disappear, than enlightenment would not be a possibility. Even impermanence can become a factor of enlightenment! Besides this it is clear that every change in a 'subject' at the same time means a change in the experienced 'object'. In this way anitya in fact becomes a universal experience.

Things are impermanent because there can be no 'permanent' substance ('soul', '*atman* ', 'self', 'ego'). The 'elements of existence' (dharma) - and therefore also the 'forms of existence' which are composed by these elements - are 'self-less' (P. *anatta*). All that exists (the world of experience) is self-less, without self, without permanence, without absoluteness. This is the main criterion of the Teaching of the Buddha.

But: if there is no 'self', than who is it that suffers? That which we call an 'individual', a 'personality', 'ego' or 'psyche', is in fact no more than a convergence of events, impulses, thought constructions, volitional actions, etc. In short, all that is conventionally understood under the term "mental activity". This collection (khandha, skandha) has no permanent substance or essence (*atman*). Just as no permanent 'house-entity' is found in a constructed house, in the same way no permanent 'entity' can be found within the different forms of existence including sentient beings. This compound nature of the forms of existence explains not only their impermanence but also their 'artificiality', their com-positeness (together + to put) (sam-skri), their polymer character.

The term 'samskara' has, as was mentioned before, a lot of meanings that can not be confused with one another. Each of these possible meanings however point to a compound nature, an aggregate; yet, the context in which the term is used can differ. Therefore it is necessary to make a clear distinction between its different uses: e.g. samskara is used to denote the fourth of the five skandha's (aggregates) in which case the connotations of 'karma' and 'will or volition' will be determining. When it is used as the second link of the pratitya samutpada (dependent co-origination), the emphasis will be put on the dynamic that runs from a (past) volitional action towards its (future) result, the fruit which conditions a future mental situation.

Every momentous 'being' is a compound of a series of ever-changing and impermanent aggregates called the 'five aggregates' (*pañca-skandha*).

- *Rupa*: form, corporeality
- *Vedana*: feeling, perception
- *Sanna*: cognition, conception

- *Samskara*: volition, karma-formations
- *Vijñana*: consciousness, discrimination

How difficult it is to give a proper translation or even an approach of these terms becomes apparent from the multitude of (sometimes contradictory) translations. These five skandha's are stages of perception, cognition and volition. They are NOT ontological elements. They give an approach of the mental process that is active in the 'psyche'. We thus can look upon them as psychological/epistemological elements.It would therefore be wrong to consider each of these skandha's as an 'entity', a 'being'. Not only are they compound (ad infinitum), they also can not exist by themselves but only in relation to and in function of the other skandha's. They are therefore without substance and without autonomy, the two prerequisites for the so-called *'atman '*. Thus there is no *'atman '*. Or to state it more clearly: concentrating on or around the idea of an *atman* is (according to Buddhist thought) an inefficient thought-error. Buddhism in all its forms and aspects is an-*atman* (*anatta*): non-self.

This strict norm is the main criterion to separate things Buddhist from things non-Buddhist.Further: the fivefold classification of the personality into skandha's and the twelve-fold classification of karmic existence (see later) are not a "scientific neurological or neuro-psychological" analysis and make no statements concerning an objective, anatomical reality. We are to look upon these classifications as empirical 'expedient means' (*upaya*) used to gain an insight into the process which leads from an 'existence characterized by suffering' (*samsara*) to a state of 'non-suffering' (*nirvana*). We are therefore clearly dealing with a soteriological methodology and not with mere psychological data or metaphysical statements.

The illusion to have or to be an *atman* - or even to take it into consideration - is the deep origin of suffering. Suffering comes to an end through the destruction of the *atman* -delusion (*avidya* = ignorance, mis-conception). This delusion leads to desire (*trisna*, P. *tanha* = thirst) and hatred (*dosa* = aversion), out of which the whole world of dissatisfaction or unsatisfactoriness, in short 'duhkha' comes into existence. The term 'desire, thirst' should not be interpreted to narrow, in the sense of merely emotional or psychological. Desire encompasses 'all beings'. So for instance we could say that 'the heart desires to beat' seeing that this is the hearts necessary function. We can even speak of a certain 'cosmic' desire, e.g. as is seen in the mutual attraction of two masses (Newton's Law). Seen as such, desire is not only the motive or drive of the individual, it can also be transposed to a collectivity, yes even cosmically as the drive or the motive of the universe.

This all leads us to conclude that 'suffering' has its origin in 'desire', which in its turn has its source in 'ignorance'. To often however this is interpreted as "my suffering has its origin in my desire which in its turn finds its source in my ignorance". Such an expression leads to irrelevant questions concerning e.g. the suffering of innocent children. This mistaken shifting of emphasis is based on the input of the concept of 'mine' there where 'it' is meant. The reduction to individuality is in contradiction with the presupposition of *anatman* or 'no-self' and leads to a methodological incoherence. In our discussion of causality we should continuously take this into account with every step in our train of thought. This makes that the Third and Fourth Noble Truths should consequently be interpreted in a purely soteriological and pragmatic (i.e. effective) way. A further consequence of the *anatman* -idea is than that all concepts, all ideas, all forms of thought are anatman, and therefore have no absolute or adequate sense, i.e. they can only be understood as being relative (i.e. in relation to).

Further: *anatman* is also applied to *anatman,* meaning even anatman is relative: it is only a form of expression in which the content is relative, interchangeable, and impermanent. From this the concept of 'emptiness' (*sunyata*) originated. However, also the concept of sunyata is a mere concept.....therefore..... Buddhist philosophy than will primarily be an epistemology, a philosophy of knowing and Buddhist soteriology will be wisdom of knowing: seeing things as they are in se, in their emptiness, and not as they appear to our existential consciousness. In relation to this we could mutatis mutandis point to an analogy with "Gestalt Psychology", which has phenomenological data (Gegebenheiten) as its basis. "We do not perceive the world as it is, but as we are." The 'perceiver' organizes his/her own world of experience out of or around his/her own attitude.

To give a structure or a soteriological efficiency to such "emptiness-thinking", we can make use of several keys or paradigms with which we can solve the apparent unacceptability's or paradoxes. Most used in relation hereto are:

1. The logical tetralemma, which forms the basis of the Buddhist four-fold logic:
   a. A is
   b. A is not
   c. A is, and is not
   d. A neither is, nor is not

   In which the final and definitive emphasis is put on (d.). Where paradoxes occur (e.g. in the question of self/no-self) the thought process should - if possible - extend to the fourth lemma (d.) i.e. "neither self, nor no-self".
2. The threefold level in relation to 'person', based on a centrifugal perspective:
   a. Personal
   b. Transpersonal
   c. Impersonal

Kant already knew that Buddhists do not believe in a creator and ruler of the universe who judges men after death, for he writes : "They reject the idea of divine providence, but they teach that vices are punished and virtues are recompensed by a fatal necessity" Kant did not yet know anything about the Buddhist doctrine of Karma and Rebirth, and his philosophy has in no way been influenced by Buddhist ideas., But the doctrine of metempsychosis appealed to him in several periods of his life Even a short time before his death, when asked by his friend hasse about the future of the individual after death Kant expressed himself in favour of the doctrine of transmigration.

On another occasion he called it one of the most attractive teachings of Oriental philosophy. He himself taught a pre - existence of the soul before man is born and he was of opinion that after death man has to continue his way to perfection in infinite progress. His ideas have. Therefore, in this point much in common with Buddhism. Kant lived at a time when Buddhist texts had not yet been studied and translated by European scholars. It was only after his death that English and French scholars began to occupy themselves with the Buddhist scriptures.

In contradistinction to Kant the German philosophers of the beginning of the nineteenth century were better informed about Buddhist philosophy. Thus we find with Schelling and Hegel some more detailed remarks on Buddhism and in later times with Nietzsche and many other philosophers. An enthusiastic admirer of the great religion of the East was Arthur Schopenhauer (1788 - 1860). Since he was introduced to Indian Wisdom as a young man of 26 years of age until his death at the age of 72 he read almost every book published on Buddhism and came to the conviction that Buddha together with Plato and Kant was of the three great illuminators of the world. He was much influenced by Buddhist thought in framing his own system of metaphysics.

He believed in a strong conformity of his doctrine with that of the Buddha. So he wrote: "If I were to take the results of my philosophy as a yardstick for the truth, I would concede to Buddhism the Preeminence of all religions of the world. In any case I can be happy to see that my teaching is in such great harmony wigh a religion which has the greatest number of adherents on earth". There are indeed, many points in which the German philosopher agrees with Buddhists; they both deny the existence of a personal God, they teach that neither a beginning nor an end of the cosmic process can be established. They both assume the existence of a plurality of world systems; they see no essential but only a gradual difference between men and animals and are therefore ardent advocates of the protection of animals against cruelty.

They do not believe in permanent immortal souls and metempsychosis, but in a rebirth caused by the will (sankara) which manifests itself in the doings of the previous existence. They both acknowledge a moral law (dharma) as the moving factor in the universe. Though they both have a pessimistic outlook on life, they are optimistic in so far, as they are both convinced of the possibility of liberation from the trammels of existence. Just as for Buddha so for Schopenhauer too the state of deliverance cannot be explained with the help of terms and words belonging to our world of phenomena. Schopenhauer's system being an original and independent outcome of his own thinking it differs, of course, in many other points, from Buddhism. This partly finds its reason in the fact that at the time of Schopenhauer Buddhism was not yet sufficiently known in Europe.

Schopenhauer was the greatest herald of Buddhist wisdom, ever arisen among the philosophers of the western world. His works had a deep influence on many other thinkers rendering them in their turn, very keen on studying the sacred writings of the Buddhist faith at least in translations. A remarkable witness of the over whelming impression that Buddhism made on him are the following words of a great musician, the famous composer Richard Wagner (1813 – 1883). He wrote: "Buddha's teaching is such a grand view of life that every other one must seem rather small when compared to it, The philosopher with his deepest thoughts, the scientist with his largest results, the artist with his most extravagant imaginations, the man with the most open heart for everything that breathes and suffers they'll find their unlimited abode in this wonderful and in comparable conception of the world."

It is an uncontested fact that Buddhism has played a very prominent role in the realm of Indian Philosophy during the one thousand five hundred years of its existence on the sub - continent. Not only because it produced a great variety of metaphysical systems many of which belong to the most elaborate and sublime ones which the fertile Indian mind has ever created. But the contribution of Buddhism is still greater. Through its very existence it has compelled the Brahmanic and Jaina Philosophers to defend their teachings and to improve and remodel them. The discussions kindled by the struggle waged between Buddhist philosophy of permanent flux and the Upanishadic philosophy of unchangeable being have raised Indian metaphysical thought to that high level which has gained it the admiration of the world.

Since the celebrated passage in *Majjhima Nikaya* 22 where Buddha argues controversially against the doctrine of the Vedanta, and Kathaka Upanishad 4, 14, where the Brahmins reject the Buddhist theories of Dharmas, the antagonism between Vedanta and Buddhism permeates the whole history of Indian philosophy, just as the fight between the conception of the world of Heraclitus and Parmenides dominates Greek philosophy.

As so often in similar cases, each of the two opponents has learned much from the other and taken over some of his ideas. To my mind the monistic Mahayana shows the deep influence which Vedanta has exerted on later Buddhism. On the other hand the lofty idealism of Yogavasishta, of Gaudapada and Shankara are indebted to Nagarjuna's and Asanga's theories on the unreality of the world.

But the contribution of Buddhism to philosophical thought is not confined to India. Buddhism has been the ariginator and promoter of philosophy in many countries that had not yet developed a philosophy of their own when the doctrine of the Buddha reached them. Buddhism has stimulated the inteligentsia in Ceylon, Burma, Siam, Kamboja, and Laos, in Korea, Japan, Tibet and Mongolia to philosophical endeavours. In China, too, which already possessed a philosophy of a high level Buddhism has greatly developed the indigenous metaphysical thought. It is well known that Taoism, at least in its later phases, has been influenced by Buddhist theories. But also Confucianism is indebted to it. It seems to me that the founder of the Neo-Confucianist school, the celebrated Chu

His (1130 - 1200), though a staunch opponent of Buddhism, much learned has therefrom. And Idealists such as Shao Yung (1011 - 1077) and Wans Yangmtn (1472 - 1528) have deeply drawn from the fountain of Mahayana.

Buddhism having had such an enormous direct and indirect influence on philosophical thought in the whole of Southern and Eastern Asia proves that it must have appealed in a high degree to Asian mentality. It is noteworthy that in contradistinction to the overwhelming importance Buddhism has had in the East, it has till now not been able to fertilize in a comparable way thought in the West. The reason for this fact may have been that its sublime doctrines were not easy to understand for Westerners, though the emperor Ashoka had already sent missions to the Greek kings. As far as our present knowledge goes it was only gradually that Buddhism unveiled its essence to the Occident. The Greeks already knew of the name of Buddha. They also knew of his supernatural birth and they were aware of the fact that the Samanaioi (sramana) were different from the brahmanical ascetics.

In the middle Ages the story of Buddha's leaving His home was known in the Christianized form of the legend of Barlam and Josaphat. Marco Polo (1254 - 1323), the famous Italian traveller, paid his tributes to the saintly life of Gautama when he wrote in his Travel Diary: "Ilec fist moult grans adbstinences, ainsi comme s'Il eust este crestien. Car s'il l'eust este. Il feust un grand saint avecnotre Seigneur Jhesucrist, a la bonne vie et honneste qu'il mena" "He lived a life of grand abstinence as if he had been a Christian. For had he been. He would have been a great saint with our Lord jesus Christ, considering the good and honest life he led".

The first European I know of who mentions an important doctrine of Buddhism which distinguishes it from the other great religions of the world was the French traveller la Loubere, who wrote in his work "Du Royaume de Siam", Published in 1691, "I think that one can establish that the Buddhists do not believe in a world - ruling deity". We are indebrted to the great English indologist Henry Thomas

Colebrooke for the first interpretation of the Buddhist theory that there is no transmigrating soul but nevertheless a rebirth caused by karmic influences. In the lecture "On Indian Sectaries", read at a public meeting of the Royal Asiatic Society, February 3, 1827, he said; there is not an eternal soul, but merely succession of thought attended with individual consciousness abiding within body".

Colebrooke also explained the 'concatenation of causes and effects" which link one existence with another. Though many European scholars have dealt with this crucial point of Buddhist metaphysics it took many years of investigation before the true basis of this doctrine was elucidated. The two Russian Scholars Theodore Stcherbatsky and his pupil Otto Rosenberg have shown that the doctrine of the "dharmas', ie. Impersonal soul forces, is the central philosophical conception which is at the bottom of all Buddhist philosophical thought. The great Belgian Indologist La Valle Poussin has dealt more minutely with the probleam in his magnificent translation of Vasubandhu's Abhidharma - kosha. We understand now why the celebrated stanza 'Ye dharmah hetuprabhavah" is the credo of all Buddhists.

It is to be regretted that most European indologists in former times have continued to occupy themselves with the doctrines of living Buddhism as they have been taught for over at least 2000 years than with speculations on the doctrine that the Buddha may have taught. Many of these scholars have tried to show that Buddha's own doctrine differed greatly from the doctrines that today form the basis of all Buddhist philosophy. It seems to me very improbable that Buddha was no philosopher at all, as some scholars think.

For in a time in which as the texts show a very highly developed philosophical life was going on in Ancient India, Buddha would not have been able to win adherents from the philosophically trained Brahmans and Kshatriyas if He had not propounded a doctrine which could hold its own in view of hairsplitting dialectics of materialists, agnostics, sceptics and the very elaborate systems of Brahmans and Jains.

Other scholars are of opinion that Buddha's teaching was a special form of Vedanta and that the monks later on changed it to its present form, I do not think that this is probable. For to maintain this assertion it would be necessary to show in detail how the anatma - doctrine of the Buddhists has developed out of the alleged atmadoctrine of the Buddha It will not do to quote some sayings of the Buddha unconnected with their context and to interpret them in the said manner. Nor is it to be understood that on the one side the texts at our disposal should be so reliable that the so - called true original Vedantic doctrine of the Buddha may be surmised therefrom, and that at the same time they should be so unreliable that most of their metaphysical contents have been fabricated by the monks of a later time.

Nor do I understand what necessity there may have been for the Buddha to teach a particular new doctrine, when it was only a re-hash of the Upanishadic teachings of His time. One may ask with Professor T.R.V. Murti in his excellent book on the Madhyamika system "If the *atman* had been a cardinal doctrine with Buddhism. Why was it so securely hidden under a bushel that even the immediate followers of the Master had no inkling of it?"

In my opinion from the point of view of objective scholarship we may acknowledge that the real doctrine of the Buddha cannot be ascertained today because we do not possess manuscripts from his own hand nor were his teachings taken down on records. All we know of Him was taken down in writing only four centuries after His *Nirvana*. If we cannot ascertain with absolute certainty the original doctrine of the Buddha we may ask: what may it most predecessor of what all Buddhists of to day agree in.

I can see two reasons for the Vedantic explanation of Buddha's teachings. One is an emotional one: the Vedantist has the natural endeavour to harmonize the teachings of the great Gautama with a system which he thinks to be the most sublime in the world. I myself having written several works on Vedanta have the greatest esteem for it. I consider Vedanta to be one of the most grandiose philosophical conceptions ever originated in the world of thought. But this admiration for the Vedanta does not carry me, as an historian of Indian Philosophy, so far as to interpret Vedantic ideas into the Buddhist texts.

The other reason why many scholars have tried to interpret the teachings of the Buddha in a Vedantic fashion is one of a view of history. It is an undoubted duty of an investigator of the history of Indian thought to show the dependence of every new system on older ones proceeding. It had to trace its very roots to contemporary ideas. Now there is no possible doubt that the sublime teachings of the Upanishads were in existence before Buddha. As Buddha's *Nirvana i*n some respect resembles the Brahma of the Vedanta it seems plausible to believe that Buddha was a sort of Vedantist. But this, In my opinion, is a delusion For Buddha's *Nirvana* is in no way like the Brahma, the absolute being which is the very foundation of the world, or out of which everything that is has developed and came to existance.

It is only that *nirvana* is a state of peace, of rest, of calm in which is may be compared to one of the aspects of the Brahma. Butthere are many different systems in the world the ultimate aim of which is such a state of redemption. But the several systems as such differ widely from advita Vedanta because they have a theistic basis, as the Mohammedan and Christian mysticism, or as Jainism. Which denies the existence of a world - ruling deity? For this reason the reference to Vedanta carries no weight. One may, of course, argue that a similar need, or requirement, is deeply rooted in many religious minds, but there is neither a necessity nor a possibility to trace all kinds of quietism to the same source.

There is yet another deliberation which speaks against the exclusive dependence of Buddha's teachings on that of the Upanishads. The Buddhism of the Theravadins and all the older schools is a pluralistic system. Now a pluralistic interpretation of the world was very common in Magadha, for Jainism was spreading there just at Buddha's time. As far as I know nobody has ever tried to deduce Jainism from the Upanishads or to interpret its doctrine in a Vedantic manner. I cannot therefore see any reasonable ground for assuming that Buddhism must have sprung from an Upanishadic fountain. In my work on the stages of development of Indian thought published in 1940 I have tried to trace the Buddhistic dharma - theory to antecedents in the Vedic time For the Brahmanas and the Vedic texts teach a pluralism of substantial factors which have a strong similarity to Buddhist Dharmas.

For in that remote period of Indian thought qualities such as love, hatred, knowledge, etc. were considered as substances which had their own quasi - independent existence, and were not regarded as inherent in any substance. Of course by this I do not mean that the dharmas of Buddhism are in any way identical with these archaic concepts of the epoch of the Brahmana texts. Between the comparatively primitive and crude concepts of this archaic mode of thinking the highly refined means of the Buddha there lay centuries of philosophical development. It may be that between these two periods other thinkers were active in shaping and perfecting these ideas and in this respect the Buddhist doctrine that there were Buddhas before Gautama may not be without foundation.

8

Buddhism of Faith and Devotion

Faith is an important constituent element of the teachings of the Buddha for all traditions of Buddhism, though the kind and nature of faith changes in the different schools. According to receive tradition, some of the first words which the Buddha 'voiced' after resolving to teach Dharma where:

"Wide opened is the door of the Immortal to all who have ears to hear; let them send forth faith [*saddha*] to meet it."

THE TREASURE, FACULTY AND POWER OF FAITH

The Pali *suttas* (scriptures) list faith as one of the Seven Treasures (*dhanas*), one of the five "spiritual faculties" (*indriyas*), one of the four "streams of merit", and one of the "spiritual powers" (*balas*). Gyatrul (b.1924), in a purport to the work of Chagmé (Wylie: karma-chags-med, fl. 17th century), rendered into English by Wallace, states:

By the power of faith, we are able to eliminate the two types of obscurations. Through the power of faith both ontological and phenomenological knowledge arises. It is also by the power of faith that both the common and uncommon *siddhis* arise.

KALAMA SUTTA

In the Kalama Sutta, Sakyamuni Buddha demonstrates "blind faith" based upon authority, tradition or specious reasoning. When a person decides to give up domestic life and live as a monk or nun, it is said to be out of faith "through faith in the Lord". First comes the 'hearing' of Dharma and then the aspirant follows the Dharma teachings and instructions on faith, reflecting upon the value of its application.

Faith is primarily faith in the Buddha himself as the Teacher of supreme spiritual realization and accomplishment. The Buddha extols such faith as befitting a "noble" Buddhist disciple:

"The ariyan [noble] disciple is of faith; he has faith in the Awakening of the Tathagata [Buddha], and thinks: He is indeed Lord, perfected one, fully Self-Awakened One, endowed with right knowledge and conduct, well-farer, knower of the world(s), matchless charioteer of men to be tamed, teacher of devas [gods] and men, the Awakened One, the Lord."

Such faith, it is said, can lead towards Liberation. Indeed, a person who is "released by faith" can well, in consequence, be "on the path to arahantship" (spiritual adeptship). It is for such reasons that faith is stated by the Buddha to be appropriate as "a person's partner" and to be "a man's best treasure". The Buddha even quotes with evident approval the god Sakka's Dharma-charged words:

... faith in the Tathagata

unshakable and well established...

... the person of intelligence,

remembering the Buddha's Teaching,

should be devoted to faith and virtue,

to confidence and vision of the Dhamma [Dharma].

ANANDA AND VAKKALI

Two disciples of Buddha in the Theravada canon exemplify faith in Buddha – Ananda and Vakkali. The power of visionary faith over skepticism is exemplified in An 3.8, a passage which more closely resembles in tone and quality many of the later Mahayana sutras. Buddha extols Ananda over the skeptic Udayi when Ananda is awed and overwhelmed by the power of the Buddha, "Ananda had asked the Blessed One how far his voice would reach in the universe. The Lord had answered that the Enlightened Ones were immeasurable and could reach further than a thousandfold world system (with a thousand suns, a thousand heavens, and a thousand brahma worlds), even further than a three-thousandfold world system. They could penetrate all those worlds with their shining splendor and reach all beings living there with their voice.

Ananda was delighted with this description, so all-encompassing and transcending all horizons, and he exclaimed: "How fortunate I am, that I have such an almighty, powerful master!" Udayi objected: "What good does it do to you brother Ananda, that your master is almighty and powerful?" The Buddha immediately took sides with Ananda with the following words:

"Not so, Udayi, not so, Udayi! Should Ananda die without being fully liberated; he would be king of the gods seven times because of the purity of his heart, or be king of the Indian subcontinent seven times. But Udayi, Ananda will experience final liberation in this very life."

Vakkali Thera was considered one of the Chief Arahants who had obtained Arahanthood through faith and love (saddhadhimuttanam) for Buddha. After seeing the Buddha, he could never tire of looking at him and became a monk just to be near him. Apart from eating and bathing, spent all his time meditating on the Buddha's appearance, to which Buddha admonished Vakkali with his famous utterence on the transcendental nature of Buddha's true Dharmakaya, "The sight of my foul body is useless; he who sees the Dhamma, he it is that seeth me".

Buddha had to command Vakkali to leave. With a heavy heart he went up to Gijjhakuta Mountains. In the Apadana Buddha is said to have spoken to him from the foot of the rock, saying "Come, monk." Filled with joy Vakkali jumped down the mountain to greet Buddha dropping a depth of many cubits but remained unhurt and realized Arahantship. Here, Buddha declared him to be amongst the foremost among those of great faith.

FAITH IS NOT BLIND

In the Buddhadharma, faith is not blind for it sees with the heart of devotion. It betokens faith in the reliability of the Sakyamuni as a truly awakened spiritual friend and faith, conviction and confidence in the Triratna. Devoted faith in some *Yana* may take the form of the Guru yoga sadhana. In the Kalama Sutta the Buddha himself argues against "blind faith" based simply on authority, tradition or specious reasoning; for even though one's own experience is emphasized in accepting Buddha and Buddhism, the counsel of the wise (implicitly meaning a Buddha, ultimately Gautama himself, or a Buddhist master well versed in Dharma) should always be depended upon - whence there remains a requirement for a degree of trusting confidence in Buddhism, essentially in the authority of Gautama as the ultimate Buddha, based on his spiritual attainment and salvational knowledge.

Faith in Buddhism centres on the authority of Gautama as a supremely Awakened being, by assenting to his unsurpassed role as teacher of both humans and gods, to the truth of his Dharma (spiritual Doctrine), and in accepting the *Sangha* (community of spiritually developed followers). Faith in Buddhism can be said to function as a form of motor, which propels the Buddhist practitioner towards the goal of Awakening (bodhi) and *Nirvana*. In Buddhism, faith is only one part of five characteristics that a Noble disciple must possess. In other words, in Buddhism faith is qualified. Blind faith is especially not treated well. In Sutta 44, Buddha questions Sariputta to which Sariputta answers, "Herein, O Lord, I do not follow the Exalted One out of faith.

Those by whom this is unknown, unseen, uncognized, unrealized and unexperienced by wisdom will herein follow others out of faith." In other words, in blind faith there is no knowledge or conviction, and one can have blind faith in anyone and such blind faith never leads to wisdom and true conviction. Only the actual experience of regular practice can lead to true faith and conviction born out of realization. "But those by whom this is known, seen, cognized, realized and experienced by wisdom, they have no uncertainty, no doubt about it that these five faculties, if cultivated and regularly practiced, lead to the Deathless, are bound for the Deathless, end in the Deathless."

FAITH IN MAHAYANA BUDDHISM

In general, the role of faith in Mahayana Buddhism is as strong as that of the Theravadin, though the depth and range of faith may be perceived as being intensified particularly in the tathagatagarbha sutras and the Pure Land literature. In the *Mahaparinirvana Sutra,* Sakyamuni Buddha is portrayed giving a foundational position to faith. Sakyamuni states: "we say that unsurpassed Awakening [*bodhi*] has faith as its cause. The causes of Awakening are innumerable, but if stated as faith, this covers everything."

Faith as understood in this sutra is belief in the teachings of the Buddha and in the Buddha's own eternality. More specifically, it is belief in such doctrines as the law of karma, in the reality and eternity of the Three Jewels (i.e. the Buddha, the Dharma, and the *Sangha*), as well as in the efficacy of the Buddhist Path. The Buddha comments:

All that is said in these Mahayana sutras is the truths of the Way [*marga*]... As I have already stated, if one believes in the Way, such a Way of faith is the root of faith. This assists the Way of Awakening... The Way begins with the root of faith....

The Buddha further notes that a person possessed of faith is superior to one lacking in it:

There are two kinds of men: one who has faith, and the other who has not. O *Bodhisattva*! Know that he with faith is one who is good, and that he who has no faith is one who is not good.

Faith in the Buddha is seen as a positive virtue as it leads to more attentive absorption in Dharma, which in turn strengthens faith still further. The Buddha remarks: "Faith arises out of listening to Dharma, and this listening is [itself] grounded in faith."

Through such faith, along with other spiritual practices, the Buddhist aspirant is enabled to attain *Nirvana*, according to this text. Faith is the first step for the *Bodhisattva* to tread along that path to *Nirvana*. It is viewed as a basic requirement, and crucially entails the understanding that the "real" Buddha is not a being of flesh and blood who can bleed and who dies, or whose Truth (Dharma) perishes with his physical body. The true Buddha and his Dharma are utterly deathless and eternal, so the *Mahaparinirvana Sutra* insists. This *Bodhisattva* is urged to believe:

"First, he [i.e. the *Bodhisattva*] is perfect in faith. How is faith perfect? This is believing deeply that the Buddha, Dharma and *Sangha* are Eternal, that all Buddhas of the ten directions [everywhere] make use of expedients [effectively to convey Dharma to the different types of being], and that beings and *icchantikas* [the most spiritually depraved of persons] all possess the *Buddha-dhatu* [Buddha-Principle, Buddha-nature]. It is not believing that the Tathagata is subject to birth, old age, illness, and death, that he has undergone austerities, and that Devadatta [Buddha's cousin] really caused blood to flow from the Buddha's body, that the Tathagata ultimately enters *Nirvana* [finally dies], and that authentic Dharma dies out. This is where we speak of the *Bodhisattva*'s being perfect in faith."

Yet faith in the Buddha should not be blind. The Mahayana not infrequently links faith with discernment and spiritual insight (*Prajna*) - spiritual penetration. The following words of the Buddha's indicate the need for a balance:

If a person does not possess faith and insight [*Prajna*], such a person increases his ignorance. If a person possesses insight, but not faith, such a person will increase [his or her] distorted views.... A person who has no faith will say, out of an angry mind: "There cannot be any Buddha, Dharma, and *Sangha*!"

TATHAGATAGARBHA LITERATURE

The *Nirvana Sutra* is not alone in according a foundational position to faith. The "Tathagatagarbha" sutra entitled, Anunatva-Apurnatva-Nirdesa ("Exposition of Non-Decrease, Non-Increase") tells of how the essence of Ultimate Truth, the Tathagatagarbha", can be perceived by means of faith. This matter of the Tathagatagarbha lies beyond the reach of the foolish, of the ordinary person, unless that person possesses faith, which will gain him or her entry into the realm of the Tathagatagarbha:

No *sravakas* [the elementary students of the Buddha] or *pratyekabuddhas* ["private" Buddhas, who usually avoid people and generally do not teach] are able to know, see or investigate this matter with their insight. How much less able to do so are foolish ordinary people, except when they directly realise it by faith! Faith is thus presented as a powerful means for the Buddhist practitioner to penetrate through to, and realise for him/herself, deep spiritual truths.

It is not only in the tathagatagarbha literature that faith is lauded. In the Prajnaparamita scriptures, too, faith is extolled. Here it is usually in connection with trust and belief in the sutra which is at that moment being expounded. Thus in the *Prajnaparamita Sutra on How Benevolent Kings May Protect Their Countries*, the Buddha declares that even if living beings were to give away the most precious substances known to humanity in a huge act of generosity, still "their merit would not be such as that of the production of one single thought of serene faith in this Sutra".

This and other *Prajnaparamita* sutras explain that such persons who naturally engender faith in these texts are those who have worshipped and revered countless Buddhas in past incarnations. Faith comes naturally to them. Moreover, faith in, and reverence towards, such sutras is tantamount to faith and reverence directed towards all Buddhas. The Buddha asserts in the *18,000-Line Prajnaparamita Sutra*:

If anyone, when this deep perfection of wisdom is being preached, feels respect, affection, and serene faith for it, then he feels respect, affection and serene faith also for the Buddhas and Lords of the past, future, and present.

Takasaki in his translation and study of the Sanskrit *Ratnagotravibhaga* (with protracted consideration of the Tibetan and Chinese traditions) renders an embedded extract of a sutra of Sakyamuni unidentified in the text that conveys the importance of faith in relation to what is known in the tradition as the 'revolution of the basis' (Sanskrit: aœrayaparivitti) of 'buddha-dhatu' (buddha-nature) to the 'Dharmakaya' (a Buddhadharma nomenclature of the ultimate truth):

O Sariputra, the ultimate truth is really approachable only by faith [in the Tathagata]. O Sariputra, the ultimate Truth is a synonym of the mass of living beings (sattva-*dhatu*). The mass of living beings is O Sariputra, nothing but a synonym of the Matrix of the Tathagata (tathagatagarbha). The Matrix of the Tathagata is Sariputra, nothing but a synonym of the Absolute Body (*dharmakaya*).

PURE LAND LITERATURE

It is perhaps in the "Pure Land" sutras that faith and devotion reach a pinnacle of soteriological importance. Here it is one's faith in the salvific compassion of the Buddha Amitabha, coupled with one's development of "roots of goodness" and the earnest wish to enter the Buddha's happy land that is said to bring deliverance into Buddha Amitabha's Western Paradise, the "land of bliss", preparatory to entry into Awakening and *Nirvana*. In the *Contemplation of Amitayus Sutra*, the Buddha tells of the types of being who gain birth in this pure land – and they are all characterised by faith:

Those born in the Western Land are of nine grades. Those who attain birth on the highest level of the highest grade are sentient beings that resolve to be born in that land, awaken the three kinds of faith and so are born there. What are the three? They are, first, the sincere faith, second, the deep faith; and third, the faith that seeks birth there by transferring one's merit. Those who have these three kinds of faith will certainly be born there. However, even in these faith-oriented sutras of "Pure Land" Dharma, faith is often linked with understanding (it is not totally "blind faith"). The Buddha of the *Smaller Pure Land Sutra* speaks of faith allied with understanding as a prerequisite for the attainment of supreme Awakening (*bodhi*), when hearing this text. Thus:

> Furthermore... if there is a good son or good daughter, whether having already heard this, or shall hear it, or who is now hearing it – once hearing this Sutra, profoundly is there born an understanding faith. Once there is born an understanding faith, a certainty about the accumulations of merit residing in the ten directions with the Buddha World-Honoured Ones, whose number is like the sands of Ten River Ganges, and they practice as instructed, all will be firmly in the supremely unexcelled Bodhi.

This teaching of faith, originally advocated in conjunction with discernment and Dharmic practice, received a new interpretation in the teachings of the Japanese Buddhist saint, Shinran Shonin (1173–1262 CE), who taught that just one recitation of the mantra, "Homage to Amida Buddha", with deep faith, would be enough to secure the faithful person entrance into the Western Paradise. Subsequent utterances of that formula would be expressions of gratitude to Buddha Amida (Amitabha). Deep understanding of the Buddha's teachings and Buddhic practice were not necessary, Shinran claimed. This interpretation of the "Pure Land" sutras represents perhaps the zenith of faith-oriented Buddhism and remains controversial, although Shinran's school of "Jodo Shinshu" is today perhaps the largest Buddhist sect in Japan.

One of the most famous of Mahayana sutras, the Lotus Sutra, also embraces the ideal of faith, but links it to discernment. The Buddha tells his audience in the *Lotus Sutra*:

If any living beings who seek after the Buddha-way either see or hear this Law-Flower Sutra [i.e. the *Lotus Sutra*], and after hearing it believe and discern, receive and keep it, you may know that they are near Perfect Enlightenment.

The same sutra asserts that the Dharma as a whole is difficult to grasp with mere words and that ultimately only those *Bodhisattva*s who believe with firm faith can penetrate its nature. The Buddha says:

This Law [Dharma] is inexpressible,

It is beyond the realm of terms;

Among all the other living beings

None can apprehend it

Except the Bodhisattvas

Who are firm in the power of faith.

Thus faith is a major element within Buddhism. While it is rarely (if ever) taught by the Buddha in any "blind" form and is often linked to discernment and understanding, it is nevertheless viewed as a powerful force which can start the Buddhist practitioner on his or her spiritual journey and convey him or her towards Awakening itself. Perhaps the most enthusiastic paean to faith can be found in the massive Avatamsaka Sutra, where, to the delight of all the Buddhas, the Bodhisattva Samantabhadra proclaims the following verses in a great eulogy of *Bodhisattva*s' Faith:

Deep faith, belief, and resolution always pure,

They [*Bodhisattva*s] honour and respect all Buddhas...

Deeply believing in the Buddha and the Buddha's teaching,

They also believe in the Way traversed by buddhas-to-be,

And believe in unexcelled great enlightenment:

Thereby do enlightening beings [*Bodhisattva*s] first rouse their will.

Faith is the basis of the Path, the mother of virtues,

Nourishing and growing all good ways,

Cutting away the net of doubt, freeing from the torrent of passion,

Revealing the unsurpassed road of ultimate peace.

When faith is undefiled, the mind is pure;

Obliterating pride, it is the root of reverence,

And the foremost wealth in the treasury of religion...

Faith is generous...

Faith can joyfully enter the Buddha's teaching;

Faith can increase knowledge and virtue;

Faith can ensure arrival at enlightenment...

Faith can go beyond the pathways of demons,

And reveal the unsurpassed road of liberation.

Faith is the unspoiled seed of virtue,

Faith can grow the seed of enlightenment.

Faith can increase supreme knowledge,

Faith can reveal all Buddhas...

Faith is most powerful, very difficult to have;

It's like in all worlds having

the wondrous wish-fulfilling pearl.

TANTRAYANA

The *Vajra Garland Explanatory Tantra* (Wylie: bShad rgyud rdo re phreng ba) evokes the metaphor of the snowlioness and her salvific milk of Dharma, hailed as a *panacea* in Traditional Tibetan medicine, rendered into English by Wallace:

Just as the milk of a lioness

Is not to be placed in an earthen container,

So is the Mahayogatantra

Not to be given to those who are not suitable vessels.

Gyatrul (b.1924), in a purport to this verse cited by Chagmé (Wylie: karma-chags-med, fl. 17th century), conveys the importance of faith as a qualification of disciples who 'listen' to the Dharma, rendered into English by Wallace:

This injunction pertains to teaching Mahayana, Vajrayana, and to Atiyoga in particular. Those without faith who are completely involved in the eight mundane concerns are not suitable vessels, and they should not be taught these kinds of Dharma.

Dudjom, *et.al* renders the 'Eight Worldly Concerns' into English, thus: profit, loss, pleasure, pain, fame, defamation, praise and blame.

CHODPA

Faith cultivated on the pilgrimage to 'The Red Citadel on the Copper Mountain' (Sangri Khamar), the cave of Machig Lapdron, redactor of a specific form of Chöd practice, Tsultrim Allione and pilgrims have to traverse the 'Great Purifier' (Tsangpo River):

As we sat next to the river, many members of the group used their own methods to see whether we would go or not...This was a very interesting moment in the pilgrimage, because the practice of Chod is all about attachment and the demons of hope and fear. Here we were on the bank of this river, close to Machig's place and thus full of hope, yet the rushing water told us death was a real possibility if we tried to cross. I decided to relax completely and to allow Machig to help us, and if that meant staying at camp, that was okay. I saw that faith is a form of relaxation, and this turned out to be one of the most powerful realizations of the pilgrimage for me. Faith is taking things one step at a time, relaxing, trusting. It is moment-to-moment opening to the wisdom beings.

9

Tantra or Magical Buddhism

The religious practices found in the Tibetan cultural world, accepted by and even conducted by the monastic orders, include the incantation of mystic, magical formulas, the exorcism and destruction of demons, divination, auguries, oracles, and symbolic sacrifice and ransom - aspects associated with Shamanism. It is this element within Tibetan Buddhism of magic and the supernatural, so remote from the original teachings and practices of Buddhism that has led to its designation as Lamaism, as if it were a separate religion or at least a separate offshoot of the original faith. In attempting to account for these apparent contradictions, scholars have sought to identify the sources of these seeming divergences from what can be claimed as the pure, original Buddhist teachings.

Buddhism was a foreign import into Tibet, but Tibet made Buddhism its own, and that encompassing system of beliefs and practices known as Tibetan Buddhism can only be understood in the full context of the country, its history, its society, and its indigenous religious and cultural practices. It is also necessary to consider particular religious currents (i.e., Tantrism) within Buddhism that ultimately affected its form in Tibet. At the core of Buddhist teachings are the four noble truths, explaining the nature and cause of suffering and the way to enlightenment: a focused approach that makes no mention of a creator and that seems in our contemporary world more a philosophy - a perspective on reality - and a guide to living, than a religion. Yet, although Tibetan Buddhism is based on those core teachings, it includes practices that extend into the supernatural realm, such as defense against omnipresent evil spirits. Thus the religion seems almost split into two paradoxical factions: the spiritual path to enlightenment, and rituals of protection against the hosts of evil.

And although the original teachings of the Buddha do not mention a creator or other deities, Tibetan Buddhism embraces a vast pantheon of divinities. These supramundane beings derive from the intersection of many sources and influences, both native and external. Only a general survey of this complex subject can be given here. Sakyamuni, which was the Buddha's family name, was born in a small Indian state in what is now southern Nepal, although the present nation of Nepal did not come into existence until the late eighteenth century. He lived in the context of Indian culture and religion, and it was in India that Buddhism took root - the original Buddhist stronghold.

In its earliest, and some argue its purist or most authentic form, Buddhism was nontheistic, keeping its focus on a way of thought and a conduct of life that would release human beings from inevitable suffering. A basic premise of Buddhism is that neither the Buddha nor any divine being interferes in human life, or acts as a savior or intercedes as a saint might do. Rather, such beings teach, expound the Dharma (law), and show the way. The concept of karma is fundamental to Buddhism. It is based on the premise of the inexorable relation of cause and effect: in familiar Western terms, you reap what you have sown. Your own actions, rather than the decision of a divine being who sits in judgment, or the intercession of any god, determine what will become of you.

Against its Hindu background, Buddhism has sometimes been seen as a reform movement analogous to the Protestant Reformation, an analogy that perhaps should not be stretched too far, and it has even been considered a revolutionary movement. Yet from its inception, and in the course of its subsequent development for many centuries, Buddhism was affected by the inevitable influence of its Hindu context, even as it was a reaction against the mother culture and religion. The Mahayana movement that flourished in the Buddhist universities of eastern India absorbed Hindu elements. These sources, Hindu and Buddhist, became interwoven and were the matrix for the later development, Vajrayana.

Tantric texts depict the defeat of Hindu deities, most importantly the great god Shiva, by the *Bodhisattva* warrior, Vajrapani; the vanquished Hindu gods were converted, pledged allegiance to Buddhism, and were renamed and incorporated into the Buddhist structure. And tantric texts introduced yet other gods, such as Mahakala, who although one of the most important tantric deities in Tibetan Buddhism, has an ancient origin in Indian cults. With the further development of Mahayana, and its cult of *Bodhisattva*s (whose numbers multiplied, along with the Buddhas with whom they were often paired), the pantheon expanded. Interweaving and building on these influences, introducing and absorbing yet more deities, Buddhism, like a living organism, continued to evolve, and the form that we would come to know as "Tibetan" grew increasingly labyrinthine.

Even that is not the end of the story. After Buddhism was first introduced into Tibet in the seventh century C.E., where it encountered a native culture, a struggle ensued between the new religion and the ancient, indigenous one. Ultimately and inevitably, Buddhism was influenced by that which it came to replace. This complex interaction developed into mutual adaptation, and the native traditions added their complement of gods to a growing Buddhist pantheon of deities and supramundane beings. A century after that first introduction, a Tibetan king summoned Padmasambhava, a mystic eighth-century yogin from an area northwest of India, now thought to be Pakistan's Swat valley, to establish the primacy of the new religion: this is known as the "first diffusion" of Buddhism in Tibet.

Padmasambhava, also known as Guru Rinpoche, is honored and revered throughout the Tibetan cultural world, and even considered a second Buddha by followers of the

Nyingma-pa sect. According to legend, this legendary master battled with and successfully overcame malevolent and hostile spirits, including the indigenous Tibetan gods, and bound them over with vows to serve the new faith.

The old gods, former enemies, became champions of Buddhism; they joined the pantheon, swelling its prodigious array of deities and supernatural beings. Yet that, too, was not yet the end of the story. When Buddhism was introduced into Tibet in the seventh century under King Songtsen Gampo, it was apparently centered in the royal court and did not, at first, put down deep roots.

Almost a century passed until it found favor again under King Trisong Detsen, who with the aid of Padmasambhava strengthened its position. But even after that "first diffusion," the new religion lost ground, and it was not until the "second diffusion" of Buddhism in the ninth and tenth centuries that it became firmly and finally established as the majority religion of Tibet. While this basic outline is not disputed, scholars have disagreed about precisely what it was that Buddhism replaced. Certainly, indigenous religious beliefs and practices dominated Tibet before even the first introduction of Buddhism in the seventh century, and during the subsequent stages of its history there. But with what did Buddhism struggle during that period between the "first" and "second" diffusions? And what were the influences that led Tibetan Buddhism to diverge so markedly from Indian Buddhism that later observers attached to it a new name - Lamaism - as to a separate, distinct cult?

The great Tibetologist, Giuseppe Tucci, called Tibet's indigenous religious beliefs and practices "the folk religion," for which R.A. Stein adopted the telling designation, "the nameless religion." Just as various Middle-Eastern and European "pagan" beliefs, deities, customs and practices were absorbed into Christianity, so in Tibet many traces of the folk religion still exist, interwoven into Buddhist practices. But besides those popular beliefs, with their local cults and magical rites, another belief system either pre-dated Buddhism in Tibet or co-existed with it, and the relation of those two has been the subject of research and controversy.

That other religion is Bon. Giuseppe Tucci, David Snellgrove, and other scholars have worked to reconstruct the theology and iconography of early Bon, and have researched the question of Bon's origins, its history, and the extent of its relation to Buddhism. Tucci and other scholars believe that Bon preceded the introduction of Buddhism into Tibet. They identify divination and exorcism as central elements of the indigenous folk religion but also of Bon, and believe that both the folk religion and the more structured Bon contributed to the undeniably shamanistic aspect of Tibetan religious practice and customs. In this view, Bon brought a multiplicity of gods, demons, and spirits of nature into the Tibetan Buddhist pantheon, where they joined the gods absorbed from Indian tantrism. Tucci attributed Bon's formal doctrinal structure to a later borrowing from Buddhism.

According to the standard history, Bon vied with Buddhism for dominance during the early centuries after the introduction of the new religion, and during the period between the first and second diffusions. In any case, Buddhism prevailed, but Bon, or some form of it, has survived in parts of Tibet as well as in remote Himalayan areas, such as Dolpo in northwestern Nepal, and there has recently been a Bon revival in the West. According to this line of thought, the Bon that has survived was so heavily influenced and infused with later adaptations and borrowings from Buddhism that its original form can no longer be definitively distinguished from what is now the majority religion. Yet Buddhism was also heavily influenced by Bon: both shared traditions of magic and exorcism, and both were influenced by the still potent "folk religion." (Tucci considers that Bon was also influenced by Persian Zoroastrianism and by Shaivism, the cult of Shiva, which reached Tibet from the states on the western edge of the Himalayas.)

David Snellgrove, in contradiction, argues that Bon is not the old indigenous religion of Tibet. He agrees with the claim of present-day Bonpos (adherents of Bon) that their religion was, from the beginning, a form of Buddhism, however heterodox. Snellgrove maintains that before the famous introduction of Buddhism to Tibet in the seventh century under royal sponsorship, forms of Buddhism that had reached Central Asia were actually familiar to some Tibetans, and that Bon developed in Western or Central Asia earlier than its arrival, as traditionally understood, in Tibet.

He points out that the Bonpos, like the orthodox sects, believe in an enlightened being, Shen-rab, analogous to Buddha, and that Shen-rab, like Sakyamuni, had previous incarnations and appears in various manifestations; he maintains, moreover, that the Bonpos also have a fully developed theology and a set of tantras that he finds corresponds with Buddhist practice. Snellgrove considers Bon much closer to the Nyingma-pa, known among the recognized orthodox Buddhist sects as the "old" school, than it is to the popular folk religion with its multitude of spirits, magical rites, divination, exorcism, auguries, etc. He argues that those supernatural aspects of the indigenous cult were accepted perforce by both Bonpos as well as Buddhists, as old, deeply ingrained customs against which it was futile to contend, however irrelevant or alien to their own beliefs.

To complicate matters, some Bonpos of the present time identify Bon as the religion that prevailed in Tibet prior to the introduction of Buddhism, a position that contradicts those who argue that Bon is merely another form of Buddhism, having developed at about the same time as Buddhism reached Tibet, if not somewhat earlier. And while Bonpos consider their religion as a form of Buddhism, present-day Tibetan Buddhists regard Bon as a distinct, different religion, not as a heterodox form of Buddhism. In light of these contending, disparate views about the origin, history, and nature of Bon, and its disputed relation to Buddhism, Per Kvaerne has thus defined the three main theories:

- Bon was the pre-Buddhist religion of Tibet, its central figure a king with sacred powers;

- Bon was a form of Buddhism that developed in western Tibet at least as early as the period in which Buddhism was introduced into Tibet, and was similar in many respects to orthodox Buddhism;
- Bon, so-called, was not a religion in its own right, but the sum of all the indigenous beliefs, cults of local gods, popular rites, etc., that were once prevalent across Tibet.

Whatever the true origin, history, and nature of Bon, Tibetan Buddhist monastic orders are broadly tolerant of the old practices, some of which have almost no recognizable affinity with Buddhist belief. These native elements, whether they derive from Bon or from a folk religion, were strongly concerned with defence against hostile or ambivalent powers, ensuring that the dead do no harm to the living. Many of the rites and practices meant to defeat such hostile powers have survived not only in the folk religion, but were even, in Buddhist guise, absorbed into orthodox Buddhist ritual.

The people of the Tibetan cultural world are profoundly, devoutly Buddhist, yet the ancient traditions of folk religion not only remain vital, but have left their indelible stamp on Tibetan Buddhism, contributing to its distinctive nature. Basically, Tibetan Buddhism is the intersection of Mahayana and of Vajrayana Buddhism, with its component of Indian Tantrism, along with traditional, pre-Buddhist beliefs, whether Bon or not. And it is clear that in Tibet, rather than opposing the folk tradition, Buddhism accepted and absorbed it - and in so doing, allowed its borders to stretch. Buddhism has never concerned itself with extirpating heresy, and has no concept of excommunication.

Like a great melting pot, Tibetan Buddhism admits a multitude of powers, some celestial, others earth-based - local deities, mountain gods, spirits of the air, water, earth and soil. Among this great pantheon of divinities and spirits, many derive from the folk religion, and others - especially the multi-headed and multi-limbed ferocious gods - derive from Tantrism and also, arguably, from Bon. The process by which local deities and pre-Buddhist beliefs and rituals were adapted by the new dominant religion was eased by certain shared aspects or resemblances between the indigenous religion and Tibetan Buddhism, since Vajrayana includes a powerful element of magic.

According to legend, many of the old native gods, some benevolent, others malignant, were vanquished and then "converted" by Padmasambhava, who bound them over through mighty oaths to serve Buddhism in new roles as protectors or defenders of the law. Local deities, such as the gods of particular mountains, lakes, etc., were also admitted to the accepted pantheon, justified by their acceptance of the law. Lesser deities, with supernatural but not supreme powers, became guardians of the entrances to sacred spaces, to defend against malicious spirits. In the hierarchy of the pantheon, these are of lower rank than the great supramundane beings, such as the *Bodhisattva*s, but could also be explained as manifestations of the more important deities.

THE FOLK RELIGION

However and whenever Buddhism came to Tibet, it found itself in a rough, mountainous country with a harsh climate: a country of struggling farmers, nomadic herdsmen, and traders whose livelihood depended on perilous journeys.

Mystery was a condition of existence, not only because of the inexplicable sicknesses against which, until modern times, all people were helpless, but also in the wild, changeable, unpredictable mountain weather that ruled their lives; when a spring hailstorm destroyed the crops or a sudden blizzard covered the grazing land and froze the animals, starvation loomed. The ordinary Tibetan believed himself or herself to be continually at the mercy of supernatural powers surrounded by multitudes of spirits, both beneficent and malicious, that needed to be appeased or destroyed. The old folk religion offered rituals, techniques with which to safeguard the home purify the village, protect the crops and animals, cure the sick, and see the souls of the dead into safety.

The challenge for Buddhism was to persuade and induce a population who believed their lives were governed by a host of invisible but omnipresent spirits, to accept a highly focused set of teachings involving a relatively abstract mental discipline. Even now, one can speak of Buddhism as it is understood by the women who weed the fields and the men who drive the yaks, a faith heavily imbued with the pre-Buddhist ideas and practices of the folk religion, and of the Buddhism understood and practiced by monks, lamas, and the learned classes, those exposed to Buddhist texts and commentaries and formal teachings. Elements of those indigenous beliefs and practices remain part of Tibetan religious life, existing alongside the liturgy of monks and lamas who expound the texts they hold authentic.

The Buddhism of the monastery proved itself flexible, accommodating to popular beliefs that in any case it could only with difficulty have tried to suppress, if not eliminate. The tantric rituals accepted by Vajrayana, with their element of magic, helped bridge the gap. Rites of sacrifice, exorcism, and ransom make up a regular part of Tibetan life. In their origin they are, however symbolically they were subsequently explained, quite alien to the original, essential Buddhist beliefs. The resemblance of many of these rites to shamanism is often undeniable. And at times, some of the old gods seem less than convincing in their new Buddhist dress. The triumph of Buddhism was its ability to adapt the ancient, ingrained beliefs and customs without compromising its own fundamental insight and precepts, while teaching the new theology to the people of Tibet and firmly establishing their acceptance and understanding of its ethical code.

10

The First Three Vajra Points

The Three Jewels

The Three Jewels, also called the Three Treasures, the Three Refuges, or the Triple Gem, are the three things that Buddhists take refuge in, and look toward for guidance, in the process known as taking refuge.

The Three Jewels are:

- Buddha (*The Enlightened* or *Awakened One*), who, depending on one's interpretation, can mean the historical Buddha, Sakyamuni, or the Buddha nature-the ideal or highest spiritual potential that exists within all beings;
- Dharma (*The Teaching*), the teachings of the Buddha.
- *Sangha* (*The Community*), the community of those who have attained enlightenment, who may help a practicing Buddhist to do the same. Also used more broadly to refer to the community of practicing Buddhists.

REFUGE FORMULA

The Three Jewels, also rendered as Three Treasures, Three Refuges or Triple Gem are the three things that Buddhists give themselves to, and in return look toward for guidance, in the process known as taking refuge. Taking refuge in the Three Jewels is central to Buddhist lay and monastic ordination ceremonies, as originated by Gautama Buddha, according to the scriptures. The practice of taking refuge on behalf of young or even unborn children is mentioned in the Majjhima Nikaya, recognized by most scholars as an early text.

Taking refuge in the Three Jewels is generally considered to make one officially a Buddhist. Thus, in many Theravada Buddhist communities, the following Pali chant, the *Vandana Ti-sarana* is often recited by both monks and lay people:

- *Buddham saranam gacchami* (I go for refuge in the Buddha).
- *Dhammam saranam gacchami* (I go for refuge in the Dharma).
- *Sangham saranam gacchami* (I go for refuge in the Sangha)

The Mahayana Chinese/Japanese version differs only slightly from the Theravada:

I take refuge in the Buddha, wishing for all sentient beings to understand the great Way profoundly and make the greatest resolve. I take refuge in the Dharma, wishing for all sentient beings to delve deeply into the Sutra Pitaka, causing their wisdom to be as broad as the sea. I take refuge in the *Sangha*, wishing all sentient beings to lead the congregation in harmony, entirely without obstruction.

The prayer for taking refuge in Tibetan Buddhism.

Sang-gye cho-dang tsog-kyi cho-nam-la (I take refuge in the Buddha, Dharma, and Sangha)

Jang-chub bar-du dag-ni kyab-su-chi (Until I attain enlightenment).

Dag-gi jin-sog gyi-pe so-nam-kyi (By the merit I have accumulated from practising generosity and the other perfections)

Dro-la pan-chir sang-gye drub-par-shog (May I attain enlightenment, for the benefit of all migrators).

IMPORTANCE

The Triple Gem is in the centre of one of the major practices of mental "reflection" in Buddhism; the reflection on the true qualities of the Buddha, Dharma and *Sangha*. These qualities are called the Mirror of the Dharma in the Mahaparinibbana Sutta and help the practitioner attain the true "mind like a mirror".

In the commentary on the Apannaka Jataka Buddha declares:

"Disciples, nowhere between the lowest of hells below and the highest heaven above, nowhere in all the infinite worlds that stretch right and left, is there the equal, much less the superior, of a Buddha. Incalculable is the excellence which springs from obeying the Precepts and from other virtuous conduct."

"By taking refuge in the Triple Gem, one escapes from rebirth in states of suffering. In forsaking such a refuge as this, you have certainly erred. In the past, too, men who foolishly mistook what was no refuge for a real refuge, met disaster."

EXPLICATION

The qualities of the Buddha, Dharma, and *Sangha* are frequently repeated in the ancient texts and are called "Mirror of the Dhamma" or "Dhamma Adassa".

- The Buddha: "The Blessed One is an Arahant, perfectly enlightened, accomplished in true knowledge and conduct, fortunate, knower of the world, unsurpassed leader of persons to be tamed, teacher of devas and humans, the Enlightened One, the Blessed One."

In some traditions the Buddha as refuge is taken to refer to the historical Buddha and also 'the full development of mind', in other words, the full development of one's highest potential, i.e. recognition of mind and the completion or full development of one's inherent qualities and activities.

- The Dharma: "The Dhamma is well expounded by the Blessed One, directly visible, immediate (eternal or not subject to time), inviting one to come and see, applicable, to be personally experienced by the wise."

Refuge in the Dharma, in the Vajrayana, tradition includes reference not only to the words of the Buddha, but to the living experience of realization and teachings of fully realized practitioners. In Tibetan Buddhism, it includes both the Kangyur (the teaching of the Buddha) and the Tengyur (the commentaries by realized practitioners) and in an intangible way also includes the living transmission of those masters, which can also be very inspiring.

- The *Sangha*: "The *Sangha* of the Blessed One's disciples is practising the good way, practising the straight way, practising the true way, practising the proper way; that is, the four pairs of persons, the eight types of individuals - This *Sangha* of the Blessed One's disciples is worthy of gifts, worthy of hospitality, worthy of offerings, worthy of reverential salutation, the unsurpassed field of merit for the world."

In the Vajrayana, a more liberal definition of *Sangha* can include all practitioners who are actively using the Buddha's teachings to benefit themselves and/or others. It can be more strictly defined as the 'Realized *Sangha*' or 'Arya-*Sangha*', in other words, practitioners and historical students of the Buddha who have fully realized the nature of their mind, also known as realized Boddhisatvas; and 'Ordinary *Sangha*', which can loosely mean practitioners and students of the Buddha who are using the same methods and working towards the same goal.

THREE JEWELS IN TIBETAN BUDDHISM

In Tibetan Buddhism there are three refuge formulations, the *Outer*, *Inner* and *Secret* forms of the Three Jewels. The 'Outer' form is the 'Triple Gem', (Sanskrit: *triratna*), the 'Inner' is the Three Roots and the 'Secret' form is the 'Three Bodies' or trikaya of a Buddha. These alternative refuge formulations are employed by those undertaking Deity Yoga and other tantric practices within the Tibetan Buddhist Vajrayana tradition as a means of recognizing Buddha Nature.

The three gems are called this because of their treasured value to Buddhists, as well as their indestructible and unchanging nature. The *Three Gems* when used in the process of taking refuge become the *Three Refuges*. In this form, the metaphors occur very frequently in the ancient Buddhist Texts, and here the *Sangha* is used more broadly to refer to either the *Sangha* of *Bhikkhus*, or the *Sangha* of *Bhikkhunis*.

"I go to Master Gautama for refuge and to the Dhamma, and to the *Sangha* of *Bhikkhus*."

DIAMOND MIND

Buddha's mind in his earth body or sambhogakaya is frequently associated with the greatest gem of all, the diamond, and the hardest natural substance. In the *Anguttara Nikaya* (3:25), Buddha talks about the diamond mind which can cut through all delusion.

RATANA-SUTTA

The expression *Three Gems* are found in the earliest Buddhist literature of the Pali Canon, besides other works there is one sutta in the Sutta-nipata, called the Ratana-sutta which contains a series of verses on the Jewels in the Buddha, Dharma, and *Sangha*.

In the *Ratana-sutta*, all the qualities of the *Sangha* mentioned are attributes of the Buddha's enlightened disciples:

- One who is irascible and very irritable, displaying anger, hatred and sulkiness; such a one is said to be a person with a mind like an open sore.
- One who understands the Four Noble Truths correctly is said to have a mind like a flash of lightning.
- One who has destroyed the mind-intoxicating defilements and realized the liberation of mind and the liberation by knowledge is said to have a mind like a diamond

IN JAINISM AND TAOISM

In Buddhism, the Triple Gem isn't a metaphor. It's actually the initiation into the Dharma that every Buddhist must take. However, it is used metaphorically in Jainism and Taoism. When Buddhism was introduced into China, *ratnatraya* was translated as *sanbao* (Chinese: pinyin: *sanbĭo*; Wade-Giles: *san-pao*; literally "three jewels/treasures"), a word that first occurs in the *Tao Te Ching*.

In his analysis of the *Tao Te Ching*, Victor H. Mair notes that the jewel metaphor was already widely used in Indian religious metaphor before the *Tao Te Ching* was written. In Jainism too,

For the Jains, the Three Jewels are a metaphor for describing conduct and knowledge:

- *Samyag-darœana* (correct perception or insight)
- *Samyag-jñana* (correct knowledge)
- *Samyag-caritra* (correct conduct).

IN ART

The compound Buddhist symbols: Shrivatsa within a triratana, over a Dharmacakra wheel, on the Torana gate at Sanchi. 1st century BCE.

The *Three Jewels* are also symbolized by the *triratna*, composed of (from bottom to top):

- A lotus flower within a circle.
- A diamond rod or vajra.
- A Gankyil.
- A trident, or trisula, with three branches, representing the threefold jewels of Buddhism: Buddha, the Dharma and the *Sangha*.

On representations of the footprint of the Buddha, the Triratna is usually also surmounted by the Dharma wheel. The Triratna can be found on frieze sculptures at Sanchi as the symbol crowning a flag standard (2nd century BCE), as a symbol of the Buddha installed on the Buddha's throne (2nd century BCE), as the crowning decorative symbol on the later gates at the stupa in Sanchi (2nd century CE), or, very often on the Buddha footprint (starting from the 1st century CE). The triratna can be further reinforced by being surmounted with three dharma wheels (one for each of the three jewels of

Buddhism: the Buddha, the Dharma and the *Sangha*). The triratna symbol is also called *nandipada*, or "bull's hoof", by Hindus.

ON COINS

There are a number of examples of the triratna symbol appearing on historical coins of Buddhist kingdoms in the Indian sub-continent. For example, the Triratna appears on the 1st century BCE coins of the Kingdom of Kuninda in the northern Punjab.

It also surmounts the depictions of stupas, on some the coins of the Indo-Parthian king Abdagases of the 1st Century, CE and on the coins of some of the Kushan kings such as Vima Kadphises, also of the 1st Century CE.

11

The Fourth Vajra Point

Tathagatagarbha

"Worldly beings take what does not exist as a self for an existing self and are attached to this self. In the shravaka tradition one counteracts this belief in an existing self through meditating on the non-existence of a self, yet only in terms of sheer voidness. These concepts, and mainly the latter one, are purified by the understanding that the fruit is a state of peace, of complete freedom from the conceptual elaboration of an existing self or the non-existence of a self. Thus it is the perfection of true self." -Khenpo Tsultrim Gyamtso Rinpoche, BN.

This point is underlined again and again. It is not that there is nothing corresponding to what we take to be our 'self' or fundamental awareness. We simply suffer a serious case of mistaken identity. The infinite is obscured by adventitious attachments to the finite. We identify a continuity of conscious states with personal existence, a specific entity, the familiar sense of me is superimposed on a stream of composite phenomena, rather in the same way that we see a whirling firebrand as a solid ring of fire. Apparent yet deceptive. Memory and perception actively support this notion. It is not that there is no fire (consciousness) at all but that we are conditioned by an incorrect perception of the true nature of this element.

We fixate on certain objects, string barbed-wire, labelling 'I' and 'mine', generating a vortex of pseudo-subjectivity, well described as karmic. Statements such as these from KTGR, where the fruit is described as a state of peace and complete freedom indicate the true nature of self or awareness. It is not simply no-self or non-existence which sounds more like death than freedom to me. Freedom implies unrestricted motion. Peace means liberation from undesirable circumstances, not death. As I read these pages and attempt to understand the import of this fourth vajra point, the one they named the book after, I am repeatedly thrown back into this great meditation: the true self is the Dharmakaya maha-guru beyond existence and non-existence, unborn fire of inconceivable bliss eternally radiant beyond all relative moments of association (life) or disassociation (death) with a body/mind.

It is this fundamental blaze, the incorruptible reality of who you are, the true self which is "like a jewel, like space, like water...."

"When viewed in the light of the *Rangtong* Madhyamaka, the dharmadhatu is nothing but emptiness in the sense of freedom from conceptual elaboration, whereas in the *gZhäntong* and Mahamudra views it is spaciousness-awareness inseparable. On the basis of sheer emptiness it could not become the cause for the attainment of Buddhahood." -Khenpo Tsultrim Gyamtso Rinpoche, BN.

Since the Buddha is essentially Dharmakaya and Dharmakaya *Sunyata* and since this *Sunyata* permeates all beings, the latter are endowed with Buddha-nature. Beings are endowed with Buddha-nature since in the Tathata of Buddhas and of sentient beings there is no differentiation into good or bad, great or small, high or low. As silver is found in and may be refined from its ore, sesame oil pressed from its seed and butter churned from milk, so in all beings may Buddhahood become a reality. -quotes from Gampopa's *"Jewel Ornament of Liberation"* translated by H V Guenther.

TEN FACETS OF DHARMADHATU

We have been looking at the fourth vajra point in some detail this week. The chapter entitled "The Element (Buddha

Nature)" is structured into ten points and nine examples, all of it an effort 'to determine the meaning of the dharmadhatu' according to Jamgon Kongtrul. The ten points are briefly considered here.

1. The principle/ invokes three primary symbols found throughout buddhist scriptures; space, a gem, water, each indicating aspects of purity, each corresponding to one of the kayas.
2. The cause/ lists the four essentials which must be present for a Buddha child to manifest the fullness of Buddha-nature and the four veils which obscure the correct view supporting effective practice. These are –
    - Sincere devotion to the Dharma, in specific, the three roots for tantrikas,
    - Prajnaparamita, non-dual mother wisdom which understands the non-inherent existence of all things.
    - The regular practice of true meditation which generates the bliss of *Samadhi* and
    - Unceasing flow of the milk of compassion.
3. The fruition/ consisting of true purity, true self, true happiness and true permanence. This bold proclamation of the third turning sounds like a far different message than the first turning emphasis on the corruption of compounded phenomena, no-self, suffering and impermanence, illustrating the radical difference between provisional and definitive teachings.
4. The function and influence/there is only one primary raison d'etre, one purpose, a singularly essential impulse, at the heart of the secret nucleus: bodhi, to awaken beings. Initially, this often manifests as weariness with the tedium of *samsara* in order to gradually wean us from the primeval dither. As indicated in the root text, were there no true nature, there would be no basis to transcend suffering or attain liberation. There would be no shame associated with non-virtue, no joyful effort, real attraction or spiritual magnetism associated with the Buddha's teachings or Dharma practice.

5. The endowments/ the blessings of the ground, path and fruit, the dynamic of realization rooted in the mature wisdom of Dharmakaya consisting of the four mind-blows listed above in point #3 (the fruition) featuring the spontaneous compassion and joy which are inseparable from this trans-mundane insight. Of course these also correspond to the kayas, or the body, speech and mind of the Buddha.

6-7. The manifestation and the phases/ both of these take three forms: as ordinary sentient beings, *Bodhisattva*s and Buddhas, corresponding in some measure to the Yogacara Trisvabhava doctrine of the imaginary, dependent and consummate levels of truth. Both of these points recount the triad of sentient beings, *Bodhisattva*s and buddhas all of which are manifestations of buddha nature in its impure, partially purified, and pure aspects this is followed by the topic of 'phases' which repeats the triad this time to indicate that not only does reality take three forms but that none of them is an end in itself as each goes through a process of mutation wherein a sentient being morphs into a *Bodhisattva* which in their turn become buddhas more on the Trisvabhava.

8. All pervasive/ again, the Element is compared to space in its sovereign purity, liberal accommodation, unbiased, non-conceptual and invariable, unchanging nature.

9. Changelessness/ this one along with the previous point are included in the description of the first vajra point but are elaborated here to accommodate points 6&7; for ordinary beings, the relative invariance of the elements define the basic stability of the system... for *Bodhisattvas*, the qualities of fruition (described in point #3 above) are defined as the transcendence of the four sufferings associated with impermanent, conditional, composite phenomena- birth, old age, sickness, death... for buddhas these same qualities are listed 'kataphatically' as per point #3 above (the fruition).

10. Indivisibility/The singular nature of the real as expressed

from various viewpoints; *Dharmakaya* (as transcendent ontology), *Tathagata* (as evolutionary thematic), *Jnana* (as one's inmost awareness), and *Nirvana* (as the end of suffering). Elsewhere in relation to this point, the text states that the illumination, radiance and purity of the sun are inseparable in the same way as analytical wisdom (S. *Prajna*, T. *sherab*), primordial wisdom (S. *jnana*/T. *yeshe*) and liberation (S. *moksha*, T. *tharpa*, *rang-drol*). Again, in the example of royal portrait (p.146), a team of artistic experts are undermined by the emigration of the fellow who does the head in the same way that generosity, morality and so forth must be complemented by Prajnaparamita in order to go beyond the generation of worldly karmas.

CHANGELESS YOU DWELL THROUGHOUT THE THREE TIMES

Recall the third among the ten points listed under the heading of The Element called Buddha Nature is Fruition, part of which is true permanence. The unchanging nature of the secret nucleus is primarily experienced by impure sentient minds as the relative stability of the four elements constituting the world and the physical body. This is why materialism is such a popular philosophy.This same unvarying equanimity is experienced by genuine *Bodhisattvas* as Dharma and the transcendence of the four primary forms of suffering articulated by Sakyamuni Buddha. While for Buddhas, this same changelessness manifests directly as absolute purity, real self, true happiness and deathlessness.

NINE METAPHORS FOR THE TRUE NATURE

Some loose associations made while reflecting on the nine metaphors of the Buddha Nature in ordinary beings, focusing on the obscurations:

1. Buddha in a lotus: (desire) impermanent beauty of the lotus, the initial attraction to color/form, and the putrid rot discovered upon closer inspection

2. Honey covered w/ bees: (anger) the cold sting and flaring pain of loveless (re-activity), the aggressive/defensive hum of egoic concern and insistent worldly distraction, the inability to yield, preoccupation with boundaries and personal security
3. Unhusked rice: (ignorance) the illusion of refinement, unpalatable fruit, compromised nourishment, impenetrable coarseness, incomplete offerings, wasted resources,
4. Gold in filth: (active *klesas*) covered in human and animal waste, biologically active and infectious. Mind still enamored by the lure of *samsara* has no energy or interest in dharma.
5. Buried treasure: (innate ignorance) very likely the long-term fate of the gold nugget mentioned above. Mind given over to the poisons in their active state is as old as the hills (hosting all kinds of terma) so that these tendencies are carried from ancient times. The thing that struck me about these last two metaphors is just how unlikely anyone would ever be to ever discover the treasure. In filling out the analogy, the text suggests clairvoyance or celestial intervention might play a part in guiding one to the prize. In all nine cases, there is something of great value within arm's reach. Something must be done or understood to discover, appreciate or recognize the treasure. All of this is in keeping with the teachings on the unique opportunity we have here, the freedoms and endowments of this precious human rebirth and the necessity of taking the guru's words to heart.
6. Thick-skinned fruit: (active klesas) emphasis on tough leathery hide of this tropical exotic, the resistance offered by the ego to deeper inquiry or vulnerability beyond socially acceptable limits; the armor of opinionatedness and the sanctity of 'prior commitments'; the combination of moisture, warmth and the pull of the sun enticing the shoot to sprout and climb starward...
7. Precious rupa in tattered rags: (innate karmas) funky and thin, beginning to rot away on their own, a multi-colored array of jewels sparkling from within the oily, dusty

shadows of fabric; easily removed as the path of meditation is traversed. The fact that it is wrapped in rags suggests a conscious attempt to hide or protect it during transport or invasion. It is as if this was something previously understood to be of value which was either lost or forgotten.

8. Wretch bearing a king: (impurities of bhumis 1-7) there is an organic gestation period involved with this one, corresponding to the subsequent length of path encountered after the first moment of attaining the path of seeing (associated with #6), where emptiness is known directly for the first time; this realization is gradually perfected on the path of meditation (associated with #7).
9. Clay-covered rupa: (impurities of bhumis 8-10) depending on how you count these, this could be the third symbolic use of a rupa in this list. On the basis of the nature of Tathagata being truly inconceivable, Khenchen Thrangu Rinpoche tends to interpret the first example of the lotus to contain an actual Buddha. The difference between this one and #7 is that here, the clay covering is extremely thin and the statue freshly cast, perhaps emphasizing something of the unborn originality, unique expression and freshness associated with full realization of the *Nirmanakaya*.

All sentient beings have the Buddha nature, or seed of Enlightenment. In the *Samadhi* Raja Sutra, the Buddha said, "All sentient beings are pervaded by the essence of the Sugata (the well-gone state). For example, silver abides in its ore, oil abides in a mustard seed, and butter abides in milk. Likewise, the seed of Enlightenment abides in every sentient being. Complete Buddhahood is *Dharmakaya*, which is all- pervading emptiness. And this emptiness pervades all sentient beings. For this reason, all sentient beings have the seed of Enlightenment." The suchness of all reality has no differentiation. The reality- suchness of the Buddha and the sentient beings is not differentiated. There is no better and no worse, no higher and lower, no larger and smaller. Therefore, all sentient beings have the essence of Enlightenment. As it is possible to extract butter from milk and oil from the sesame seed, so it is possible for sentient beings to achieve Enlightenment.

To seek Buddha, see the self-nature!

Self-nature is Buddha!

Buddha is being in himself; doingless and creationless one!

Without seeing self-nature, no matter how hard you look for Buddha, day and night, it is absolutely impossible (to see).

Even though we might say there say there is originally not a thing to be attained, if you do not yet understand it, you must, with sincere effort and work, find and meet a Master to open your mind. Life-and-death is a great puzzle. Do not spend your life in vain. Deceiving yourself does not help you in anyway,

".....known as the Tathagata Garbha or "The Essence of Buddhahood Sutra", in these Sutras the Buddha explains the nature of our mind. In these Sutras the Buddha explains that the negative aspects of our minds such as afflictive emotions, desire, hatred, greed, anger and also our cognitive states, are not something which are innate aspects of our mind but rather they are adventitious, in that mental states arise within our mental continuum as a consequence of circumstantial conditions. They are not essential or intrinsic to our mind, whereas pristine clarity, the mere nature of awareness and luminosity are things which are innate aspects of our mind. The negative aspects of mind, afflictive emotions such as anger, hatred, desire and so forth, because they are not innate aspects of our mind, they can be removed from the basic continuum of our mind. This point has been underlined in the Sutras that are related to the third public sermon."

The Buddha exclaims in Avatamsaka-sutra: "How wonderful, how surprising! All beings are already endowed with the wisdom of the Buddha! They already have all Buddha-qualities! How mysterious it is!"

The idea of the Tathagatagarbha is encountered in a number of Mahayana Buddhist scriptures, notably the

"Mahaparinirvana Sutra" (the Buddha's final Mahayana sutra), the "Tathagatagarbha Sutra", the "Srimaladevisimhanada Sutra", and the "Mahayana Angulimaliya Sutra". It expresses the notion of an ultimate, uncreated and immortal core spiritual Reality in all living creatures - an indestructible, omniscient, eternal, infinite, pure, benevolent, nurturing and blissful Buddha Essence in each and every being (animals included), which empowers each being to become a Buddha. In some Tathagatagarbha sutras (notably the Angulimaliya Sutra), this spiritual Essence is taught to inhere in, and form the foundation of, all phenomena without exception and to contain all good and true qualities. Thus this teaching complements the doctrine of the "emptiness" of worldly phenomena: worldly things are empty of an eternally unchanging, individual identity of their own, but not of the perfect virtues of the everywhere-present Buddha.

The virtue-replete "Tathagatagarbha" is in fact no less than the Buddha-generating Potency itself - the state of spiritual Awake-ness or Knowing-ness ("Bodhi" or "Buddha-jnana") concealed within the deeps of each person's and each creature's profoundest mind. A similar teaching can be found in the Tibetan Buddhist 'Dzogchen' texts and traditions. It is vital to understand from the outset that the doctrine of the Buddha Nature is overwhelmingly presented by the Buddha in the core Tathagatagarbha sutras as definitive and absolute truth (not as an elementary, provisional or "relatively true" teaching).

The Tathagatagarbha is viewed by these sutras as supreme, virtue-filled, totally pure and immutable spiritual Reality. Contrary to a mass of disinformation circulating on the Internet and elsewhere on this subject, the Tathagatagarbha is not simply Emptiness (devoid of all positive qualities), or merely a more attractive way of speaking about Emptiness (again construed in a purely negative sense), or just conditioned chains of onward-flowing "dependent origination". The key Tathagatagarbha sutras make it abundantly clear that in its ultimate nature the Buddha Matrix is an unconditioned, changeless, virtuous, eternal, ineffable, spiritual Essence unshackled by the confines of time, place and process. And when it is termed "the Self" (as in the "Mahaparinirvana

Sutra"), that does NOT refer to the mutable, conditioned, worldly ego (as some Tathagatagarbha commentators, who author essays on the "significance" of the Tathagatagarbha doctrine, misleadingly imply), but equates with the eternal, changeless Self of Buddha (found in all beings), which is one with Great *Nirvana* (according to the Buddha himself in the "Mahaparinirvana Sutra").

The Tathagatagarbha is nowhere taught by the Buddha to be a mere ruse without genuine truth behind it, or to be merely some form of fictitious, purely metaphorical, concessionary phantasm or doctrinal crutch for spiritually retarded or immature students, or "for the masses at a given time" - as certain writers on Buddhism, out of whatever motive, are happy to have people erroneously believe. The very opposite of this is the case.

This Buddha-Garbha (Buddha Matrix or Essence) is revealed by the Buddha to his ADVANCED students as the unchanging and peaceful Buddhic Quintessence within each being (the "svabhava" or "*atman* " - the infinite, ego-less, unitary "Soul" of the Buddha), but which also actively functions as the seed of all positive spiritual qualities and underlies the thirst for *Nirvana*, and which indeed makes the obtention of *Nirvana* possible (since *Nirvana*, through the Tathagatagarbha, is already present within us). Thus the Tathagatagarbha is dipolar, possessing both a quiescent, calm and motionless mode (as indicated by the "Vajrasamadhi Sutra", for instance) and a dynamic, active mode of nurturing and liberating all suffering beings.

This richness of the combined ontic being and salvific function of the Tathagatagarbha seems to baffle some Western scholars, who cling to the mistaken view that the one precludes the other - yet that is the wonder of the Tathagatagarbha, that it is both quiescent in the nirvanic realm and salvationally active within the world of samsaric being. The Tathagatagarbha is on occasion called by the Buddha the True Self ("*satya-atman* ") or the Buddha-Principle ("Buddha-dhatu"), and it is indestructible. It knows no death, only life eternal. Indeed, it is the "life-principle" ("jivaka") itself, according to the Tibetan version of the "Mahaparinirvana Sutra".

This is in keeping with the definition of 'soul' found in Merriam-Webster's Collegiate Dictionary (2002): 'the immaterial essence, animating principle of an individual life; the spiritual principle embodied in human beings, all rational and spiritual beings, or the universe.' This Buddha-Soul is present everywhere, as the Buddha states in the full 'Mahaparinirvana Sutra': 'I also teach, for the sake of all beings, that, in truth, there is the Soul / the Self ('*Atman*') in all things'. This is the unified Buddha-Self, all 'of one taste'. In the Faxian version of the '*Nirvana* Sutra', the Buddha says: "The Tathagata-dhatu cannot be killed. Those who die are said to be short-lived, while the Tathagta-dhatu is stated to be the true life-principle." Although present within *samsara* (the sphere of reincarnation), this Self or Tathagatagarbha yet essentially transcends all negative samsaric qualities and is replete with wondrous virtues.

When considering the Tathagatagarbha, one must at all times be mindful of the caveat that the Tathagatagarbha is ultimately incomprehensible and inexplicable to the un-Awakened mind - so to define it as mere "Emptiness" or as merely a function of Buddhist practice (rather than as a truly real, sustaining internal presence), as some commentators are pleased to claim, is to fail to do justice to this transcendental phenomenon.

The fact is that whatever one says about the Tathagatagarbha cannot fully capture its plenitude of mystery and perfection, since words are ultimately inadequate to the task and there is nothing in the world that can truly be compared to it (this is explicitly stated in the "Angulimaliya Sutra", as well as in the "Mahaparinirvana Sutra" - the lengthiest sutra dealing with the Tathagatagarbha). The Tathagatagarbha constitutes the inconceivable realm or sphere ("visaya") of the perfect, all-knowing Buddhas themselves and nurtures each person in whom it is found (i.e. every single being). Only when it is seen and truly known by profound inward introspection and purified spiritual vision can it be fully understood. And at that point - one has become a perfect Buddha!

There are several key scriptures which contain this teaching. They include the "Tathagatagarbha Sutra" ("Buddha-Matrix Sutra"), the "Srimaladevisimhanada Sutra" ("Queen Srimala Lion's Roar Sutra"), the "Anunatva-Apurnatva Nirdesa" Sutra ("The Teaching on Non-Decrease, Non-Increase" Sutra), the "Lankavatara Sutra" ("Descent into Lanka Sutra"), and the "Angulimaliya Sutra" ("Angulimala" is the central Buddha-inspired and Buddha-guided teacher of this very vigorous and vital sutra).

12

The Fifth and Sixth Vajra Points
The Bodhi and the Guna

THE FIFTH AND SIXTH VAJRA POINTS

NATURE

The nature of Buddhahood is defined as *the two purities:*

1. Pure in itself /suchness
2. Pure in the world/ becoming.

These correspond to the two kayas, formless dharmakaya realized during meditation (*jnana/yeshe*) and the *Rupakaya* 'between sessions' (*Prajna/sherab*) as well as *vimuktikaya/ dharmakaya* or *svabhavikakaya/jnana dharmakaya*). In accordance with the *gZhantong* view, *dharmakaya* is to be understood as the joint manifestation of the realization of space-like essence (emptiness *sTong pa nyid*) and the liberated primordial wisdom of awareness (T. *rigpa yeshe*). Unlike the 'emptiness only' rendering of dharmakaya according to the *Rangtong* view, this union or coalescence is called dharmakaya (from *gZhantong* perspective). The form kayas spontaneously arise within this dharmakaya.

CAUSE

The cause of Buddhahood is the perfection of tranquility (S. *samatha* T. *zhi-né*) and insight (S. *vipassana* T. *lhag tong*). All Buddhist practices can be divided into either one or both of these, which also correspond to the two accumulations, those of wisdom (non- conceptual virtue) and merit (virtue with concepts). Keep meditating.

FRUIT

Realization of the secret nucleus translates as freedom from all emotional and mental defilement, perfect enjoyment of the four mindblows (true purity, spontaneous identification with the essential reality or self, incorruptible happiness, eternal life).

FUNCTION

Overcoming the four primary sufferings (birth, old age, sickness and death) the causes which originally moved Sakyamuni to begin wandering across the plains of northern India, 2500 yrs. ago.

ENDOWMENTS

Completely beyond concept and measurement, primordially pure (in itself) and free of all conditional defilement (in the world) empowered with the perfection of wisdoms knowing correctly [profound, suchness] and completely [vast, things in their relations] and transcendent freedoms.

MANIFESTATION

In the form of the three *kayas*- unchanging, unceasing, and undeluded, replete with extraordinary qualities.

Permanence of the kayas in the following manner- the permanence and unchanging quality of the absolute nature, the permanence of the perfect enjoyment body is not its unchangingness, but of the unblocked flow of awareness, of the continuity of appearances.

Having received teachings and meditated extensively on the all-pervading impermanence of the relative world, the mere notion of permanence should quickly point one in the direction of inconceivability.

INCONCEIVABILITY

First among the 15 endowments, that pervades all others. Buddhahood is not attainable by thoughts or conceptual thinking, beyond intellectual modeling or the subtlest of relative designations.

VAJRA POINT VI: BUDDHA QUALITIES

The 32 aspects detailing the qualities of a fully awakened Buddha relate directly to excellence in teaching and leading other sentient beings to perfect happiness; the main symbols associated with this chapter are:

- Vajra is noted for its indestructibility and capacity to destroy all obstacles.
- Lion is noted for his fearless presence, proclaiming the dharma deep in the jungles of samsaric views.
- Space is unmixed with the dynamics of the other elements while allowing for their expression in the same way that the 18 qualities of body, speech and mind are unique to Buddhas while supporting worldly beings, sravakas, pratyekas, and *Bodhisattvas* in their respective levels of present refinement. These last four are symbolized by earth, water, fire, and air. As for Buddhas, the text states, (p. 235) "Away from the features of the worldly and of those being beyond the world, they are similar to space."
- Moon in the water represents the two aspects of the Buddha's teaching; the moon itself represents the *dharmakaya* and the reflection symbolizes the form (*rupa*) kayas; the wisdom knowing correctly and the wisdom which knows completely.

The chapter also includes a detailed list of the 32 physical marks of the supreme *Nirmanakaya* which is as close to unbelievable as it gets for me. This is not the form taken by all those who awaken but is an extremely rare emanation displayed in one like Sakyamuni Buddha who was of the special class known as supreme *Nirmanakaya*. Khenpo Tsultrim Gyamtso Rinpoche comments: A supreme *Nirmanakaya* in all his beautiful signs and marks is only seen by a sentient being who has purified the veil of negative karma, whereas to someone whose mind is still obscured by former very negative actions he may appear in a very ordinary or even revulsive form, just as the clear reflection of the moon is only seen unpolluted water. [BN 385-6]

Khenchen Thrangu Rinpoche's commentary on The Uttara Tantra delineates the qualities of enlightenment in two ways, those with value for oneself which he relates to the absolute truth and the *Dharmakaya*, and value for others, which he relates to the relative truth and the *Samboghakaya* and *Nirmanakaya*. He explains that the qualities related to value for one relates to freedom and the qualities of value for others relate to maturity. Together they give fulfillment for oneself and others. I have listed what he says are the qualities with value for oneself. This is not a commentary; these are simply notes for study.

The first *kaya* which relates to value for oneself has 32 qualities of Freedom: ten powers, four fearlessnesses and eighteen distinctive qualities the ten powers:

1. Perfect knowledge of the appropriate and inappropriate,
2. Full understanding of karma,
3. Being able to gauge the intelligence of persons so that they may be taught according to their level,
4. Knowing the temperaments of beings so as to know which remedies to suggest,
5. Knowing the interests of beings so that they know which teachings will help them,
6. Knowing which path leads to less suffering, which to happiness in the here/now, and which leads to eternal happiness,
7. Knowing the correct and incorrect way to meditate,
8. Remembering former lifetimes, attained through the practice of virtue,
9. Being able to see the future,
10. Knowing that all impurities have been perfectly eliminated.

The four fearlessnesses:

1. Fearless because they know they have nothing more to purify,
2. Fearless of contradiction because they know they have a correct understanding,
3. Fearless because they know that the path is the way to complete enlightenment,
4. Fearless because they have had no pride when teaching and the 18 distinctive qualities.

In relation to behaviour:

1. It is not possible for their action to be a mistake,
2. They do not speak meaninglessly or uselessly,
3. Their mindfulness never diminishes,
4. They rest perpetually in meditation,
5. They never think of deceiving others,
6. They always act carefully, never casually relative to understanding,
7. They never lose their aspiration to help other beings,
8. They never lose their diligence,
9. Their memory never decreases,
10. Their understanding never becomes distorted,
11. Their perfect liberation does not change,
12. They never lose their jñana as related to qualities of activity,
13. Their physical activities are preceded and followed by jñana,
14. Their speech is preceded and followed by jñana,
15. Their thoughts are preceded and followed by jñana as related to qualities of jñana,
16. Their jñana is unhindered by the past,
17. Their jñana is unhindered by the present,
18. Their jñana is unhindered by the future.

These qualities are the result of freedom from obscurations, and manifest as knowledge of how-it-is and variety. "Around 1976 a new form of Buddhist ritual came to public notice. It was a form of *Buddha pûja* devised, and at that time generally conducted, by a young monk called Panadure Ariyadhamma [gestorben 1986]. The Venerable Ariyadhammais a forest-dwelling monk who began his meditation training, while still a layman, at Kanduboda and received his higher ordination there.

His *Buddha pûja* revitalizes a traditional form of *Buddha pûja*, almost obsolete, in which offerings of the kind usual at 6 P.M. - flowers, lamps, incense, etc. - were made before images of the twenty-eight Buddhas (twenty-seven former ones and Gotama) to the recitation of a few Pali verses. Another traditional element that the ritual revives is the custom of honoring the *bô* or Bodhi tree as a symbol of the Buddha's Enlightenment. The latter element led rapidly to the new ritual's becoming known as *Bodhi pûja*. In August 1978 a month of Bodhi pijds held in Galle culminated with a crowd reliably estimated at nearly 100,000.

In 1979 Gombrich wrote, "It is not yet possible to say whether the service can become popular without [Ariyadhamma's] participation as its leader." Events have proved that the *Bodhi pûja* has indeed become popular but, in spreading, has changed its form and its meaning to the participants with astonishing rapidity. Its story vividly illustrates the principle that innovations stem from individuals, but what becomes of them is what the many other individuals who constitute society make of them and often has little to do with the intention of the original innovator.

In this case the *Bodhi pûja* has been adapted to become something of a bridge between Buddhism proper and the spirit religion, which was not Ariyadhamma's intention. This will be fully illustrated below in a case history that thus neatly straddles our expository distinction between the spirit religion and Buddhism. First, however, we must briefly recapitulate our account of Ariyadhamma's original invention while referring the reader to the published material for the full version of his text, and then indicate the general lines along which the institution has been changing. We have referred to the *Bodhi pûja* as a "service" advisedly. Its form is quite new.

A traditional *Buddha pûja* involves the participation only of the person, whether monk or layman, who is making the offering; he recites (often *sotto voce*) a few set Pali verses. There is almost no set ritual and the event takes only a couple of minutes. The new *Bodhi pûja,* by contrast, takes well over an hour, and throughout that time the congregation are actively involved; they are reciting words, both Pali and Sinhala, after or along with the person who conducts the service. They also know what to recite because the words of the *Bodhi pûja* are recorded in readily available printed pamphlets. It is clear that many people already know the words of this fairly long liturgy by heart. We shall see below, however, that important variants have rapidly crept even into the published texts.

In Sinhala Buddhism it is an innovation to have an actively participating congregation at all. A crowd may come to hear a monk preach, but their only role is to listen and express approbation. Another new feature in the *Bodhi pûja* is that the leader, who early on was always the Venerable Ariyadhamma or another monk, positions himself so as to appear one of the congregation. Normally when a monk preaches or administers the precepts he faces the laity, is seated on a higher level, and is treated with great formal respect. The monk conducting the *Bodhi pûja* sits as a member of the congregation, like them facing the Buddha image in an attitude of humility.

In this respect he behaves more like a Muslim prayer leader in a mosque than a traditional monk. This is not to say that either Islam or Christianity has supplied a conscious model for the *Bodhi pûja*. However, it is possible that Ariyadhamma was influenced by the Christian service without being aware of it, since Panadura, Ariyadhamma's home, had a powerful Protestant elite and also churches and Christian schools, and moreover, was the venue for the famous controversy between Christians and Buddhists. The most fundamental innovation, which affects both form and content, is the use of Sinhala and traditionally only Pali has been used in Buddhist liturgy.

Though most laymen certainly have a general idea of what is being said, hardly any of them actually know Pali so that the words in that language can have no emotional immediacy for them. The *Bodhi pûja* uses not only Sinhala prose but also Sinhala verses of the traditional type, which are not spoken but chanted melodically. In fact the most famous feature of the original *Bodhi pûja* was the Venerable Ariyadhamma's mellifluous chanting of the verses he had composed. This is not to say that their content was not of the greatest importance; but his presentation gave them an aesthetic as well as a purely emotional appeal.

He told us that his motive for composing the service was a desire to offer young people an attraction to compete with films and pop songs. In this he certainly enjoyed at least a brief success. While he agreed, when we put it to him, that the comfort people derive from the *Bodhi pûja* might meet the needs that drive them to worship the gods, the spirit religion was not in his mind when he composed it. Already when we interviewed him in 1978 he was unhappy about the uses to which his invention was being put.

It has been the innovation in content, itself the main reason for the *Bodhi pûja*'s initial success that has contained the seeds from which these other growths have sprouted. The Sinhala text of the service has been used to express emotions hitherto unexpressed by the congregation in Sinhala public ritual of any kind. Everyday emotion may be expressed in everyday language in traditional rituals of the spirit religion, but only by the officiants; and in Buddhist ritual, we have seen, the language is Pali. In the *Bodhi pûja* everyone present expresses *adara*, the ordinary word for love, for all creatures and the hope to be forgiven for all faults. The Buddha is referred to in emotional language as both father and mother. And the most famous passage is a pair of Sinhala verses that express the hope for comfort and consolation:

To see the Lord Buddha's statue is consolation to the eyes,

To bow before the Lord Buddha is consolation to the limbs,

To think of the Lord Buddha's virtues is consolation to the mind,

To take the path the Lord took is consolation for becoming.

In life there is trouble truly every day

And to death we approach ever a little closer,

Only doing good is at least a little appropriate;

For all of us it is *nirvana* that is the consolation.

These verses are followed by the words "May all beings be happy," repeated several times, first by the monk and then by the congregation, each time a little softer, till they die away in a whisper. There is a profound silence, as everyone attempts to suffuse his own thoughts, and thence the whole world, with kindness. The silence is finally broken, on the monk's cue, with a loud exclamation of "*Sa!*" and everyone breaks into a loud, fast repetition in a monotone of the *Metta Sutta*, the scriptural and thus the traditional liturgical form given to the same sentiments.

The Venerable Ariyadhamma told us that when Maha Pajapati, the Buddha's stepmother, became a nun, she said to him, "You are now my Buddha mother and give me the milk of immortality"; the story makes him weep with emotion. The words constantly on his lips and featuring prominently in his service are kindness, compassion, pity, and above all comfort and consolation. He also frequently mentions equability, both as a quality of the Buddha and as a condition to aspire to. But it has been his genius to realize that between the laymen walking in off the street and this ideal state of calm there lays a gap that requires some emotional bridge. Not innovating, but bringing into unwanted prominence an element from the tradition, he stresses both the parental love that the Buddha felt for all suffering creatures and that we may legitimately still project onto him and the love, of the same quality, that we in our turn must cultivate.

In recalling these qualities of the Buddha, he said to us, people's thoughts become broader and open out like a flower blossoming. The main message of the sermon we heard him give at a *Bodhi pûja* was that everyone should meditate daily on the qualities of the Buddha and practice kindness. We recall here that the same meditation - recollection might be a better word - on kindness has been made part of the daily routine of Sinhala schoolchildren. The same traditional value embodied in the same meditative practice can become almost unrecognizable as its context changes. Of this the *Bodhi pûja* affords a dramatic example.

The element in the Bodbi pijd that first led to its popular reinterpretation is the series of Sinhala verses in which the worshipper contemplates the Bodhi tree. The tree under which the Buddha attained Enlightenment by defeating Mara, the personification of death and desire, has always been a popular symbol in Sinhala Buddhism. Immediately after the Enlightenment, the Buddha is supposed to have remained a week in the bliss of meditation and then a second week in unwinking contemplation of the *bô* tree, as an expression of gratitude.

There is a tradition, going back to ancient India that all important trees are inhabited by spirits, and this naturally applies also to *b*ô trees. We saw that the Venerable Balangoda Ananda Maitreya believes that he was the spirit (*devatava*) in the original *bô* tree at the time of the Enlightenment. This spirit is never explicitly identified with the Buddha, but our material will disclose a close psychological connection between the two, a connection perhaps originally fostered by the fact that in early Indian representations of the Enlightenment only the tree is shown, not the Buddha.

The Sinhala chronicles record that soon after Buddhism itself was brought to the island a cutting of the original *bô* tree was planted in Anuradhapura and that cuttings from that tree in turn were then planted in temples all over the island. The Anuradhapura *bô* tree is still one of the most important national shrines. Virtually every temple has a *bô* tree; in fact, its presence- for some grow wild- often determines the site of a temple. In a temple it is customary to build a low protective rampart around the tree, sometimes in two tiers, and to pave or at least flatten the ground around the rampart so that worshippers can circumambulate the tree; it is also often adorned with pennants.

However, the ancient custom of ritually watering the tree by bathing its roots in scented milk or water was, for the most part, obsolete before the Bodhi pûja revived it. The verses in the Bodhi pûja celebrate in turn the original bô tree, the Anuradhapura *bô* tree, and the local *bô* tree - for religiously all are one. They do not explicitly mention the deity in the *bô* tree - though it would not have been unorthodox to do so - but the *bô* tree is personified in this stanza:

I pass to and fro on this enclosure,

I tread on the roots and leaves of the Bo tree;

Forgiving me, it does away with my sin;

The king Bô tree grants me permission [to worship it}.

The Venerable Ariyadhamma assured us that he envisaged no special regard for the *bô* tree deity. His attitude to all the gods is that there must be mutual respect, but he asks no favors of them and merely follows the normal custom of offering merit to all of them without distinction. He regarded *Bodhi pûja* as a misnomer for his service and did not approve of the ritual worship of the tree which, he was aware, was already tending to accompany it. In the services he conducted, the only offerings made were of flowers and incense before images of the twenty-eight Buddhas (or fewer, standing for the twenty-eight) and of the traditional "eight requisites" to members of the *Sangha* present at the end of the service. Nor did the service have to be held in the vicinity of a *bô* tree; the tree is addressed in imagination only.

THE METAMORPHOSIS OF THE BODHI PÛJA

The *Bodhi pûja* diffused extremely rapidly. In the late 1970s the Venerable Ariyadhamma's tours, on which he held series of *Bodhi pûja*s in large towns, received a lot of newspaper publicity. The congregations tended to be young and middle class so that tape recordings of the services began to circulate. Meeting demand, several new editions of the text were soon printed - three of them are in our possession. Such *Bodhi pûja* leaflets are now on sale in stalls and on pavements at pilgrimage centers, to some extent superseding the Sinhala verse versions of *Jataka* stories and similar popular ballad literature, which seem to have gone out of fashion.

These leaflets did not have to be, and surely were not, authorized by the Venerable Ariyadhamma. The ritual instructions and glosses they contain would certainly not have met with his approval, for they instruct worshippers how to use the *Bodhi pûja* for worldly ends. At the same time, the *Bodhi pûja* has become something of a national ritual for Sinhala Buddhists. By this we do not mean that it forms part of civic religion or is associated with the state. We mean that while its emotional appeal makes it attractive to almost all Sinhala Buddhists; it has no association with any particular status group or faction within the society, but seems to belong to all Sinhala Buddhists equally.

From this point of view it is not surprising, though deeply ironic, that services have been held with the express purpose of bringing success to the Sinhala army waging war against the Tamils in the north and east. But some officiants consider this very wrong. The incumbent of the Sat Bodhi temple in Narahenpita in Colombo told us:

"That principle [performing the *Bodhi pûja* for military success] is all wrong. All of mankind is the same. The Lord Buddha did not divide people in terms of race, or of upcountry and low, or of tall and short, or of American and English. Humankind is distinguished in terms of goodness. Goodness is goodness whether it exists in the Catholic, the Muslim, or among gods and laymen. Gold does not change, whoever wears it. To do a *Bodhi pûja* to win a war with the Tamils or Muslims - that is flatly opposed to the Dhamma of the Buddha. Such actions also do not befit a civilized mind."

This monk did not, of course, derive his moral stance from the *Bodhi pûja*, but from his upbringing as a Buddhist and his training as a monk. Yet he sees the *Bodhi pûja* as a fine means to communicate Buddhist values and has therefore introduced it in his temple. He has, however, profoundly modified it in a conservative direction by using only Pali. The problem that this change is designed to meet is the use of music. All members of the *Sangha* must, ideally, abstain from witnessing displays of dancing, singing, and instrumental music, and those who take the eight precepts on *poya* days make the same vow. Pali verses are always chanted, not sung.

There is of course no clear line between chanting and singing; but the Venerable Ariyadhamma's rendition of the Sinhala verses in his service comes closer to singing. It has even been suggested that his style has been influenced by that of a certain popular singer. In his view there is no music in the service because it does not employ instruments. One might add that he breaks up the quatrains into separate lines, each being repeated by the congregation, which enhances the liturgical effect. Moreover, in traditional acts of public worship at Buddhist temples there is always a certain amount of drumming and other instrumental music performed by hereditary specialists and no one objects to that. Nevertheless, some monks do see the singing of the Sinhala verses as a problem. The incumbent at Narahenpita was aware that by restricting to Pali the *Bodhi pûja* that he introduced as part of his temple's daily evening service he was sacrificing immediacy, but felt constrained by his tradition.

One might ask whether less scrupulous officiants may not move in the opposite direction and abolish Pali altogether. We are, however, not aware of an instance of a text entirely in Sinhala. Pali sounds sonorous and impressive; as the traditional language of Theravadin liturgy its use imparts dignity, even solemnity. We recall the pseudo-Pali compositions of Uttama Sadhu's disciples. No version of the *Bodhi pûja* has similar Pali-sounding gibberish; but one of our pamphlets has added, for example, the following verse in a kind of dog Pali to be recited while circumambulating the *bô* tree.

Buddham Buddham Buddham vande (I worship the Buddha, the Buddha, and the Buddha)

Dhamma*m* Dhamma*m* Dhamma*m vande* (I worship the Dhamma, the Dhamma, and the Dhamma)

Sangham Sangham Sangham vande (I worship the Sangha, the Sangha, and the Sangha)

Cetim Bodhim sambham vande (I worship every stupa, every *bô* tree).

If on the one hand the *Bodhi pûja* has been taken up by Sinhala Buddhists as a nation to serve their common purposes, it is on the other being still more commonly used specifically by individuals to serve their private worldly ends. It is being simultaneously universalized and parochialized. We now turn to the latter. The *Bodhi pûja* is increasingly being performed for clients by priests of the spirit religion, whether old-style *kapurala* or new-style *Sami*, at their shrines. Of this we shall give an illustration in the case of Jayanta, reported below. The service is being adapted to the traditions of Sinhala spirit worship. Most strikingly, it no longer requires public participation, but may be performed for individuals or groups of clients.

Its instrumental character is moreover clearly explained in the leaflets. In effect it has become for many a rite of worship of the *bô* tree for particular ends, a piece of white magic. At the same time, as we shall see, it has not lost but rather enhanced its expressive character, so that it has a two-sided appeal. The ritual procedure laid down in our three pamphlets is basically the same, though there are minor variations in such details as the quantity and type of ingredients to be used. Typically the worshipper is instructed to bring baskets of flowers and coconut or mustard oil for lamps, these items being for the worship of Buddha images; and for the worship of the tree, the same plus panic grass, sesame oil, white sandalwood, parched rice, colored pennants, and white sand to sprinkle on the ground.

In the early days of enthusiasm some people revived the practice of bathing the tree in milk, but it has been decided that this is bad for the tree and is now actively discouraged, so our texts do not mention it. The worshipper is instructed to come first to the compound in which the tree stands and to clean and tidy it up. He is then to go to the temple and offer flowers and light lamps before the Buddha image or images there. He is to take the Three Refuges and five precepts (in Pali, as usual), and return to the tree. He is now to bathe it in water perfumed with various prescribed ingredients and pour pots of water over its roots. Trays of flowers and the other offerings are to be placed at the foot of the tree.

One then recites (repeats after the officiant) Pali and Sinhala verses from the *Bodhi pûja* text. (As a line in one of our printed texts has it, "Ghosts (preta) and demons quake on seeing the Bodhi.") One then remains silent in a meditative posture and repeats a wish (*prarthanava*) in Sinhala. We reproduce part of the prayer given in one of our texts. "The Bodhi tree that helped the Buddha of the three worlds to attain omniscience; the tree that protected the *Bodhisattva* from the enemies known as the moral defilements (*klesa*)... this *Bô* tree, descended from the glorious Great Bodhi of India, which protected the Lord Buddha; may it banish all our sufferings and sorrows, the ill effects of planets, the evil eye and evil mouth, illnesses and the machinations of enemies; and may it fulfill our wishes and give us boundless wealth."

After circumambulating the tree, the worshipper is then to take home the items that have been offered to the tree (insofar as they are recoverable) to use them for further protective rites. Here are some of the instructions for these.

- For misfortunes caused by demons and pretax recite the Ratana Sutta over the white sand and then sprinkle it around the house.
- For diseases recite the *Metta* Sutta over the panic grass and put it under the patient's pillow.
- For nightmares follow the same procedure but put the grass in the patient's hands.

- For appointments with government officials, for court cases, for taking part in public meetings, rub the sandalwood on a stone to make a paste of it, recite the Maha Mangala Sutta over it, and make a mark with it on the center of your forehead.
- For your rice crop recite the *Metta* Sutta over the mustard oil and sprinkle it on the paddy field.
- To scare away snakes, or beetles attacking coconut trees, follow the same procedure.
- To counteract sorcery recite the *pirit* text of the twenty-eight Buddhas over the mustard oil, sesame oil, and panic grass and put them in small pots at the four corners of the house.

Similar instructions are given for:

- Planetary troubles,
- Sores,
- Stomachaches,
- Eczema,
- Fear of demons,
- Epilepsy,
- Domestic disharmony,
- Sprains,
- House construction, and
- Reuniting separated families.

The *Bodhi pûja* thus covers every contingency requiring white magic for which it has been customary to use the spirit religion. This change has been accepted by many Sinhala people. The chief monk at Narahenpita, whom we mentioned above, told us that *Bodhi pûja* is for well-being (*yahapata*) in this world and specifically referred to protection from planetary evil, divine anger, and infectious diseases. There is of course a Sinhala Buddhist tradition of using the recitation of sacred texts for such protective purposes: the very word *pirit* etymologically means "protection."

Moreover, while there is a much longer classical collection of *pir*it texts for large ceremonies, the quintessential texts (collectively known as *Maha pirita*, "The Great Pirit") are just three: the Ratana, *Metta*, and Maha Mangala Suttas. So we see that the author of the above instructions is consciously tagging onto an ancient tradition. The recital of the *Metta* Sutta is already part of Ariyadhamma's *Bodhi pûja*, and it is quite natural that those three famous texts should be reprinted in *Bodhi pûja* pamphlets. The list of names of the twenty-eight Buddhas, which is not a traditional *pirit* text, is derived from the same source.

A traditional *pirit* ceremony consecrates water and thread that are then used for protective purposes. People may wear the thread around their wrists and sprinkle the water on themselves and around their houses. Are there then any important differences between the Bodhi p*i*jd as laid down in our pamphlets and the traditional use of *pirit*?

Pirit is traditionally a public ceremony and normally recited by monks - usually several of them. It is often held in private houses, but everyone around is free to come and participate and so gain merit. Moreover, though the occasion for holding a *pirit* ceremony is almost always quite specific, it is deemed to work in a general, unspecific way. About how it works there are several, mutually compatible theories. The most sophisticated and perhaps also the most impeccably orthodox is that the texts are in fact sermons being preached to convert malign spirits to Buddhist ethics so that they will give up doing harm.

Another orthodox theory simply assimilates the recital and hearing of the scriptural texts into the general category of meritorious actions: the merit gained by the participants is offered to the gods in a formula at the end, and in return they afford their protection. Other theories, pan-Indian rather than specifically Buddhist in origin, ascribe automatic efficacy to the sacred word or to the power of enunciated truth (*satyakriya*). Some texts of the Bodhi *pûja* and many people we have interviewed use the latter type of theory to account for its efficacy, it has "power vibrations" (*balavegaya*) that derive from the fact that the tree sheltered the Buddha during his fight for Enlightenment. But in its magical use it has moved from the *pirit* to the spirit religion model.

It is more laicized than *pirit* and more specific. It is being performed by priests for clients and in this form is a more private affair than *pirit*. Instead of the unspecific use of water and thread, highly specific ingredients from the magical tradition here appear. For example, the scattering of mustard seed to ward off demons seems to be a pan-Indian magical practice; here we have mustard oil as a local variant. However, the greatest difference between the *Bodhi pûja* and *pirit* lies in the appeal of the former to the emotions.

To this expressive aspect of the text we shall return below after further considering its functional use. Because of this appeal the more orthodox *Bodhi pûja* too, the one employing monks and a public congregation, is eroding the sphere of *pirit* on such occasions as the birthdays of public figures and events of more serious national concern. There seems to be a widespread feeling that the *Bodhi pûja* is a particularly appropriate remedy when one's troubles are due to the planets, that is, to a bad horoscope. Traditionally the countermeasure for such trouble is a rather elaborate ritual known as *bali* performed by specialists, but in many parts of the country *bali* rituals have become scarce.

In our earlier chapter we reported that already in 1978 a woman had seen in her daughter's horoscope that the daughter was about to pass through an unlucky period, so to avert misfortune she had watered a Bodhi tree with milk perfumed with turmeric and sandal every day for a week and given the merit to her daughter. This again illustrates the mechanism by which the *Bodhi pûja* is deemed to work: its performance creates good *karma*, a fund of merit that can be called on at need. Some printed editions of the *Bodhi pûja* include a text called *Nava Guna Santiya*, "The Blessing of the Nine Virtues," which is for warding off the bad influence of the nine planets by invoking the Buddha's nine virtues or qualities.

This has strong roots in tradition. The nine virtues are the Buduguna, a Pali formula. A passage in the original *Bodhi pûja* text dwells on the same formula, so the connection is evident. What appears to be new is again certain specificity, matching the virtues to the planets? The first three virtues *araham, sammasambuddho, vijja-carana-sampanno* (the meanings are not relevant here). The first three verses of the *Nava Guna Santiya* translate:

By the virtues of the araham Buddha

May the Sun's ill effects disappear;

Without fear of disease or pain

May happiness and joy approach me

By the effulgent power of samm*a*-sambuddho

May the Moon's ill effects disappear;

May deathly hindrances be prevented

And my wishes be fulfilled.

By the power of vijja-carana

May Saturn's ill effects disappear;

The effects of poison verses and calamities [brought by] enemies

May they not approach me.

This use of the *Bodhi pûja* is justified in an English-language newspaper article [Sunday Observer, 8 July 1984] by a learned monk, the Venerable Kaduvalle Dhirananda. "The Trinity of Brahma, Vishnu and Maheshwara preside over Time, according to the science of astrology," he writes. Each god takes his turn in controlling the universe for a twenty-year period known as *vimsatiya*.

The *vimsatiya* of Brahma is uniformly propitious, that of Visnu contains both good and bad, but the sway of Isvara is so maleficent that it even cancels out the benign results produced by his predecessors. The year 1984 is an especially bad part of Isvara's *vimsatiya*.

This year is described in astrology as a dark period of upheaval and destruction marked by murders, kidnappings, rapes, civil strife, droughts, famines, floods, robberies, lootings, drug abuse, instability of religious institutions, disaffection with gods, manifestations of divine wrath and inhuman acts resulting from hate, cruelty and vengeance.... Following in the steps of the Buddha, Ven. Meeti-yagala Gunaratana, the chief *Sangha* Nayaka of Jayawardhanapura, inaugurated the 1095 *Bodhi poojas* commencing on May 1 to ward off calamities and protect the people from inexplicable harm.... Astrology stipulates that a *Bodhi pooj*a is a vital and essential "*shanti karma*" [rite of blessing] for overcoming malefic planetary influences, the wrath of the gods and achieving one's cherished ambitions.

Having invented an astrological charter for the *Bodhi pûja*, the Venerable Dhirananda turns to its Buddhist side:

"It should be remembered that the Buddha was the first ever to hold the *Bodhi pooja*... during the second week after Enlightenment... as a mark of gratitude to the tree that helped him in his quest. It was unique because it was a week-long visual concentration on an inanimate object."

Dhirananda thus adds a mythical Buddhist justification to his astrological pseudotradition (note "stipulates") and in so doing legitimizes a blatantly Hinduized astrological doctrine, perhaps also a recent invention, by connecting it with Buddhism, despite the Buddha's well-known injunction to monks to steer clear of such "beastly arts."

We have mentioned that the success of the *Bodhi pûja* has led to its being taken up by priests of the gods and adapted to their own traditions. Some of them have reduced the rite to the literal meaning of its popular title, "Worship of the Bo Tree," and have dispensed with the text altogether. When a client comes with a problem, the priest simply makes offerings to the *bô* tree, bathes it, returns to the god's shrine, transfers the merit to the god, and utters a traditional invocation asking the god to help his devotee with the problem.

The Venerable Dhirananda's theorizing has brought a Hindu touch into Sinhala Buddhism; the practice of *kapuralas* has had an even more Hinduizing effect. By tradition all Buddhist *sacralia* are accessible to both sexes at all times, and menstruating women are not ritually impure when it comes to Buddhist worship, as they are in Hindu culture and in Sinhala tradition for the purposes of the spirit cults. Now a notice has appeared at the great *bô* tree behind the main shrine at Kataragama forbidding women access to the inner rampart around the tree, and this restriction is being emulated at other sites.

This is a drastic, and to our knowledge completely unprecedented, infringement of the Buddhist principle of sexual equality in worship. It seems that the deity in the tree objects not merely to menstrual pollution, as other gods do, but to the presence of women altogether. If this trend spreads, we shall have to change the view we have expressed above that the *Bodhi pûja* "seems to belong to all Sinhala Buddhists equally" and rewrite "Buddhists" as "Buddhist males." However, some *kapuralas* are emphatic that the exclusion of women is wrong, and one will have to wait to see which party carries the day.

Having described the current ritual uses of the *Bodhi pûja*, we return to consider the texts and the emotions they express. If the *Bodhi pûja* is tending to supersede *pirit*, we have suggested, that is largely due to the appeal of the text. The *pirit* texts, besides being in Pali, are not devotional in tone and never evoke the image of the Buddha. By contrast a line in one of the Venerable Ariyadhamma's Sinhala verses says, "I make my heart into a cool Fragrant Hut," the term Fragrant Hut being a technical term for wherever the Buddha is staying. The sentiment is not new to the literature: an older Pali verse that is used in the service says much the same; but the point is that now it is expressed in the speaker's mother tongue.

In Ariyadhamma's text the worship is directed to all twenty-eight Buddhas, but this does not affect the emotional tone. We quote a few sample verses from the newer printed versions that elaborate on this theme.

- 1. With the power of alms-merit he brought blessings on the world, Sage Tanhamkara, I worship you. Sadhu!
- 3. Giving away his children as alms, he defeated Mara. Sage Saranamkara, I worship you. Sadhu!
- 14. Removing doubt, he opened the way to liberation. Royal Sage Sumedha, I worship you. Sadhu!
- 21. He defeated the assembled host of Mara. Sage Phussa, I worship you. Sadhu!

However, when Gautama, "our" Buddha, is addressed in these texts, the tone becomes still warmer:

The world is bathed in the lovely rays of the Buddha;
The Buddha monk uttered such good sermons.
With full heart I offer lights at your blessed feet.
My sorrow and sin destroyed, may I inherit content.
Like the full moon seen from the mountain top,
Wearing a golden robe and giving forth light,
Showing compassion to the three worlds,
Behold the beauty of our Lord Buddha.

Another short sequence from one of our variant versions expresses traditional Buddhist themes in simple language; it states the purposes of the ritual:

To spread compassion to beings in all the worlds,
To release from suffering those near and far,
To obtain happiness for all in this world,
For my mother and father to achieve *nirvana.*
To live without trouble from our enemies,
To live in harmony with our friends,
To live in happiness forever-
May our friends and enemies achieve *nirvana.*
To be born in an honorable caste (kula),
To possess as much wealth as one wishes,

To build stupas without limit

May I be born like King Dahamsonda.

King Dahamsonda, "Dharma Addict," was, according to an apocryphal story, the future Buddha Gautama in one of his former births. He was so avid to hear the Dhamma preached that he gave his life for it, though luckily the sacrifice proved to be illusory. In a similar vein this version goes on with verses in which the devotee asks to have the wisdom of Mahausadha (the Buddha in another former birth), the health of the monk Bakkula, and the divine eye (clairvoyance) of the Buddha's disciple Mugalan.

The less traditional themes in our variant versions are three: references to the magical and almost exorcistic uses of the ritual dealt with above; the focusing of worship on the tree; and adoration of the Buddha as a mother figure. The first two of these themes cannot be entirely disentangled in our examples. The text used by Jayanta has a series of stanzas addressed to the *bô* tree that are strongly reminiscent of exorcistic verse. In that tradition it is customary to expel the badness (*dosa*) from the patient, moving systematically from his head down to his feet.

O Lord Bô, who gave [the Buddha] tenfold power and wisdom,

By the merit of past births we have come to worship here.

May all planetary ills and calamities be banished

From the face, ears, and tongue.

O Lord Bô, who gave tenfold power and wisdom,

We worship you to calm the fires of sorrow.

Through the two legs and from the soles

May all planetary ills and calamities disappear.

O Lord Bô, who gave tenfold power and wisdom,

We have come to deck you with lovely flowers and worship you.

From the waist, intestines, kidneys, and so on

May all planetary ills and calamities disappear.

O Lord Bô, who gave tenfold power and wisdom,

We have come to offer you lights and lovely flowers.

Such things as poisons, venoms, and tying [by black magic],

May such bad planetary ills and calamities be banished.

Expel and banish badness caused by the nine planets.

May we be blessed by the power of the ninefold *Sangha*.

O Lord Bô, who destroyed the power of Mara,

May we obtain the help (*pihita*) of the Fully Enlightened One.

We mentioned above that at the climax of Ariyadhamma's service everyone repeats several times, "May all beings be happy." The predicate of the sentence, *suvapat vetva*, is so vague as to be hard to translate; one might also translate it, for example, as "attain bliss." Jayanta, however, has given that point in the service a decided twist by inserting the word "physical" (*kayika*) at one of the repetitions; one would therefore translate the climax of his service as "May all beings be well, / May all beings be physically well, / Be well, be well."

Everyone we have interviewed maintains the traditional theory that the Buddha cannot directly intercede in current affairs or help the worshipper and equally maintains that the *Bodhi* tree is a king by virtue of the divinity living in it and presiding over it. Clearly if there is an agency that can grant the worshipper's requests, it can only, according to the doctrine, be that divinity.

But the last stanza cited above shows that in this context the tree, the tree spirit, and the Buddha himself have all but merged in the mind of the devotee. The standard traditional formula is "The Buddha for refuge, the gods for help"; yet in the verse above the same term "help" from that formula is used to request assistance from the Buddha.

In many verses (we choose three separate ones at random) the *bô* tree is said to shine with the Buddha's own halo or effulgence (*ras*):

By simply gazing our eyes awaken [to truth],

By worship and offerings the roots of sin are washed,

By hearing his name the path to liberation unfolds,

The Buddha's rays shine in the compound of the glorious victorious Bodhi.

In every house may there be a Buddha image

And may it shine with scented flowers and lamps,

And may I get the comfort and protection of the gods,

And may the Buddha rays shine from the King Bô.

May the power of the blessed Gautama Buddha appear,

May the blessed Lord Bô protect this country,

May the power of the *Bodhisattva*s here appear

And may the Buddha rays radiate from the blessed Tooth Relic.

We mentioned above that already in the original text by the Venerable Ariyadhamma the Buddha is referred to as both father and mother. This is somewhat unusual. In Sinhala the Buddha is usually referred to as "lord" or "king," much less frequently as "father." We are not aware that in the Pali liturgy he is ever referred to by a kinship term. Gombrich has published elsewhere a premodern Sinhala text of uncertain date in which the Buddha is compared to a mother in an elaborate metaphor, but this was worth drawing attention to precisely because it was exceptional.

As pointed out in that chapter, it is much less unusual to attribute to one's mother the qualities (namely, the compassion) of the Buddha. Occasionally the compassion of the mother is attributed to the Buddha. Thus in the Buddha legend as recorded in the thirteenth-century Sinhala text *Pûjavaliya* a repentant person addresses the Buddha as "compassionate mother." But in public utterance the Buddha has always been referred to and addressed with a certain distance and formality.

Now we find Jayanta singing, with his audience as chorus:

O Mother, the mother guru of all the worlds,

O Mother, the mother guru of human beings,

O Mother, full of goodness and truth,

Worship the fully Enlightened Buddha-Mother.

Here what was hitherto a private emotion in Sinhala culture has been given public expression. In the traditional pantheon there was only one important goddess, namely Pattinî, so she was the only being onto whom the Sinhala worshipper could project maternal feelings. Her cult is now in decline for other reasons, and her place as a good mother is not being taken by the ambivalent Kali. Possibly, though we would not wish to press the point, the Buddha is here moving into an emotional gap left by Pattinî's withdrawal. Be that as it may, the officiants of the *Bodhi pûja* are, as Levi-Strauss has argued, abreacting their own past and opening a breach in the public culture by permitting the emotion of mother love to emerge from individual consciousness into the public cult of the Buddha. We should perhaps add, at the risk of saying the obvious, that none of the worshippers is denying that the Buddha is male; his "motherhood" is metaphorical. It is nonetheless felt for that.

In the *Bodhi pûja* texts (including that of Ariyadhamma) we also find the word *bhakti*, "devotion," which though not unknown to the Theravadin tradition is hardly typical of it. In devotional Hinduism *bhakti* is passionate love of God; as in Christian mystical tradition the model, implicit or explicit, is often sexual love. The *bhakti* in the *Bodhi pûja* lacks sexual connotations; it refers to the mother's warmth and nurturance and the child's grateful dependence. The Hindu analogue of this Buddhist sentiment is the feeling for the cow. It may be no accident that one printed text of the *Bodhi pûja* tells the worshipper not to eat beef, though it enunciates no other food taboo or more general injunction to vegetarianism.

We sum up the emotional development of the Bodhi pûja with an illustration. Any offering of flowers before a Buddha image is normally accompanied by a Pali stanza that naturally almost everyone knows by heart. It means:

"I make offering to the Buddha with this flower, and by this merit may there be release. Just as this flower fades, so my body goes towards destruction."

In other words the offering is made an occasion for recalling the cardinal Buddhist principle of impermanence. The Sinhala equivalent of this verse given in one printed version preserves the main idea but strikes a more hopeful note:

Like these flowers may my mind be pure;

May these flowers make me aware of the body [as impermanent];

May these flowers become an offering for the Sage,

And like these flowers may my mind blossom to *nirvana.*

Yet another Sinhala verse now current says:

Brimming with the scent of goodness,

To the fully Enlightened Buddha-Mother (*amma Sambudunhata*),

Overflowing with scent and color

I offer these flowers. Sadhu! Sadhu! "

13

The Seventh Vajra Point

The Krtya-kriya of the Tathagata

The example involving the lapis lazuli ground is interesting and multi- leveled. This is apparently derived from a tradition of 'scrying' or gem gazing for oracular and visionary purposes, the clarity of the vision being equivalent to the mind purified of obstructions. In such a crystal/mind, the exotic abode of Lord Indra was believed to become visible. Once mortals see the various splendors of his realm, they are motivated to practice virtuous deeds and pray to attain such a rebirth for themselves. The text notes that it is of no import that these sentient beings do not have full knowledge of the absolute mode of existence (as emptiness-awareness) of this appearance or even that such experiences are impermanent; beings are effectively inspired by these visions to practice with the aim of attaining rebirth in the realm of the gods.

It is underscored that the extraordinary qualities of Buddha activity are not accompanied by any self-conscious intention to benefit other but manifest as spontaneously as reflections in a mirror. The pre-requisite of purification for this sublime perception suggests another dimension of activity in the analogy. The vision of Indra's abode serving as a contributory cause attracting others to the practice of virtue corresponds to the activity of the *Bodhisattva*. Without clinging to artifice for recognition or leaning too far forward, the pure energy of true *Sangha* is naturally attractive and inspiring to other sentient beings, so that they are magnetized toward a life of graceful discipline wherein the cultivation of loving-kindness and true wisdom are uppermost.

Kasyapa said to the Buddha: "O World-honoured One! Is there any self in the twenty-five existences or not?" The Buddha said: "O good man! 'Self' means 'tathagatagarbha.' Every being has the Buddha Nature. This is self. Such a self is, since the very beginning, under cover of innumerable illusions. That is why man cannot see it. O good man! There is here a poor woman. She has in her house the true gold hidden. But none of the people of the house, big or small, know it. But there is a stranger, who, by expediency, speaks to the poor woman: 'I shall employ you. You now weed the land!' The woman answers: 'I cannot do it now. If you let my son see where the gold is hidden, I will soon work for you.' The man says, 'I know the way. I will show it to your son.'

The woman says again: 'No people of my house, big or small, know. How can you?' The man says: 'I will now make it clear.' The woman says again: 'I desire to see. Pray let me.' The man digs out the gold that lay hidden. The woman sees it, is glad, and begins to respect the person. O good man! The same is the case with the Buddha Nature that man has. Nobody can see it. This is as in the case of the gold the poor woman possessed and yet could not see. O good man! I now let persons see the Buddha Nature that they possess, which is overspread by illusions. This is as in the case of the poor woman who cannot see the gold, even possessing it. The Tathagata now shows all beings the storehouse of enlightenment, which is the so-called Buddha Nature. If all beings see this, they are glad and will take refuge in the Tathagata. The good expediency is the Tathagata and the poor woman is all the innumerable beings, and the cask of true gold is the Buddha Nature.

"Also, next, O good man! For example, a woman has a child, who, yet very young, is taken by illness. Worried by this, the woman seeks a good doctor. A good doctor comes and mixes up three medicines, which are the butter, milk and rock candy. This he gives her, to have it taken by the child. Then, he says to the woman: 'When the child has taken the medicine, do not give milk to the child for some time. When the medicine has worked out its way, you, then, may give milk.' Then, the woman applies a bitter thing to the nipple and says to the child: 'Do not touch it. The nipple is poisoned.' The child is dying for the milk and wants to have it. Hearing of poison, it runs away. When the medicine has done the work, the mother washes the nipple, calls the child in, and gives it. The hungry child, having heard of poison, does not come to it.

The mother says again: 'Just to give you the medicine, I put on it poison. As you have already taken the medicine, I have washed it off. Come! Have the nipple. It is no more bitter.' Hearing this, the child slowly comes back and takes it. O good man! The same is the case with the Tathagata. To save beings, he gives them the law of no-self. Having thus practiced the Way, the beings make away with the mind that clings to self and gain *nirvana*. All this is to make away with the wrong concept of the people, to show them the way and make them stand above, to show them that they stick to self, that what goes in the world is all false and not true, and make then practice no-self and purify their own self. This is as in the case of the woman who puts bitter things to the nipple for love of the child. The same is the case of the Tathagata. For practicing the void, I say that all do not have the self.

This is as in case of the woman who washed the nipple, calling for the child to partake of the milk. The same is the case with me too. I speak of the tathagatagarbha. Because of the, the bhikshus do not entertain fear. The same goes with the child who hears its mother, slowly comes back, and take the milk. The same is the case with the bhikshus.

They should well know that the Tathagata hides nothing." At one time the Buddha achieved Samyak-Sambodhi (Correct Peerless Enlightenment) under the Bodhi-tree in Magadha state. The Bodhi-tree's name is Ahsipah, its root was deep in the soil, its trunk was tall, straight and had no knot, like a sandalwood column. Whenever birds approach, they had to fly back because they could not fly over the tree. The tree's skin was fine and glossy, with various interlaced colors, just like damasks. The tree was branchy and the crown of it was bushy and green.

Around the tree, there were many beautiful and lovely flowers blooming and emanating fragrance. They were much more beautiful than all other flowers except the Kovidars and Parijatas. Around the tree, there were also many shorter trees. This Bodhi-tree, the king of trees, was splendid and handsome. It was like the Sumeru Mountain, which is the king of all mountains. It was so tall that even the people beyond 1 Yojana could see it. Its fragrance flows all around and its halo shines all around. People who saw it far away at night would suspect that it is a group of huge fires. The area under the tree was majestic, beautiful, spacious, and flat, like the happy garden, with luxuriant fragrant grass. It was like the neck of the peacock king, beautiful and fragrant, people do not tire of watching it.

At such a place, the Tathagata sat rightly and divinely, with many beings around him, just like a moon surrounded by stars. At that time, coming from other directions, there were Buddhas as many as the atoms of ten Buddha-Worlds. In order to make the Bodhi-manda (site of enlightenment) of Vairocana more sublime, those Buddhas appeared as *Bodhisattva*s and joined the congregation. The names of their leaders are: Avalokitesvara (Contemplator of the World's Sounds) Bodhisattva, Manjusri Bodhisattva, Ksitigarbha (Earth Store) Bodhisattva, Akasagarbha (Space Store) Bodhisattva, Vajragarbha Bodhisattva, Vimalakirti Bodhisattva, Virtuous mighty light Bodhisattva, Extinguish all eclipses Bodhisattva, Ratna-Pani (Treasure Hand) Bodhisattva, Mahamati (Great Wisdom) Bodhisattva, Samantabhadra (Universal Goodness) Bodhisattva, and so on.

Moreover, hundred billions of *Bodhisattva*s appeared as Sravakas and came to join the congregation. The names of their leaders are: Sariputra, Maha-Maudgalyayana, Subhuti, Rahula, Ajnata-Kaundinya, Maha-Kasyapa, Upali, Aniruddha, Revata, Ananda, Devadatta, Upandanda, and so on. All of them had practiced the Six-*Paramitas* for a long time, and had already been very close to the Bodhi of Buddhas. In order to enlighten living beings, they appeared as Sravakas in this defiled world. There were also innumerable Bhikshunis headed by Maha-Prajapati. All of them had already accomplished the meritorious virtues of great and wise men, in order to soothe the inferior living beings, they appeared as women.

There were also innumerable Sakra Devanam Indras, Brahmas, guardian gods, Devas, dragons, Yaksas, Gandharvas, Asuras, Garudas, Kinnaras, Mahoragas, human and nonhuman beings. They were all great *Bodhisattvas*; none of them was mundane person.

At that time, the Bhagavan (World Honored One), who was sitting under the Bodhi-tree, was sublime, pure, refined and wonderful, like the Wish-fulfilling pearl under the Citta tree. With the immovable Correct-Mindfulness, he was like the Sumeru Mountain. In order to make all *Bodhisattva*s and living beings understand the mighty and holy power of Buddhas' profound and secret Dhyana (Zen)s, he entered a *Samadhi* named Tathagata's Unimaginable State. Suddenly, each mark of the 32 marks of the Bhagavan revealed infinite Buddha-Worlds and Buddhas of the ten directions, just like a bright mirror reflecting various colors. Moreover, each mark of the 80 minor marks of the Bhagavan revealed his previous *Bodhisattva*-practices. From the Radiance king to the final incarnation at the place of Dipamkara (Burning Lamp) Buddha, all the difficult and arduous practices, the history that he completely donated all his heads, eyes, bodies, skins, fleshes, arms, legs, wives, servants, and the kingships, palaces, and so on.

This *Samadhi* has the great mighty power, all Buddhas are always in this *Samadhi* when they are eating, walking, teaching Dharmas, and even in *Nirvana*. Why? Because all Buddhas rely on this *Samadhi* to achieve boundless great mighty sacrosanct power, as far as to realize-and-prove (pravista) the vacuum nature of all dharmas, so they can manifest various unrestricted things at all Buddha-Worlds of the ten directions.

For example, a person visualizes various fantastic things in his dream, but when he wakes up, all those things disappear. Likewise, for the mundane persons, because of the dreams of ignorance, they mistakenly think that all things are entities; meanwhile, all Buddhas are awakened and do not cling to anything, thus they can freely show infinite Buddha-Activities (Buddha-karya) within one infinitesimal thought, to profit all living beings and make them succeed, to help them comprehend innumerable abstruse and wonderful Liberation-Gates.

At that time, Virtue Store *Bodhisattva,* who had not yet achieved the perfection of Bodhi-Practices, asked Samantabhadra *Bodhisattva*: "What is the name of the *Samadhi* that the Tathagata entered into just now? How can he freely show various Buddha-Activities in all the worlds of the ten directions to rescue living beings?" Then Samantabhadra Bodhisattva spoke to Virtue Store *Bodhisattva*: "Listen carefully and I'll tell you." At that time, all *Bodhisattva*s looked at them intently and reverently, and glorified together with one voice: "What an excellent question! How profound, delicate and wonderful! Arya (sage) Samantabhadra, who knows everything, is going to preach now." Instantly, the earth shook in six different ways, heaven rained down exquisite flowers, all living beings suffering from afflictions and distresses were relieved for a while.

Then Samantabhadra Bodhisattva said: "Buddha-Son, this *Samadhi*'s name is Tathagata's Unimaginable State, namely, the Bodhi of all Buddhas, because all Buddhas always rely on and stay in it. Since the Bhagavan has been awarded the prediction of coming Buddhahood by Dipamkara Buddha, he has been always in this *Samadhi*. He always does nothing, and simultaneously, he naturally shows infinite Buddha-Activities as responses to all living beings."

"Say, inside one single hair-tip in the space, there are Buddha-worlds as many as the atoms of all Buddha-Worlds. Inside those worlds, the Bhagavan may appear as being born in the Tushita Heaven; may appear have gone down from that heaven and entered his mother's womb; may appear as a newborn, have taken 7 steps and said that 'I am now on the margin of birth and death'; may appear as being in the palace, may appear as leaving home or practicing austerities; may appear as subduing demons, or achieved the Correct-Awakening, or turning the wonderful Dharma-wheel; may stay in the world for countless kalpas, rescue all living beings and make them get away from the suffering; may appear as in *Nirvana*; may reveal that all kalpas (eons) are in one kshana(moment), or one Kshana includes all kalpas, kalpas and kshanas do not increase or decrease, thus all living beings have not been extricated yet. From kshana to kshana, and universally in all worlds, the Bhagavan is constantly doing such various Buddha-Activities and never rest, but in fact he always does nothing."

"Such as, inside that single hair-tip in the space, there are infinite worlds. In those worlds, each infinitesimal thought of the Bhagavan universally reveals various majesties and principles of all Buddhas, and meanwhile he does nothing. Likewise, inside all hair-tips that spread over all universes, there are infinite worlds. For all atoms of those worlds, each atom contains worlds much more than the atoms of all Buddha-Worlds. In one kshana, in all those worlds, the various majesties and activities of all Buddhas are naturally and universally revealed.

For example, may be born in heaven, may be in *Nirvana*, may have extricated innumerable Asamkhyeyas of living beings. In such a way, infinitesimal thought after infinitesimal thought unto the endless future, Bhagavans are constantly performing Buddha-Activities to benefit all living beings, never resting, even at the ultimate end of universes, and at the ultimate end of realms of all living beings. Meanwhile, the Buddha-Worlds do not decrease, the atoms do not increase. Why? Because all dharma (thing)s are like illusive flame, are unstable."

"For example, in this congregation, the great *Bodhisattva*s as many as atoms of ten Buddha-Worlds, are staying together in this area of 12 yojanas in Magadha state, but do not squeeze each other. Likewise, each of those atoms contains infinite Buddha-Worlds. Those Buddha-Worlds, some are upward, some are downward, some are face to face, some are back to back, some are side by side, some are interpenetrating, and yet do not obstruct each other."

"For example, people in dream see many things at a same place, because they are not real, they do not obstruct each other. Likewise, all the universes are shown by the heart (Alaya). Living beings may see kalpa-fire, or see the fire burned out everything; may see the world is made by wind, may see clean or dirty things, may see the world with no Buddha. Each of them sees different scenes, all because of the karma of their own heart."

"For example, driven by hunger and thirst, the hungry ghosts go to the Ganges-river. When they arrive, some of them may see water, some of them may see that the river is filled up with dusts, purulence, blood, dung, and other dirty things." "Likewise, every living being, which is affected by his own karmas, may see the Buddha's land is clean or dirty;

May see the Buddha is living, or the Buddha is in *Nirvana*;

May see the Buddha is teaching the public at the site of enlightenment;

May hear about the foremost truth, or hear the praises for generosity and charity.

May see the Buddha is walking or standing still;

May see the Buddha is sitting or taking food;

May see the Buddha is one time or seven times or one yojana times taller then normal people, or even hundreds, thousands yojana times taller;

May see that the majestic light of Buddha looks like the rising sun or the full moon;

May be born in a period that the Buddha has been in *Nirvana* long before because of the hindrances of karma;

May be unable to hear the names of Buddhas, just like those hungry ghosts, see no water in Ganges-river but only various dunghills;

May see many Buddhas come from their own pure-land, with great and dignified *Bodhisattva*-bodies, enter into this congregation or a world, while other living beings only see that the kalpa-fire is burning;

Maybe a world is full of living beings and all of them can see Buddhas;

May see the Tathagata collect all worlds and put them into one Buddha-World, or insert one Buddha-World into all worlds.

Just like some people with eye-diseases, they stay at a same place but see different scenes, and those scenes do not interfere each other. They cannot see the reality, all because of their eye-diseases. Likewise, the Dharma-Nature of everything is unimpeded, but because of various minds and relationships, the living beings are hoodwinked so that they do not have correct view, and unable to know the truth."

"Buddha-Son, now I am going to tell you in brief the method of staying in this *Samadhi*. Just like the Buddha, the Bhagavan who is staying in this *Samadhi*, by one infinitesimal thought, he universally permeates through infinite Buddha-Lands inside the hair-tips that spread over all universes. For all the atoms of those Buddha-Lands, each of them contains worlds as many as all atoms of the Dharma-Realm. In order to profit all living beings, kshana by kshana, he universally permeates through all worlds, reveals the expedient means, majesties, and activities of the Buddhas as many as atoms of ten Buddha-Worlds, in such a way, unto the time that all living beings have attained Bodhi, the Buddha-Activities never interrupt. Also, for one Buddha, two Buddhas, three Buddhas... up to all Buddhas of the ten directions, the great mighty and virtuous powers shown by each of them are just like that."

Having heard the teaching, Virtue Store Bodhisattva immediately acquired this *Samadhi* on his seat. Suddenly, he sees those infinite Buddhas and knows all the mighty, virtue and expedient means of them. With the power of this *Samadhi*, he can also rescue living beings in the same way. At the same time, each of the Hundreds of Ganges-river-sands *Bodhisattva*s in the congregation also had acquired various *Samadhi*s, ksanti (forbearance)s, and different Bhumi(stage)s. As for Avalokitesvara *Bodhisattva* and other great *Bodhisattva*s of the tenth Bhumi, because all the meritorious virtues and wonderful practices of them are perfected, they had acquired this *Samadhi* eons before.

They can also gather all kalpas and put them into one kshana, store infinite worlds into one atom, permeate through all worlds by one infinitesimal thought, liberate innumerable living beings and always do nothing, because of their abilities of showing all Buddha-Activities naturally. Thus, although they heard this Dharma, they gained no improvement by that, just like the bottles filled with water, which will not receive even one extra drop of water in a rain.

At that time, the Bhagavan in the *Samadhi* emitted a light named Great-Apocalypse from the position between his eyebrows (urna). For all the *Bodhisattva*s practicing with effort and had not yet acquired the tenth Bhumi, once they had been illuminated by that light, they immediately saw infinite Buddha-Worlds in all hair-tips of universes and the Buddha-Worlds in all atoms, just like a vitreous bottle filled with white mustard seeds, the observer can clearly see the inside. Likewise, those *Bodhisattva*s saw infinite Buddha-Worlds in atoms, saw all Buddhas in those worlds, and saw all Buddha-Bodies inside each Buddha-Body. Each Buddha has infinite names, for sake of every single living being. Infinitesimal thoughts by infinitesimal thoughts, they constantly and naturally appear in every Buddha-world, in Anuttara-Samyak-Sambodhi.

For example, the Wish-fulfilling pearl on the high streamer can rain various treasures naturally according to the wishes of living beings. Likewise, the Tathagatas, who are manifesting that they had achieved the Correct-Awakening in various worlds, can liberate innumerable living beings naturally, and various living beings of those worlds do not obstruct each other. Just like the one with transcendental power, can travel through spaces, mountains, rivers, rocks, and cliffs with no impediment. Why? Because all destinies are like illusive fire, are unstable. Having witnessed that, each of those *Bodhisattva*s saw that his body permeates through all worlds and stays in front of each Buddha with one infinitesimal thought, and respectfully offers and sustains those Buddhas for one kalpa, two kalpas, three kalpas, or up to hundreds, thousands kalpas, or for one moment, or one muhurta (split-second).

They may hear that the Bhagavan is preaching the Dharma-Gates of various *paramitas* and Dharanis, or explaining levels of Bhumis, or showing supernatural transformations, or gathering all kalpas into one infinitesimal thought. Thus they aroused a thought that it's wonderful and hard to encounter, and pondered: "Why is the Bhagavan so superbly powerful, so virtuous and unrestricted? Within one kshana, he can make us accomplish virtuous roots and meritorious virtues of infinite kalpas, so we can quickly acquire the great mighty divine powers of the Tathagata's Unimaginable State *Samadhi*." At that time, in order to profit all living beings, Virtue Store Bodhisattva continued to ask Samantabhadra Bodhisattva: "For anyone who wish to acquire this *Samadhi*, what meritorious virtues, donations and wisdom are needed?"

Then Samantabhadra Bodhisattva, who manifests himself being the Correct-Awakening One (Buddha)s universally in all pure-worlds of the ten directions and are enlightening living beings, told Virtue Store *Bodhisattva*: "Buddha-Son, to acquire this *Samadhi*, one should firstly cultivating blessings and develop his virtuous roots. Such as, to constantly offer and sustain Buddhas, Dharmas, *Sangha*s, and parents; to rescue and teach all the penniless, anguished, helpless, homeless, and pitiful living beings, and never abandon them. Do not be selfish even for the body and flesh of oneself."

"Why? Because the one who offers and sustains Buddhas will gain great felicities and virtues, will quickly attain

Anuttara-Samyak-Sambodhi, will make all living beings restful and pleased. The one who supports Dharmas will have his wisdom increased, will prove the Dharma of absoluteness, will be able to fully realize the true nature of all dharmas. The one who offers and sustains *Sangha*s will gain innumerable accumulation (sambhara)s of felicities and wisdoms, will achieve the Buddhahood quickly."

"One should also offer and sustain his parents, teachers, all the people who had helped him, and all the people that he had relied on. He should think of repaying them doubly. Why? Because the one who remembers kindness of others will not lose his virtuous roots even if he is in the cycle of birth and death; and the unthankful one will lose his virtuous roots and do much villainy."

"Thus, all Tathagatas praise the appreciation of kindness, criticize the unthankful ones, and constantly take pity on and relieve the suffering living beings. By that, *Bodhisattva*s never lose their immeasurable virtuous roots. If one can diligently nurtures meritorious virtues, constantly be thankful, and takes pity on living beings, then the Bodhi is already in his hand."

"We should know that Buddhas say, offering and sustaining on each of those three fields can achieve innumerable virtuous roots." "Secondly, Virtue Store, we should know that, *Bodhisattva*s (anyone who wish to acquire this *Samadhi*. Because of his great wishes and practices, he's called "*Bodhisattva*") should plant the great seed, because this seed sprouts buds of *Samadhi*s, and grows up into fruit of Bodhi. The method of planting it is, to respectfully offer and sustain the present Buddhas or statues/images of Buddhas with multifarious beautiful flowers, vanillas, paste incenses, ground incenses, and various performances and music, and imagine as mentioned above: 'Universally in infinite worlds inside all hair-tips and all atoms of universes, for all majestic Buddhas and *Bodhisattva*s in all Buddha-congregations, I widely offer and sustain them absorbedly with correct mindfulness.

Because the Dharma-nature of one Buddha I offer and sustain is the Dharma-nature of all Buddhas, thus if I am offering and sustaining one Tathagata, it's same as offering and sustaining all Tathagatas. By the sacrosanct powers of every those Buddhas, I can gather numbers of kalpas into one infinitesimal thought, then that's same as having offered and sustained the Tathagatas for so many kalpas.'"

"If any living being can believe and understand this method, plant the great seed, then he will get the great *Samadhi* of Tathagata's Unimaginable State. So good man, you should practice this method, offer and sustain day to day. Because even one bow in front of Buddhas can make this seed grow and sprout buds of *Samadhis*. Also, you should irrigate it with the water of charity, observing precepts, great vows and wisdoms. When a *Bodhisattva* is practicing donations for irrigating the *Samadhi,* he should not discriminate merit-fields, enemies, relatives, well-doers, wrong-doers, those keep precepts, those breaking rules, rich ones, or poor ones. He should think: "Though the donations to the rich would be useless, I still should practice charity." And also, *Bodhisattva* should keep precepts purely, when seeing those who are breaking rules, he should take great pity on them, should not loathe them."

"And also, *Bodhisattva* should make great Bodhi vows from deep inside his heart: 'From thought to thought, for worlds that inside the hair-tips spread all over the universes, for worlds that inside every atom of all Buddha-Worlds, I must attain the Impartial-Correct-Awakening universally in those infinite worlds, and turn the wonderful Dharma-Wheel to enlighten all living beings, same as what the present Bhagavan Vairocana do, without vyapara; gathers infinite kalpas into one infinitesimal thought, within each world in those kalpas, reveals the majesties of the Buddhas as many as all atoms of Buddha-Worlds, each majesty enlightens Ganges-River-Sands living beings and make them detach from suffering. In such a manner, unto the ultimate of universes and realms of living beings, I will never rest.'"

"Buddha-Son, listen with single-mind and I am going tell you how to develop wisdom. If any good man or good woman wishes to acquire this *Samadhi* for the perfection of unsurpassed Bodhi, he should in advance develop his wisdom, because this *Samadhi* must be acquired by wisdom." "The one who developing wisdom should keep away from false speeches, frivolous speeches, gossips, distractions, and all meaningless things, although he arouses great compassionate heart for all living beings, his mind is concentrated, without pollution or distraction."

"Then he should go to a sublime-abode to watch a statue of Buddha. The body of Buddha is golden and sublime, the characteristics of Buddha's body are perfectly beautiful, innumerable nirmana (miraculously created) Buddhas in *Samadhi* are sitting one by one in the halo."

"Then the practitioner should bow to the Buddha's feet in front of the statue and think: 'I know that the infinite Buddhas of the ten directions, who exist presently are: Perfection of all meanings Buddha, Amitabha Buddha, Ratna-ketu (Treasure streamer) Buddha, Aksobhya Buddha, Vairocana Buddha, Ratna-candra (Treasure moon) Buddha, Ratna-prabha (Treasure light) Buddha, and so on.'" Then he should respectfully arouse great pure belief in whichever Buddha he like, and meditate on the image of the Buddha. He should regard the image as the real body of the Tathagata, with respect and worship. He should meditate on the image according to the Buddha statue in front of him; look up and down carefully, with concentration."

"Then he should stay in an unoccupied place, sit rightly and visualize the image of Buddha, as if the Buddha is in front of him within one arm's length. He should constantly meditate on the image of Buddha, never forget or lose it. If he temporarily forgets or loses the image, he should go back to the sublime-abode and watch the Buddha statue again."

"When watching the statue, he should greatly respect and worship it as if the real body of Buddha is in front of him, watches it in detail, and do not treat it as a statue any longer. When he has seen that, he should respectfully circle clockwise around the Buddha, offer and sustain the Buddha with exquisite flowers, ground incenses, paste incenses, and various materials." "He should always watch in such a way, with single-mind, as if the Bhagavan is staying in front of him. 'The Buddha, the Bhagavan who sees all, hears all, knows all, and must completely know my heart.' By thinking that, when the visualization has been completed, he should go back to the unoccupied place, visualize the Buddha in front of him, never forget or lose the image."

"With single-mind, Practice that diligently for 21 days, if the felicities and virtues that he has accomplished are enough, he will immediately see the Tathagata appear in front of him. If he cannot see the Tathagata due to the karma-obstacles that caused by the evildoings in his previous lives, then if he can diligently keep practicing with single-mind, do not regress, and think nothing else, then he still will see the Tathagata quickly." "Why? Because if one endeavors for unsurpassed Bodhi absorbedly practices one dharma will surely succeed. Conversely, if one is not undaunted and regresses again and again in what he practices, he cannot liberate even himself, how can he liberate all suffering living beings? If one encountered this correct and true shortcut to Bodhi but cannot practice diligently, then he is merely a heavy burden of the mother earth."

"For example, in sea, if one drank the seawater scooped up with both hands just once, then he has already drunk the water of all rivers in Jambudvipa. Likewise, if *Bodhisattva* practices this Bodhi-sea, then he has already practiced all *Samadhis*, forbearances, Bhumis, Dharanis. Thus, one should constantly and diligently practice it without laziness or dissipation, be concentrated, set his mind on seeing the Buddha in front of him."

"Practices in such a way, when one sees the Buddha for the first time, one would think: 'Is this a real Buddha, or only an image?' If he know what he see is a real Buddha, then he should kneel down in front of the Buddha, join his palms, worship and think: 'Inside all hair-tips that spread over the universes, inside all atoms, there are infinite Buddhas. Their powers and virtues are boundless. Because of their great compassion, now they appear as one and come in front of me.

I should request, Bhagavan, please teach me the great *Samadhi* Dharma of Tathagata's Unimaginable State.' If he hears any teaching from the Tathagata, he should decisively and completely believe in everything the Buddha says, do not be doubtful, then he will immediately acquire this *Samadhi* at that place."

"If one cannot ask the Buddha due to his karma-obstacles, he should think: 'All dharma (phenomenon)s are like illusions, like flames, like nebulas, like shadows, like images, like dreams. Meditate in such a way; know that the dharma-nature is void and tranquil.

Although Tathagata realizes that all dharmas are like illusions and dreams, the essential nature of Tathagata is neither illusion nor dream, just like the spaces. So the Bhagavan can appear in front of me by his wisdom and compassion. Bhagavan, please emit the great compassionate bright light for me, to extinguish all my suffering.'

Thereupon, the Buddha will emit a ray called 'Green flame' from the position between his eyebrows. As soon as the ray shines him, all his suffering will be extinguished, and then he will acquire the Dharma-Light Kshanti by Dhyana; will be able to realize innumerable *Samadhi*s. At the seventh night, in his dream, the Tathagata will award him the prediction of Anuttara-Samyak-Sambodhi."

"If he knows what he sees is an image, he should think: 'All Buddhas and living beings are also like images are appearing along with thoughts, without substantiality. Known that the Tathagata is like illusion, like nirmana, like dream, like mirage, then the Buddha appear naturally in front of me is also like the things in dream, is not an entity, no birth thus be born, does not vanish thus vanishes, does not go thus goes, does not perceive thus perceives, does not do anything thus shows many doings, does not speak thus speaks all Dharmas, not me not other living ones, not living being not foster, not intermediate state, not thought not action, not cognize not eat, not with *Skandha* not in *Skandha* thus shows all *Skandhas*. Likewise, unto the ultimate, all are not existent and also not non-existent. Thus, all dharmas and Buddhas are truly equal, are with a same character, just like that mirages are with a same character.'"

"'All living beings, all Buddhas and worlds, are all shown by consciousnesses and thoughts of one's own heart. All phenomena that are caused by consciousnesses and thoughts are not existent after all. Tathagata has been away from all consciousnesses and thoughts, thus I should not seek him through appearance.

Knowing that the Buddha image that I see is shown by heart, then also, all real Buddha inside hair-tips that spread over universes are shown by heart, are like the space, and are equal and with no difference. If I discriminate, then I see the Buddha; if I am away from discrimination, then I see nothing. The heart creates Buddhas, away from the heart there is no Buddha. Likewise, all Buddhas of the triple world of past, present and future are without substantiality is created by the heart (Alaya).'"

"Once *Bodhisattva* realized that all Buddhas and all dharmas are shown by thoughts of heart, he will acquire the accordance Kshanti, or enter the first Bhumi, after his present life he will be reborn quickly in the Wonderful-Joyances world, or be reborn in the Utmost-Happiness pure Buddha-Land, then he will always see the Tathagata, offer and sustain the Tathagata personally."

Then Virtue Store Bodhisattva asked Samantabhadra Bodhisattva again: "If any living being hear this Dharma-Gate, accept, uphold, recite, chant, explain, and write it, then how many felicities would he gain?"

Samantabhadra Bodhisattva answered: "Buddha-Son, listen carefully. Suppose that one can accept all living beings of the Three-Realms, make them get away from birth and death, and make all of them become Arhats; Suppose that one had offered and sustained each of those Arhats with heavenly exquisite clothes, beddings, drinks, foods, soups, and various materials for a hundred kalpas, and built seven-treasures towers for each of them after their *Nirvana*, offers and sustains the towers respectfully; Suppose that there is another one, who had kept observing precepts purely for a hundred kalpas, or practices forbearance, diligence and Dhyana (Zen).

The ones mentioned above would gain innumerable felicities, but if someone else hears this Dharma-Gate, believes and accepts it respectfully without slandering, then his bliss will surpass the bliss of those former ones, and he will achieve the Correct-Awakening quickly."

At that time, infinite Buddhas of all worlds of the ten directions emerged by themselves and praised Samantabhadra Bodhisattva: "Excellent, excellent, Buddha-Son, just as what you said."

Then Sakyamuni Tathagata emitted innumerable varicolored rays from his face, universally shone three kinds of existence, rained down multifarious flowers, melodious music was playing by itself, the ground quaked slightly. In the rays, Sakyamuni Buddha spoke a Gatha (verse):

"If one hears this Dharma with the pure heart,

He will acquire Bhumis, *Samadhis*, and Dharanis.

With the power of observing precepts, forbearances, and unrestricted supernatural abilities,

He will quickly achieve the unsurpassed Bodhi of Buddhas,

And turn the great wonderful Dharma-Wheel,

Just as what the previous Maharsi (great immortal being) do.

Gathers innumerable kalpas into one infinitesimal thought,

And reveals infinite worlds from within one atom

Innumerable living beings are sinking in the Three-Realms,

Constantly be tortured by various sufferings,

Being bound by erroneous views, they lose the correct way,

This one will liberate all of them from thought to thought."

Because Samantabhadra Bodhisattva had achieved this Dharma-Gate eons before, after his preaching, billions of gods crossed over all suffering, and reached the level of no-regression of Anuttara-Samyak-Sambodhi. Virtue Store Bodhisattva and all other *Bodhisattva*s, gods, dragons, Asuras, and the others, were all greatly pleased, and they received it with faith and respectfully practice it.

14

The Advantage of Having Faith in the Tathagata-Garbha Teaching

There is a teaching (dharma) which can awaken in us the root of faith in the Mahayana, and it should therefore be explained. The explanation is divided into five parts. They are (1) the Reasons for Writing; (2) the Outline; (3) the Interpretation; (4) on Faith and Practice; (5) the Encouragement of Practice and the Benefits Thereof.

REVELATION OF TRUE MEANING

ONE MIND AND ITS TWO ASPECTS

The revelation of the true meaning of the principle of Mahayana can be achieved by unfolding the doctrine that the principle of One Mind has two aspects. One is the aspect of Mind in terms of the Absolute (tathata; Suchness), and the other is the aspect of Mind in terms of phenomena (*samsara*; birth and death). Each of these two aspects embraces all states of existence. Why? Because these two aspects are mutually inclusive.

Mind in Terms of the Absolute

The Mind in terms of the Absolute is the one World of Reality (*dharmadhatu*) and the essence of all phases of existence in their totality. That which is called "the essential nature of the Mind" is unborn and is imperishable. It is only through illusions that all things come to be differentiated. If one is freed from illusions, then to him there will be no appearances (*lakshana*) of objects regarded as absolutely independent existences; therefore all things from the beginning transcend all forms of verbalization, description, and conceptualization and are, in the final analysis, undifferentiated, free from alteration, and indestructible. They are only of the One Mind; hence the name Suchness.

All explanations by words are provisional and without validity, for they are merely used in accordance with illusions and are incapable of denoting Suchness. The term Suchness likewise has no attributes which can be verbally specified. The term Suchness is, so to speak, the limit of verbalization wherein a word is used to put an end to words. But the essence of Suchness itself cannot be put an end to, for all things in their Absolute aspect are real; nor is there anything which needs to be pointed out as real, for all things are equally in the state of Suchness. It should be understood that all things are incapable of being verbally explained or thought of; hence the name Suchness.

If they understand that, concerning all things, though they are spoken of, there is neither that which speaks, nor that which can be spoken of, and though they are thought of, there is neither that which thinks, nor that which can be thought of, then they are said to have conformed to it. And when they are freed from their thoughts, they are said to have entered into it. Next, Suchness has two aspects if predicated in words. One is that it is truly empty (*sunya*), for this aspect can, in the final sense, reveal what is real. The other is that it is truly non-empty (*a-sunya*), for its essence itself is endowed with undefiled and excellent qualities.

Truly Empty

Suchness is empty because from the beginning it has never been related to any defiled states of existence, it is free from all marks of individual distinction of things, and it has nothing to do with thoughts conceived by a deluded mind. It should be understood that the essential nature of Suchness is neither with marks nor without marks; neither not with marks nor not without marks; nor is it both with and without marks simultaneously; it is neither with a single mark nor with different marks; neither not with a single mark nor not with different marks; nor is it both with a single and with different marks simultaneously. In short, since all unenlightened men discriminate with their deluded minds from moment to moment, they are alienated from Suchness; hence, the definition "empty"; but once they are free from their deluded minds, they will find that there is nothing to be negated.

Truly Nonempty

Since it has been made clear that the essence of all things is empty, i.e., devoid of illusions, the true Mind is eternal, permanent, immutable, pure, and self-sufficient; therefore, it is called "nonempty". And also there is no trace of particular marks to be noted in it, as it is the sphere that transcends thoughts and is in harmony with enlightenment alone.

THE MIND IN TERMS OF PHENOMENA

The Storehouse Consciousness

The Mind as phenomena (*samsara*) is grounded on the Tathagata-garbha. What is called the Storehouse Consciousness is that in which "neither birth nor death (*nirvana*)" diffuses harmoniously with "birth nor death (*samsara*)", and yet in which both are neither identical nor different. This Consciousness has two aspects which embrace all states of existence and create all states of existence. They are: (a) the aspect of enlightenment, and (b) the aspect of nonenlightenment.

THE ASPECT OF ENLIGHTENMENT

Original Enlightenment

The essence of Mind is free from thoughts. The characteristic of that which is free from thoughts is analogous to that of the sphere of empty space that pervades everywhere. The one without any second, i.e. the absolute aspect of the

World of Reality (dharmadhatu) is none other than the undifferentiated Dharmakaya, the "Essence-body" of the Tathagata. Since the essence of Mind is grounded on the Dharmakaya, it is to be called the original enlightenment. Why? Because "original enlightenment" indicates the essence of Mind (a priori) in contradistinction to the essence of Mind in the process of actualization of enlightenment; the process of actualization of enlightenment is none other than the process of integrating the identity with the original enlightenment.

THE PROCESS OF ACTUALIZATION OF ENLIGHTENMENT

Grounded on the original enlightenment is nonenlightenment. And because of nonenlightenment, the process of actualization of enlightenment can be spoken of. Now, to be fully enlightened to the fountainhead of Mind is called the final enlightenment; and not to be enlightened to the fountainhead of Mind, nonfinal enlightenment. What is the meaning of this? An ordinary man becomes aware that his former thoughts were wrong; then he is able to stop (nirodha) such thoughts from arising again. Although this sometimes may also be called enlightenment, properly it is not enlightenment at all because it is not enlightenment that reaches the fountainhead of Mind.

The followers of Hinayana, who have some insight, and those *Bodhisattva*s who have just been initiated become aware of the changing state (*anyathatva*) of thoughts and are free from thoughts which are subject to change [such as the existence of a permanent self (*atman*), etc.]. Since they have forsaken the rudimentary attachments derived from unwarranted speculation (*vikalpa*), their experience is called enlightenment in appearance. *Bodhisattva*s who have come to the realization of *Dharmakaya* become aware of the temporarily abiding state (*sthiti*) of thoughts and are not arrested by them. Since they are free from their rudimentary false thoughts derived from the speculation that the components of the world are real, their experience is called approximate enlightenment.

Those *Bodhisattvas* who have completed the stages of a *Bodhisattva* and who have fulfilled the expedient means needed to bring forth the original enlightenment to the fullest extent will experience the oneness with Suchness in an instant; they will become aware of how the inceptions of the deluded thoughts of the mind arise (*jati*), and will be free from the rise of any deluded thought. Since they are far away even from subtle deluded thoughts, they are able to have an insight into the original nature of Mind.

The realization that Mind is eternal is called the final enlightenment. It is, therefore, said in a sutra that if there is a man who is able to perceive that which is beyond thoughts he is advancing toward the Buddha wisdom. Though it is said that there is an inception of the rising of deluded thoughts in the mind, there is no inception as such that can be known as being independent of the essence of Mind. And yet to say that the inception of the rising of deluded thoughts is known means that it is known as existing on the ground of that which is beyond thoughts [i.e., the essence of Mind].

Accordingly, all ordinary people are said not to be enlightened because they have had a continuous stream of deluded thoughts and have never been freed from their thoughts; therefore, they are said to be in a beginningless ignorance. If a man gains insight into that which is free from thoughts, then he knows how those thoughts which characterize the mind [i.e., deluded thoughts] arise, abide, change, and cease to be, for he is identical with that which is free from thoughts. But, in reality, no difference exists in the process of the actualization of enlightenment, because the four states [of arising, abiding, etc.] exist simultaneously and each of them is not self-existent; they are originally of one and the same enlightenment [in that they are taking place on the ground of original enlightenment, as its phenomenal aspects]. And, again, original enlightenment when analyzed in relation to the defiled state [in the phenomenal order], presents itself as having two attributes. One is the "Purity of Wisdom" and the other is the "Suprarational Functions".

PURITY OF WISDOM

By virtue of the permeation (*vasana*, perfuming) of the influence of dharma [i.e., the essence of Mind or original enlightenment], a man comes to truly discipline himself and fulfills all expedient means of unfolding enlightenment; as a result, he breaks through the compound consciousness [i.e., the Storehouse Consciousness that contains both enlightenment and nonenlightenment], puts an end to the manifestation of the stream of deluded mind, and manifests the *Dharmakaya* [i.e., the essence of Mind], for his wisdom (*Prajna*) becomes genuine and pure. What is the meaning of this? All modes (*lakshana*) of mind and consciousness under the state of nonenlightenment are the products of ignorance. Ignorance does not exist apart from enlightenment; therefore, it cannot be destroyed [because one cannot destroy something which does not really exist], and yet it cannot not be destroyed [insofar as it remains].

This is like the relationship that exists between the water of the ocean [i.e., enlightenment] and its waves [i.e., modes of mind] stirred by the wind [i.e., ignorance]. Water and wind are inseparable; but water is not mobile by nature, and if the wind stops the movement ceases. But the wet nature remains undestroyed. Likewise, man's Mind, pure in its own nature, is stirred by the wind of ignorance. Both Mind and ignorance have no particular forms of their own and they are inseparable. Yet Mind is not mobile by nature, and if ignorance ceases, then the continuity of deluded activities ceases. But the essential nature of wisdom [i.e., the essence of Mind, like the wet nature of the water] remains undestroyed.

Suprarational Functions

He who has fully uncovered the original enlightenment is capable of creating all manner of excellent conditions because his wisdom is pure. The manifestation of his numberless excellent qualities is incessant; accommodating himself to the capacity of other men he responds spontaneously, reveals himself in manifold ways, and benefits them.

THE CHARACTERISTICS OF THE ESSENCE OF ENLIGHTENMENT

The characteristics of the essence of enlightenment have four great significances that are identical with those of empty space or that are analogous to those of a bright mirror. First, the essence of enlightenment is like a mirror which is really empty of images. It is free from all marks of objects of the mind and it has nothing to reveal in itself, for it does not reflect any images. Second, it is like a mirror influencing (vasana) all men to advance toward enlightenment. That is to say, it is truly nonempty; appearing in it are all the objects of the world which neither go out nor come in; which are neither lost nor destroyed.

It is eternally abiding One Mind. All things appear in it because all things are real. And none of the defiled things are able to defile it, for the essence of wisdom [i.e., original enlightenment] is unaffected by defilements, being furnished with an unsoiled quality and influencing all men to advance toward enlightenment. Third, it is like a mirror which is free from defiled objects reflected in it.

This can be said because the nonempty state [of original enlightenment] is genuine, pure, and bright, being free from hindrances both affectional and intellectual, and transcending characteristics of that which is compounded [i.e., the Storehouse Consciousness]. Fourth, it is like a mirror influencing a man to cultivate his capacity for goodness, serving as a coordinating cause to encourage him in his endeavors. Because the essence of enlightenment is free from defiled objects, it universally illumines the mind of man and induces him to cultivate his capacity for goodness, presenting itself in accordance with his desires [as a mirror presents his appearance].

THE ASPECT OF NONENLIGHTENMENT

Because of not truly realizing oneness with Suchness, there emerges an unenlightened mind and consequently, its thoughts. These thoughts do not have any validity to be substantiated;

therefore, they are not independent of the original enlightenment. It is like the case of a man who has lost his way: he is confused because of his wrong sense of direction. If he is freed from the notion of direction altogether, then there will be no such thing as going astray. It is the same with men: because of the notion of enlightenment, they are confused. But if they are freed from the fixed notion of enlightenment, then there will be no such thing as nonenlightenment.

Because there are men of unenlightened, deluded mind, for them we speak of true enlightenment, knowing well what this relative term stands for. Independent of the unenlightened mind, there are no independent marks of true enlightenment itself that can be discussed. Because of its nonenlightened state, the deluded mind produces three aspects which are bound to nonenlightenment and are inseparable from it. First is the activity of ignorance. The agitation of mind because of its nonenlightened state is called activity. When enlightened, it is unagitated. When it is agitated, anxiety (*Dukkha*) follows, for the result [anxiety] is not independent of the cause [the agitation contingent upon ignorance].

Second is the perceiving subject. Because of the agitation that breaks the original unity with Suchness, there appears the perceiving subject. When unagitated, the mind is free from perceiving. Third is the world of objects. Because of the perceiving subject, the world of objects erroneously appears. Apart from the perceiving, there will be no world of objects. Conditioned by the incorrectly conceived world of objects, the deluded mind produces six aspects.

First is the aspect of the discriminating intellect. Depending on the erroneously conceived world of objects, the mind develops the discrimination between liking and disliking.

Second is the aspect of continuity. By virtue of the discriminating function of the intellect, the mind produces an awareness of pleasure and pain with regard to things in the world of objects. The mind, developing deluded thoughts and being bound to them, will continue uninterrupted. Third is the aspect of attachment. Because of the continuity of deluded thoughts, the mind, superimposing its deluded thoughts on the world of objects and holding fast to the discriminations of liking and disliking develops attachments to what it likes. Fourth is the aspect of the speculation (*vikalpa*) on names and letters [i.e., concepts]. On the basis of erroneous attachments, the deluded mind analyzes words which are provisional and therefore devoid of reality. Fifth is the aspect of giving rise to evil karma. Relying on names and letters [i.e., concepts which have no validity, the deluded mind] investigates names and words and becomes attached to them, and creates manifold types of evil karma. Sixth is the aspect of anxiety attached to the effects of evil karma. Because of the law of karma, the deluded mind suffers the effects and will not be free. It should be understood that ignorance is able to produce all types of defiled states; all defiled states are aspects of nonenlightenment.

THE RELATIONSHIPS BETWEEN ENLIGHTENMENT AND NONENLIGHTENMENT

Two relationships exist between the enlightened and nonenlightened states. They are:

Identity

Just as pieces of various kinds of pottery are of the same nature in that they are made of clay, so the various magic-like manifestations (*maya*) of both enlightenment (*anasrava*: nondefilement) and nonenlightenment (*avidya*: ignorance) are aspects of the same essence, Suchness. For this reason, it is said in a sutra that "all sentient beings intrinsically abide in eternity and are entered into *nirvana*.

The state of enlightenment is not something that is to be acquired by practice or to be created. In the end, it is unobtainable [for it is given from the beginning]." Also it has no corporeal aspect that can be perceived as such. Any corporeal aspects [such as the marks of the Buddha] that are visible are magic-like products of Suchness manifested in accordance with the mentality of men in defilement. It is not, however, that these corporeal aspects which result from the suprarational functions of wisdom are of the nature of nonemptiness [i.e., substantial]; for wisdom has no aspects that can be perceived.

Non-identity

Just as various pieces of pottery differ from each other, so differences exist between the state of enlightenment and that of nonenlightenment, and between the magic-like manifestations of Suchness manifested in accordance with the mentality of men in defilement, and those of men of ignorance who are defiled [i.e., blinded] as to the essential nature of Suchness.

THE CAUSE AND CONDITIONS OF MAN'S BEING IN SAMSARA

That a man is in *samsara* (birth and death) results from the fact that his mind (*manas*) and consciousness (*vijnana*) develop on the ground of the Storehouse Consciousness (*citta*). This means that because of the aspect of nonenlightenment of the Storehouse Consciousness, he is said to be in possession of ignorance [and thus is bound to remain in *samsara*].

Mind

The mentality which emerges in the state of nonenlightenment, which incorrectly perceives and reproduces the world of objects and, conceiving that the reproduced world of objects is real, continues to develop deluded thoughts, is what we define as mind. The mind has five different names. The first is called the "activating mind", for, without being aware of it, it breaks the equilibrium of mind by the force of ignorance. The second is called the "evolving mind", for it emerges contingent upon the agitated mind as the subject that perceives incorrectly. The third is called the "reproducing mind", for it reproduces the entire world of objects as a bright mirror reproduces all material images. When confronted with the objects of the five senses, it reproduces them at once. It arises spontaneously at all times and exists forever reproducing the world of objects in front of the subject.

The fourth is called the "analytical mind", for it differentiates what is defiled and what is undefiled. The fifth is called the "continuing mind", for it is united with deluded thoughts and continues uninterrupted. It retains the entire karma, good and bad, accumulated in the immeasurable lives of the past, and does not permit any loss. It is also capable of bringing the results of the pain, pleasure, etc., of the present and the future to maturity; in doing so, it makes no mistakes. It can cause one to recollect suddenly the things of the present and the past and to have sudden and unexpected fantasies of the things to come.

The triple world, therefore, is unreal and is of mind only. Apart from it there are no objects of the five senses and of the mind. What does this mean? Since all things are, without exception, developed from the mind and produced under the condition of deluded thoughts, all differentiations are no other than the differentiations of one's mind itself. Yet the mind cannot perceive the mind itself; the mind has no marks of its own that can be ascertained as a substantial entity as such.

It should be understood that the conception of the entire world of objects can be held only on the basis of man's deluded mind of ignorance. All things, therefore, are just like the images in a mirror which are devoid of any objectivity that one can get hold of; they are of the mind only and are unreal. When the deluded mind comes into being, then various conceptions (dharma) come to be; and when the deluded mind ceases to be, then these various conceptions cease to be.

Consciousness

What is called "consciousness (*vijnana*)" is the "continuing mind". Because of their deep-rooted attachment, ordinary men imagine that are real and cling to them in their illusions. As soon as objects are presented, this consciousness rests on them and discriminates the objects of the five senses and of the mind. This is called "vijnana [i.e., the differentiating consciousness]" or the "separating consciousness". The propensity for discrimination of this consciousness will be intensified by both the intellectual defilement of holding fast to perverse views and the affectional defilement of indulgence in passion. That the deluded mind and consciousness arise from the permeation of ignorance is something that ordinary men cannot understand.

The followers of the Hinayana, with their wisdom, likewise fail to realize this. Those *Bodhisattvas*, who, having advanced from the first stage of correct faith by setting the mind upon enlightenment through practicing contemplation, have come to realize the Dharmakaya, can partially comprehend this. Yet even those who have reached the final stage of *Bodhisattva*hood cannot fully comprehend this; only the Enlightened Ones have thorough comprehension of it. Why? The Mind, though pure in its self-nature from the beginning, is accompanied by ignorance.

Being defiled by ignorance, a defiled state of Mind comes into being. But, though defiled, the Mind itself is eternal and immutable. Only the Enlightened Ones are able to understand what this means. What is called the essential nature of Mind is always beyond thoughts. It is, therefore, defined as "immutable". When the one World of Reality is yet to be realized, the Mind is mutable and is not in perfect unity with Suchness. Suddenly, a deluded thought arises; this state is called ignorance.

Defiled States of Mind

Six kinds of defiled states of mind conditioned by ignorance can be identified. The first is the defilement united with attachment to *atman* (self), from which those who have attained liberation in Hinayana and those *Bodhisattvas* at the "stage of establishment of faith" are free. The second is the defilement united with the "continuing mind", from which those who are at the "stage of establishment of faith" and who are practicing expedient means to attain enlightenment can gradually free themselves and free them completely at the "stage of pure-heartedness".

The third is the defilement united with the discriminating "analytical mind", from which those at the "stage of observing precepts" begin to be liberated and finally are liberated completely when they arrive at the "stage of expedient means without any trace". The fourth is the subtle defilement disunited from the represented world of objects, from which those at the "stage of freedom from the world of objects" can be freed. The fifth is the subtler defilement disunited from the "evolving mind that perceives" [i.e., the defilement existing prior to the act of perceiving], from which those at the "stage of freedom from evolving mind" are freed. The sixth and most subtle is the defilement disunited from the basic "activating mind", from which those *Bodhisattva*s who have passed the final stage and have gone into the "stage of Tathagatahood" are freed.

Comments on the Terms Used in the Foregoing Discussion

On the expression "the one World of Reality is yet to be realized": From this state those *Bodhisattva*s who have advanced from the "stage of the establishment of faith" to the "stage of pure-heartedness", after having completed and severed their deluded thoughts, will be more and more liberated as they advance, and when they reach the "stage of Tathagatahood", they will be completely liberated. On "united": By the word "united" appearing in the first three defilements is meant that though difference [i.e., duality] exists between the mind (subject) and the datum of the mind (object), there is a simultaneous relation between them in that when the subject is defiled the object is also defiled, and when the subject is purified the object is also purified.

On "disunited": By the word "disunited" is meant that the second three subtle and fundamental defilements are the aspects of nonenlightenment on the part of the mind existing prior to the differentiation into the subject and object relationship; therefore, a simultaneous relation between the subject and object is not as yet established. On the expression "defiled state of mind": It is called "the hindrance originating from defilements", for it obstructs any fundamental insight into Suchness.

On "ignorance": Ignorance is called the "hindrance originating from misconceptions of objects", for it obstructs the wisdom that functions spontaneously in the world. Because of the defiled state of mind, there emerges the subject that perceives [incorrectly; i.e., the evolving mind] and that which reproduces [the reproducing mind] and thus one erroneously predicates the world of objects and causes oneself to deviate from the undifferentiated state of Suchness. Though all things are always in quiescence and devoid of any marks of rising, because of the nonenlightenment due to ignorance, one erroneously strays from the dharma [i.e., Suchness]; thus one fails to obtain the wisdom that functions spontaneously by adapting oneself to all circumstances in the world.

THE CHARACTERISTICS OF BEINGS IN SAMSARA

In analyzing the characteristics of beings in *samsara,* two categories may be distinguished. The one is "crude", for those who belong to this category are united with the crude activities of the defiled mind; the other is "subtle", for those who belong to this category are disunited from the subtle activities of the defiled mind. Again, each category may in turn be subdivided into the cruder and the subtler. The cruder of the crude belongs to the range of mental activity of ordinary men; the subtler of the crude and the cruder of the subtle belong to that of *Bodhisattvas*; and the subtler of the subtle belongs to that of Buddhas.

These two categories of beings in the phenomenal order come about because of the permeation of ignorance; that is to say, they come about because of the primary cause and the coordinating causes. By the primary cause, "nonenlightenment" is meant; and by the coordinating causes, "the erroneously represented world of objects". When the primary cause ceases to be, then the coordinating causes will cease to be. Because of the cessation of the primary cause, the mind disunited from the represented world of objects, etc. will cease to be; and because of the cessation of the coordinating causes, the mind united with the attachment to *atman,* etc. will cease to be.

Question: If the mind ceases to be, what will become of its continuity? If there is continuity of mind, how can you explain its final cessation? Answer: What we speak of as "cessation" is the cessation of the marks of the deluded mind only and not the cessation of its essence. It is like the case of the wind which, following the surface of the water leaves the marks of its movement. If the water should cease to be, then the marks of the wind would be nullified and the wind would have no support on which to display its movement. But since the water does not cease to be, the marks of the wind may continue. Because only the wind ceases, the marks of its movement cease accordingly. This is not the cessation of water. So it is with ignorance; on the ground of the essence of Mind there is movement.

If the essence of Mind were to cease, then people would be nullified and they would have no support. But since the essence does not cease to be, the mind may continue. Because only stupidity ceases to be, the marks of the stupidity of the mind cease accordingly. It is not that the wisdom [i.e., the essence] of Mind ceases. Because of the four kinds of permeation, the defiled states and the pure state emerge and continue uninterrupted. They are (1) the pure state, which is called Suchness; (2) the cause of all defilements, which is called ignorance; (3) the deluded mind, which is called "activating mind"; (4) the erroneously conceived external world, which is called the "objects of the five senses and of mind".

The meaning of permeation: Clothes in the world certainly have no scent in themselves, but if a man permeates them with perfumes, then they come to have a scent. It is just the same with the case we are speaking of. The pure state of Suchness certainly has no defilement, but if it is permeated by ignorance, then the marks of defilement appear on it. The defiled state of ignorance is indeed devoid of any purifying force, but if it is permeated by Suchness, then it will come to have a purifying influence.

Permeation of Ignorance

How does the permeation of ignorance give rise to the defiled state and continue uninterrupted? It may be said that, on the ground of Suchness [i.e., the original enlightenment], ignorance [i.e., nonenlightenment] appears. Ignorance, the primary cause of the defiled state, permeates into Suchness. Because of this permeation a deluded mind results. Because of the deluded mind, deluded thoughts further permeate into ignorance. While the principle of Suchness is yet to be realized, the deluded mind, developing thoughts fashioned in the state of nonenlightenment, predicates erroneously conceived objects of the senses and the mind.

These erroneously conceived objects of the senses and the mind, the coordinating causes in bringing about the defiled state, permeate into the deluded mind and cause the deluded mind to attach itself to its thoughts, to create various evil karma, and to undergo all kinds of physical and mental suffering. The permeation of the erroneously conceived objects of the senses and the mind is of two kinds.

One is the basic permeation by the "activating mind", which causes *Arhats, Pratyeka-buddhas,* and all *Bodhisattva*s to undergo the suffering of *samsara*, and the other is the permeation which accelerates the activities of the "object-discriminating consciousness" and which makes ordinary men suffer from the bondage of their karma. The permeations of ignorance are of two kinds. One is the basic permeation, since it can put into operation the "activating mind", and the other is the permeation that develops perverse views and attachments, since it can put into operation the "object-discriminating consciousness".

Permeation of Suchness

How does the permeation of Suchness give rise to the pure state and continue uninterrupted? It may be said that there is the principle of Suchness, and it can permeate into ignorance. Through the force of this permeation, Suchness causes the deluded mind to loathe the suffering of *samsara* and to aspire for *nirvana*. Because this mind, though still deluded, is now possessed with loathing and aspiration, it permeates into Suchness in that it induces Suchness to manifest itself. Thus a man comes to believe in his essential nature, to know that what exists is the erroneous activity of the mind and that the world of objects in front of him is nonexistent, and to practice teachings to free himself from the erroneously conceived world of objects.

He knows what is really so - that there is no world of objects in front of him - and therefore with various devices he practices courses by which to conform himself to Suchness. He will not attach himself to anything nor give rise to any deluded thoughts. Through the force of this permeation of Suchness over a long period of time, his ignorance ceases. Because of the cessation of ignorance, there will be no more rising of the deluded activities of mind. Because of the nonrising of the deluded activities of mind, the world of objects as previously conceived ceases to be; because of the cessation of both the primary cause (ignorance) and the coordinating causes (objects), the marks of the defiled mind will all be nullified.

This is called "gaining *nirvana* and accomplishing spontaneous acts". The permeation of Suchness into the deluded mind is of two kinds. The first is the permeation into the "object-discriminating consciousness". Because of this permeation, ordinary men and the Hinayanists come to loathe the suffering of *samsara*, and thereupon each, according to his capacity, gradually advances toward the highest enlightenment. The second is the permeation into mind. Because of this permeation, *Bodhisattva*s advance to *nirvana* rapidly and with aspiration and fortitude. Two kinds of permeation of Suchness into ignorance can be identified. The first is the "permeation through manifestation of the essence of Suchness", and the second is "the permeation through external influences".

Permeation through Manifestation of the Essence of Suchness

The essence of Suchness is, from the beginningless beginning, endowed with the "perfect state of purity". It is provided with suprarational functions and the nature of manifesting itself (literally, the nature of making the world of object). Because of these two reasons it permeates perpetually into ignorance. Through the force of this permeation it induces a man to loathe the suffering of *samsara*, to seek bliss in *nirvana*, and, believing that he has the principle of Suchness within himself, to make up his mind to exert himself.

Question: If this is so, then all sentient beings are endowed with Suchness and are equally permeated by it. Why is it that there are infinite varieties of believers and nonbelievers, and that there are some who believe sooner and some later? All of them should, knowing that they are endowed with the principle of Suchness, at once make an effort utilizing expedient means and should all equally attain *nirvana*. Answer: Though Suchness is originally one, yet there are immeasurable and infinite shades of ignorance. From the very beginning ignorance is, because of its nature, characterized by diversity, and its degree of intensity is not uniform. Defilements, more numerous than the sands of the Ganges, come into being because of the differences in intensity of ignorance, and exist in manifold ways; defilements, such as the belief in the existence of *atman* and the indulgence in passion, develop because of ignorance and exist in different ways.

All these defilements are brought about by ignorance, in an infinitely diversified manner in time. The Tathagatas alone know all about this. In Buddhism there is a teaching concerning the primary cause and the coordinating causes. When the primary cause and the coordinating causes are sufficiently provided, there will be the perfection of a result. It is like the case of wood: though it possesses a latent fire nature which is the primary cause of its burning, it cannot be made to burn by itself unless men understand the situation and resort to means of actualizing fire out of wood by kindling it.

In the same way a man, though he is in possession of the correct primary cause, Suchness with permeating force, cannot put an end to his defilements by himself alone and enter *nirvana* unless he is provided with coordinating causes, i.e., his encounters with the Buddhas, *Bodhisattva*s, or good spiritual friends. Even though coordinating causes from without may be sufficiently provided, if the pure principle [i.e., Suchness] within is lacking in the force of permeation, then a man cannot ultimately loathe the suffering of *samsara* and seek bliss in *nirvana*.

However, if both the primary and the coordinating causes are sufficiently provided, then because of his possession of the force of permeation of Suchness from within and the compassionate protection of the Buddhas and *Bodhisattva*s from without, he is able to develop a loathing for suffering, to believe that *nirvana* is real, and to cultivate his capacity for goodness. And when his cultivation of the capacity for goodness matures, he will as a result meet the Buddhas and *Bodhisattva*s and will be instructed, taught, benefited, and given joy, and then he will be able to advance on the path to *nirvana*.

PERMEATION THROUGH INFLUENCES

This is the force from without affecting men by providing coordinating causes. Such external coordinating causes have an infinite number of meanings. Briefly, they may be explained under two categories: namely, the specific and the general coordinating causes.

The Specific Coordinating Causes

A man, from the time when he first aspires to seek enlightenment until he becomes an Enlightened One, sees or meditates on the Buddhas and *Bodhisattva*s as they manifest themselves to him; sometimes they appear as his family members, parents, or relatives, sometimes as servants, sometimes as close friends, or sometimes as enemies. Through all kinds of deeds and incalculable performances, such as the practice of the four acts of loving-kindness, etc., they exercise the force of permeation created by their great compassion, and are thus able to cause sentient beings to strengthen their capacity for goodness and are able to benefit them as they see or hear about their needs.

This specific coordinating cause is of two kinds. One is immediate and enables a man to obtain deliverance quickly; and the other is remote and enables a man to obtain deliverance after a long time. The immediate and remote causes are again of two kinds: the causes which strengthen a man in his practices of expedient means to help others, and those which enable him to obtain enlightenment.

The General Coordinating Causes

The Buddhas and *Bodhisattvas* all desire to liberate all men, spontaneously permeating them with their spiritual influences and never forsaking them. Through the power of the wisdom which is one with Suchness, they manifest activities in response to the needs of men as they see and hear them. Because of this indiscriminately permeating cause, men are all equally able, by means of concentration (*Samadhi*), to see the Buddhas. This permeation through the influence of the wisdom whose essence is one with Suchness is also divided into two categories according to the types of recipients.

The one is yet to be united with Suchness. Ordinary men, the Hinayanists, and those *Bodhisattvas* who have just been initiated devote themselves to religious practices on the strength of their faith, being permeated by Suchness through their mind and consciousness. Not having obtained the indiscriminate mind, however, they are yet to be united with the essence of Suchness, and not having obtained the perfection of the discipline of free acts, they are yet to be united with the influence of Suchness.

The other is the already united with Suchness: *Bodhisattvas* who realize *Dharmakaya* have obtained undiscriminating mind and are united with the essence of the Buddhas; they, having obtained free acts, are united with the influence of the wisdom of the Buddhas. They singly devote themselves with spontaneity to their religious disciplines, on the strength of Suchness within; permeating into Suchness so that Suchness will reclaim itself, they destroy ignorance.

Again, the defiled principle (dharma), from the beginningless beginning, continues perpetually to permeate until it perishes by the attainment of Buddhahood. But the permeation of the pure principle has no interruption and no ending. The reason is that the principle of Suchness is always permeating; therefore, when the deluded mind ceases to be, the *Dharmakaya* [i.e., Suchness, original enlightenment] will be manifest and will give rise to the permeation of the influence of Suchness, and thus there will be no ending to it.

ESSENCE AND ATTRIBUTES OF SUCHNESS: MEANINGS OF MAHA

The Greatness of the Essence of Suchness

The essence of Suchness knows no increase or decrease in ordinary men, the Hinayanists, the *Bodhisattva*s, or the Buddhas. It was not brought into existence in the beginning nor will it cease to be at the end of time; it is eternal through and through.

The Greatness of the Attributes of Suchness

From the beginning, Suchness in its nature is fully provided with all excellent qualities; namely, it is endowed with the light of great wisdom, the qualities of illuminating the entire universe, of true cognition and mind pure in its self-nature; of eternity, bliss, Self, and purity; of refreshing coolness, immutability, and freedom. It is endowed with these excellent qualities which outnumber the sands of the Ganges, which are not independent of, disjointed from, or different from the essence of Suchness, and which are suprarational attributes of Buddhahood. Since it is endowed completely with all these, and is not lacking anything, it is called the Tathagata-garbha when latent and also the *Dharmakaya* of the Tathagata.

Question: It was explained before that the essence of Suchness is undifferentiated and devoid of all characteristics. Why is it, then, that you have described its essence as having these various excellent qualities? Answer: Though it has, in reality, all these excellent qualities, it does not have any characteristics of differentiation; it retains its identity and is of one flavor; Suchness is solely one. Question: What does this mean? Answer: Since it is devoid of individuation, it is free from the characteristics of individuation; thus it is one without any second. Question: Then how can you speak of differentiation [i.e., the plurality of the characteristics of Suchness]? Answer: In contrast to the characteristics of the phenomena of the "activating mind" the characteristics of Suchness can be inferred. Question: How can they be inferred? Answer: All things are originally of the mind only; they in fact transcend thoughts.

Nevertheless, the deluded mind, in nonenlightenment, gives rise to irrelevant thoughts and predicates the world of objects. This being the case, we define this mentality as "the state of being destitute of wisdom (*avidya*: ignorance)". The essential nature of Mind is immutable in that it does not give rise to any deluded thoughts, and therefore, is the very opposite of ignorance; hence, it is spoken of as having the characteristic of "the light of great wisdom". When there is a particular perceiving act of the mind, objects other than the objects being perceived will remain unperceived. The essential nature of Mind is free from any partial perceiving; hence, Suchness is spoken of as having the characteristic of "illuminating the entire universe".

When the mind is in motion [stirred by ignorance], it is characterized by illusions and defilements, outnumbering the sands of the Ganges, such as lack of true cognition, absence of self-nature, impermanence, blisslessness, impurity, fever, anxiety, deterioration, mutation, and lack of freedom. By contrast to this, the essential nature of Mind, however, is motionless [i.e., undisturbed by ignorance]; therefore, it can be inferred that it must have various pure and excellent qualities, outnumbering the sands of the Ganges. But if the mind gives rise to irrelevant thoughts and further predicates the world of objects, it will continue to lack these qualities. All these numberless excellent qualities of the pure principle are none other than those of One Mind, and there is nothing to be sought after anew by thought. Thus, that which is fully endowed with them is called the Dharmakaya when manifested and the Tathagata-garbha when latent.

The Greatness of the Influences of Suchness

The Buddha-Tathagatas, while in the stages of Bodhisattvahood, exercised great compassion, practiced *Paramitas,* and accepted and transformed sentient beings. They took great vows, desiring to liberate all sentient beings through countless aeons until the end of future time, for they regarded all sentient beings as they regarded themselves. And yet, they never regarded them as separate sentient beings. Why? Because they truly knew that all sentient beings and they themselves were identical in Suchness and that there could be no distinction between them. Because they possessed such great wisdom which could be applied to expedient means in quest of enlightenment, they extinguished their ignorance and perceived the original *Dharmakaya*.

Spontaneously performing incomprehensible activities, exercising manifold influences, they pervade everywhere in their identity with Suchness. Nevertheless, they reveal no marks of their influences that can be traced as such. Why? Because the Buddha-Tathagatas are no other than the *Dharmakaya* itself and the embodiment of wisdom. They belong to the realm of the absolute truth, which transcends the world where the relative truth operates. They are free from any conventional activities. And yet, because of the fact that sentient beings receive benefit through seeing or hearing about them, their influences [i.e., of Suchness] can be spoken of in relative terms.

The influences of Suchness are of two kinds. The first is that which is conceived by the mind of ordinary men and the followers of Hinayana [i.e., the influence of Suchness as reflected] in the "object-discriminating consciousness". This is called the influence of Suchness in the form of the "Transformation-body" (*Nirmanakaya*). Because they do not know that it is projected by the "evolving mind", they regard it as coming from without; they assume that it has a corporeal limitation because their understanding is limited. The second is that which is conceived by the mind of the *Bodhisattvas*, from the first stage of aspiration to the highest stage, [i.e., the influence of Suchness as reflected] in the mentality which regards external objects as unreal.

This is called the influence of Suchness in the form of the "Bliss-body" (*Sambhogakaya*). It has an infinite number of corporeal forms, each form has an infinite number of major marks, and each major mark has an infinite number of subtle marks. The land where it has its abode has innumerable adornments. It manifests itself without any bounds; its manifestations are inexhaustible and free from any limitations. It manifests itself in accordance with the needs of sentient beings; and yet it always remains firm without destroying or losing itself. These excellent qualities were perfected by the pure permeation acquired by the practice of *paramitas* and the suprarational permeation of Suchness. Since the influence is endowed with infinite attributes of bliss, it is spoken of as the "Bliss-body".

What is seen by ordinary men is only the coarse corporeal forms of the manifestation of Suchness. Depending upon where one is in the six transmigratory states, his vision of it will differ. The visions of it conceived by the unenlightened beings are not in a form of Bliss; this is the reason why it is called the "Transformation-body" [i.e., the body appearing in the likeness of the conceiver]. The *Bodhisattvas* in their first stage of aspiration and the others, because of their deep faith in Suchness, have a partial insight into the nature of the influence of Suchness. They know that the things of the Bliss-body, such as its corporeal forms, major marks, adornments, etc., do not come from without or go away, that they are free from limitations, and that they are envisioned by mind alone and are not independent of Suchness.

These *Bodhisattvas*, however, are not free from dualistic thinking, since they have yet to enter into the stage where they gain complete realization of the *Dharmakaya*. If they advance to the "stage of pure-heartedness", the forms they see will be subtler and the influences of Suchness will be more excellent than ever. When they leave the last stage of Bodhisattvahood, they will perfect their insight into Suchness.

When they become free from the "activating mind" they will be free from the perceiving of duality.

The Dharmakaya of the Buddhas knows no such thing as distinguishing this from that. Question: If the Dharmakaya of the Buddhas is free from the manifestation of corporeal form, how can it appear in corporeal form? Answer: Since the Dharmakaya is the essence of corporeal form, it is capable of appearing in corporeal form. The reason this is said is that from the beginning corporeal form and Mind have been nondual. Since the essential nature of corporeal form is identical with wisdom, the essence of corporeal form which has yet to be divided into tangible forms is called the "wisdom-body".

Since the essential nature of wisdom is identical with corporeal form, the essence of corporeal form which has yet to be divided into tangible forms is called Dharmakaya pervading everywhere. Its manifested corporeal forms have no limitations. It can be freely manifested as an infinite number of *Bodhisattvas*, Buddhas of Bliss-body, and adornments in the ten quarters of the universe.

Each of them has neither limitation nor interference. All of these are incomprehensible to the dualistic thinking of the deluded mind and consciousness, for they result from the free influence of Suchness.

FROM SAMSARA TO NIRVANA

Lastly, how to enter into the realm of Suchness from the realm of *samsara* will be revealed. Examining the five components, we find that they may be reduced to matter (object) and mind (subject). The objects of the five senses and of the mind are in the final analysis beyond what they are thought to be. And the mind itself is devoid of any form or mark and is, therefore, unobtainable as such, no matter where one may seek it. Just as a man, because he has lost his way, mistakes the east for the west, though the actual directions have not changed place, so people, because of their ignorance, assume Mind (Suchness) to be what they think it to be, though

Mind in fact is unaffected even if it is falsely predicated. If a man is able to observe and understand that Mind is beyond what it is thought to be, then he will be able to conform to and enter the realm of Suchness.

THE CORRECTION OF EVIL ATTACHMENTS

All evil attachments originate from biased views; if a man is free from bias, he will be free from evil attachments. There are two kinds of biased view: one is the biased view held by those who are not free from the belief in *atman* [i.e., ordinary men]; the other is the biased view held by those who believe that the components of the world are real [i.e., the Hinayanists].

THE BIASED VIEWS HELD BY ORDINARY MEN

There are five kinds of biased views held by ordinary men which may be discussed. Hearing that it is explained in the sutra that the Dharmakaya of the Tathagata is, in the final analysis, quiescent, like empty space, ordinary men think that the nature of the Tathagata is, indeed, the same as empty space; for they do not know that the purpose of the sutra is to uproot their adherence. Question: How is this to be corrected? Answer: The way to correct this error is to understand clearly that "empty space" is a delusive concept, the substance of which is nonexistent and unreal. It is merely predicated in relation to its correlative corporeal objects. If it is taken as a being termed nonbeing, a negative being, then it should be discarded, because it causes the mind to remain in *samsara.*

In fact there are no external corporeal objects, because all objects are originally of the mind. And as long as there are no corporeal objects at all, "empty space" cannot be maintained. All objects are of the mind alone; but when illusions arise, objects which are regarded as real appear. When the mind is free from its deluded activities, then all objects imagined as real vanish of themselves. What is real, the one and true Mind, pervades everywhere.

This is the final meaning of the Tathagata's great and comprehensive wisdom. The *Dharmakaya* is, indeed, unlike "empty space". Hearing that it is explained in the sutra that all things in the world, in the final analysis, are empty in their substance, and that *nirvana* or the principle of Suchness is also absolutely empty from the beginning and devoid of any characteristics, they, not knowing that the purpose of the sutra is to uproot their adherence, think that the essential nature of Suchness or *nirvana* is simply empty.

Question: How is this to be corrected? Answer: The way to correct this error is to make clear that Suchness or the Dharmakaya is not empty, but is endowed with numberless excellent qualities. Hearing that it is explained in the sutra that there is no increase or decrease in the Tathagata-garbha and that it is provided in its essence with all excellent qualities, they, not being able to understand this, think that in the Tathagata-garbha there is plurality of mind and matter.

Question: How is this to be corrected? Answer: They should be instructed that the statement in the sutra that "there is no increase or decrease in the Tathagata-garbha" is made only in accordance with the absolute aspect of Suchness, and the statement that "it is provided with all excellent qualities" is made in accordance with the pluralistic outlook held by the defiled minds in *samsara*. Hearing that it is explained in the sutra that all defiled states of *samsara* in the world exist on the ground of the Tathagata-garbha and that they are therefore not independent of Suchness, they, not understanding this, think that the Tathagata-garbha literally contains in itself all the defiled states of *samsara* in the world.

Question: How is this to be corrected? Answer: In order to correct this error it should be understood that the Tathagata-garbha, from the beginning, contains only pure excellent qualities which, outnumbering the sands of the Ganges, are not independent of, severed from, or different from Suchness; that the soiled states of defilement which, outnumbering the sands of the Ganges, are not independent of, severed from, or different from Suchness; that the soiled states of defilement which, outnumbering the sands of the Ganges, merely exist in illusion; are, from the beginning, nonexistent; and from the beginningless beginning have never been united with the Tathagata-garbha.

It has never happened that the Tathagata-garbha contained deluded states in its essence and that it induced itself to realize Suchness in order to extinguish forever its deluded states. Hearing that it is explained in the sutra that on the ground of the Tathagata-garbha there is *samsara* as well as the attainment of *nirvana*, they, without understanding this, think that there is a beginning for sentient beings. Since they suppose a beginning, they suppose also that the *nirvana* attained by the Tathagata has an end and that he will in turn become a sentient being. Question: How is this to be corrected? Answer: The way to correct this error is to explain that the Tathagata-garbha has no beginning, and that therefore ignorance has no beginning. If anyone asserts that sentient beings came into existence outside this triple world, he holds the view given in the scriptures of the heretics. Again, the Tathagata-garbha does not have an end; and the *nirvana* attained by the Buddhas, being one with it, likewise has no end.

THE BIASED VIEWS HELD BY THE HINAYANISTS

Because of their inferior capacity, the Tathagata preached to the Hinayanists only the doctrine of the nonexistence of *atman* and did not preach his doctrines in their entirety; as a result, the Hinayanists have come to believe that the five components, the constituents of samsaric existence, are real; being terrified at the thought of being subject to birth and death, they erroneously attach themselves to *nirvana*. Question: How is this to be corrected? Answer: The way to correct this error is to make clear that the five components are unborn in their essential nature and, therefore, are imperishable - that what is made of the five components is, from the beginning, in *nirvana*. Finally, in order to be completely free from erroneous attachments, one should know that both the defiled and the pure states are relative and have no particular marks of their own-being that can be discussed. Thus, all things from the beginning are neither matter nor mind, neither wisdom nor consciousness, neither being nor non-being; they are ultimately inexplicable.

And yet they are still spoken of. It should be understood that the Tathagatas, applying their expedient means, make use of conventional speech in a provisional manner in order to guide people, so that they can be free from their deluded thoughts and can return to Suchness; for if anyone thinks of anything as real and absolute in its own right, he causes his mind to be trapped in *samsara* and consequently he cannot enter the state filled with true insight [i.e., enlightenment].

THE MEANINGS OF YANA

All *Bodhisattva*s aspire to the enlightenment (*bodhi*; Chinese, *tao*) realized by all the Buddhas, disciplining themselves to this end, and advancing toward it. Briefly, three types of aspiration for enlightenment can be distinguished. The first is the aspiration for enlightenment through the perfection of faith. The second is the aspiration for enlightenment through understanding and through deeds. The third is the aspiration for enlightenment through insight.

THE ASPIRATION FOR ENLIGHTENMENT THROUGH THE PERFECTION OF FAITH

Question: By whom and through what kind of discipline can faith be perfected so that the aspiration for enlightenment may be developed? Answer: Among those who belong to the group of the undetermined, there are some who, by virtue of their excellent capacity for goodness developed through permeation, believe in the law of retribution of karma and observe the ten precepts. They loathe the suffering of *samsara* and wish to seek the supreme enlightenment. Having been able to meet the Buddhas, they serve them, honor them, and practice the faith. Their faith will be perfected after ten thousand aeons. Their aspiration for enlightenment will be developed either through the instruction of the Buddhas and the *Bodhisattvas*, or because of their great compassion toward their suffering fellow beings, or from their desire to preserve the good teaching from extinction.

Those who are thus able to develop their aspiration through the perfection of faith will enter the group of the determined and will never retrogress. They are called the ones who are united with the correct cause for enlightenment and who abide among those who belong to the Tathagata family. There are, however, people among those who belong to the group of the undetermined whose capacity for goodness is slight and whose defilements, having accumulated from the far distant past, are deep-rooted.

Though they may also meet the Buddhas and honor them, they will develop the potentiality merely to be born as men, as dwellers in heaven, or as followers of the Hinayana. Even if they should seek after the Mahayana, they would sometimes progress and sometimes regress because of the inconsistent nature of their capacity. And also there are some who honor the Buddhas and who, before ten thousand aeons have passed, will develop an aspiration because of some favorable circumstances.

These circumstances may be the viewing of the Buddhas' corporeal forms, the honoring of monks, the receiving of instructions from the followers of the Hinayana, or the imitation of others' aspiration. But these types of aspiration are all inconsistent, for if the men who hold them meet with unfavorable circumstances, they will relapse and fall back into the stage of attainment of the followers of the Hinayana. Now, in developing the aspiration for enlightenment through the perfection of faith, what kind of mind is to be cultivated? Briefly speaking, three kinds can be discussed.

The first is the mind characterized by straightforwardness, for it correctly meditates on the principle of Suchness. The second is the mind of profoundness, for there is no limit to its joyful accumulation of all kinds of goodness. The third is the mind filled with great compassion, for it wishes to uproot the sufferings of all sentient beings. Question: Earlier it has been explained that the World of Reality is one, and that the essence of the Buddhas has no duality. Why it is that people do not meditate of their own accord on Suchness alone, but must learn to practice good deeds? Answer: Just as a precious gem is bright and pure in its essence but is marred by impurities, so is a man. Even if he meditates on his precious nature, unless he polishes it in various ways by expedient means, he will never be able to purify it. The principle of Suchness in men is absolutely pure in its essential nature, but is filled with immeasurable impurity of defilements.

Even if a man meditates on Suchness, unless he makes an effort to be permeated by it in various ways by applying expedient means, he certainly cannot become pure. Since the state of impurity is limitless, pervading throughout all states of being, it is necessary to counteract and purify it by means of the practice of all kinds of good deeds. If a man does so, he will naturally return to the principle of Suchness. As to the expedient means, there are, in short, four kinds: The first is the fundamental means to be practiced. That is to say, a man is to meditate on the fact that all things in their essential nature are unborn, divorcing himself from deluded views so that he does not abide in *samsara*.

At the same time he is to meditate on the fact that all things are the products of the union of the primary and coordinating causes, and that the effect of karma will never be lost. Accordingly he is to cultivate great compassion, practice meritorious deeds, and accept and transform sentient beings equally without abiding in *nirvana*, for he is to conform himself to the functions of the essential nature of Reality (*dharmata*) which knows no fixation. The second is the means of stopping evils. The practice of developing a sense of shame and repentance can stop all evils and prevent them from growing, for one is to conform oneself to the faultlessness of the essential nature of Reality. The third is the means of increasing the capacity for goodness that has already been developed.

That is to say, a man should diligently honor and pay homage to the Three treasures, and should praise, rejoice in, and beseech the Buddhas. Because of the sincerity of his love and respect for the Three Treasures, his faith will be strengthened and he will be able to seek the unsurpassed enlightenment. Furthermore, being protected by the Buddha, the Dharma, and the *Sangha,* he will be able to wipe out the hindrances of evil karma. His capacity for goodness will not retrogress because he will be conforming himself to the essential nature of Reality, which is free from hindrances produced by stupidity. The fourth is the means of the great vow of universal salvation.

This is to take a vow that one will liberate all sentient beings, down to the last one, no matter how long it may take to cause them to attain the perfect *nirvana,* for one will be conforming oneself to the essential nature of Reality which is characterized by the absence of discontinuity. The essential nature of Reality is all-embracing, and pervades all sentient beings; it is everywhere the same and one without duality; it does not distinguish this from that, because it is, in the final analysis, in the state of quiescence. When a *Bodhisattva* develops this aspiration for enlightenment through faith, he will be able, to a certain extent, to realize the *Dharmakaya.*

Because of this realization of the *Dharmakaya,* and because he is led by the force of the vow that he made to liberate all sentient beings, he is able to present eight types of manifestation of himself for the benefit of all sentient beings. These are: the descent from the Tushita heaven; the entrance into a human womb; the stay in the womb; the birth; the renunciation; the attainment of enlightenment; the turning of the wheel of the Dharma (doctrine); and the entrance into *nirvana.* However, such a *Bodhisattva* cannot be said to have perfectly realized the *Dharmakaya,* for he has not yet completely destroyed the outflowing evil karma which has been accumulated from his numberless existences in the past. He must suffer some slight misery deriving from the state of his birth.

However, this is due not to his being fettered by karma, but to his freely made decision to carry out the great vow of universal salvation in order to understand the suffering of others. It is said in a sutra that there are some *Bodhisattva*s of this kind who may regress and fall into evil states of existence, but this does not refer to a real regression. It says this merely in order to frighten and stir the heroism of the newly initiated *Bodhisattvas* who have not yet joined the group of the determined, and who may be indolent. Furthermore, as soon as this aspiration has been aroused in the *Bodhisattvas*, they leave cowardice far behind them and are not afraid even of falling into the stage of the followers of the Hinayana. Even though they hear that they must suffer extreme hardship for innumerable aeons before they may attain *nirvana*, they do not feel any fear, for they believe and know that from the beginning all things are of themselves in *nirvana*.

THE ASPIRATION FOR ENLIGHTENMENT THROUGH UNDERSTANDING AND DEEDS

It should be understood that this type of aspiration is even more excellent than the former. Because the *Bodhisattvas* who cherish this aspiration are those who are about to finish the first term of the incalculable aeons since the time when they first had the correct faith, they have come to have a profound understanding of the principle of Suchness and to entertain no attachment to their attainments obtained through discipline. Knowing that the essential nature of Reality is free from covetousness, they, in conformity to it, devote themselves to the perfection of charity. Knowing that the essential nature of Reality is free from the defilements which originate from the desires of the five senses, they, in conformity to it, devote themselves to the perfection of precepts.

Knowing that the essential nature of Reality is without suffering and free from anger and anxiety, they, in conformity to it, devote themselves to the perfection of forbearance. Knowing that the essential nature of Reality does not have any distinction of body and mind and is free from indolence, they, in conformity to it, devote themselves to the perfection of zeal. Knowing that the essential nature of Reality is always calm and free from confusion in its essence, they, in conformity to it, devote themselves to the perfection of meditation. Knowing that the essential nature of Reality is always characterized by gnosis and is free from ignorance, they, in conformity to it, devote themselves to the perfection of wisdom.

THE ASPIRATION FOR ENLIGHTENMENT THROUGH INSIGHT

As for the *Bodhisattvas* of this group, who range from the "stage of pure-heartedness" to the "last stage of Bodhisattvahood", what object do they realize? They realize Suchness. We speak of it as an object because of the "evolving mind", but in fact there is no object in this realization that can be stated in terms of a subject-object relationship. There is only the insight into Suchness transcending both the seer and the seen; we call this the experience of the Dharmakaya. The *Bodhisattvas* of this group can, in an instant of thought, go to all worlds of the universe, honor the Buddhas, and ask them to turn the wheel of the Dharma. In order to guide and benefit all men, they do not rely on words. Sometimes, for the sake of weak-willed men, they show how to attain perfect enlightenment quickly by skipping over the stages of the *Bodhisattva*.

And sometimes, for the sake of indolent men, they say that men may attain enlightenment at the end of numberless aeons. Thus they can demonstrate innumerable expedient means and suprarational feats. But in reality all these *Bodhisattvas* are the same in that they are alike in their lineage, their capacity, their aspiration, and their realization of Suchness; therefore, there is no such thing as skipping over the stages, for all *Bodhisattvas* must pass through the three terms of innumerable aeons before they can fully attain enlightenment. However, because of the differences in the various beings, there are also different ways of teaching them what to practice. The characteristics of the aspiration for enlightenment entertained by a *Bodhisattva* belonging to this group can be identified in terms of the three subtle modes of mind.

The first is the true mind, for it is free from false intellectual discrimination. The second is the mind capable of applying expedient means, for it pervades everywhere spontaneously and benefits sentient beings. The third is the mind subject to the influence of karma operating in subconsciousness, for it appears and disappears in the most subtle ways. Again, a *Bodhisattva* of this group, when he brings his excellent qualities to perfection, manifests himself in the heaven of Akanishta (the highest heaven in the world of form according to the cosmology of Indian Buddhism) as the highest physical being in the world. Through wisdom united with original enlightenment of Suchness in an instant of thought, he suddenly extinguishes ignorance.

Then he is called the one who has obtained all-embracing knowledge. Performing suprarational acts spontaneously, he can manifest himself everywhere in the universe and benefit all sentient beings. Question: Since space is infinite, worlds are infinite. Since worlds are infinite, beings are infinite. Since beings are infinite, the variety of their mentalities must also be infinite.

The objects of the senses and the mind must therefore be limitless, and it is difficult to know and understand them all. If ignorance is destroyed, there will be no thoughts in the mind. How then can a comprehension that has no content be called "all-embracing knowledge"? Answer: All objects are originally of One Mind and are beyond thought determination. Because unenlightened people perceive objects in their illusion, they impose limitations in their mind. Since they erroneously develop these thought determinations, which do not correspond to Reality (*dharmata*), they are unable to reach any inclusive comprehension.

The Buddha-Tathagatas are free from all perverse views and thoughts that block correct vision; therefore, there are no corners into which their comprehension does not penetrate. Their Mind is true and real; therefore, it is no other than the essential nature of all things. The Buddhas, because of their very nature, can shed light on all objects conceived in illusion. They are endowed with an influence of great wisdom that functions as the application of innumerable expedient means. Accommodating themselves to the capacity of understanding of various sentient beings, they can reveal to them the manifold meanings of the doctrine. This is the reason they may be called those who have "all-embracing knowledge".

Question: If the Buddhas are able to perform spontaneous acts, to manifest themselves everywhere, and to benefit all sentient beings, then the sentient beings should all be able, by seeing their physical forms, by witnessing their miracles, or by hearing their preachings, to gain benefit. Why is it then that most people in this world have not been able to see the Buddhas? Answer: The *Dharmakaya* of all the Buddhas, being one and the same everywhere, is omnipresent. Since the Buddhas are free from any fixation of thought, their acts are said to be "spontaneous". They reveal themselves in accordance with the mentalities of all the various sentient beings. The mind of the sentient being is like a mirror. Just as a mirror cannot reflect images if it is coated with dirt, so the Dharmakaya cannot appear in the mind of the sentient being if it is coated with the dirt of defilements.

ON FAITH AND PRACTICE

Having already discussed interpretation, we will now present a discussion of faith and practice. This discussion is intended for those who have not yet joined the group of beings who are determined to attain enlightenment.

ON FOUR FAITHS

Question: What kind of faith should a man have and how should he practice it? Answer: Briefly, there are four kinds of faith. The first is the faith in the Ultimate Source. Because of this faith a man comes to meditate with joy on the principle of Suchness. The second is the faith in the numberless excellent qualities of the Buddhas. Because of this faith a man comes to meditate on them always, to draw near to them in fellowship, to honor them, and to respect them, developing his capacity for goodness and seeking after the all-embracing knowledge.

The third is the faith in the great benefits of the Dharma (Teaching). Because of this faith a man comes constantly to remember and practice various disciplines leading to enlightenment. The fourth is the faith in the *Sangha* (Buddhist Community) whose members are able to devote themselves to the practice of benefiting both themselves and others. Because of this faith a man comes to approach constantly and with joy the assembly of *Bodhisattvas* and to seek instruction from them in the correct practice.

ON FIVE PRACTICES

There are five ways of practice which will enable a man to perfect his faith. They are the practices of charity, observance of precepts, patience, zeal, and cessation of illusions and clear observation. Question: How should a man practice charity? Answer: If he sees anyone coming to him begging, he should give him the wealth and other things in his possession in so far as he is able; thus, while freeing himself from greed and avarice, he causes the beggar to be joyful. Or, if he sees one who is in hardship, in fear, or in grave danger, he should, according to his ability and understanding, explain it by the use of expedient means.

In doing so, however, he should not expect any fame, material gain, or respect, but he should think only of benefiting himself and others alike and of extending the merit that he gains from the practice of charity toward the attainment of enlightenment. Question: How should he practice the observance of precepts? Answer: He is not to kill, to steal, to commit adultery, to be double-tongued, to slander, to lie, or to utter exaggerated speech. He is to free himself from greed, jealousy, cheating, deceit, flattery, crookedness, anger, hatred, and perverse views. If he happens to be a monk or nun who has renounced family life, he should also in order to cut off and suppress defilements keep himself away from the hustle and bustle of the world and always residing in solitude, should learn to be content with the least desire and should practice vigorous ascetic disciplines.

He should be frightened and filled with awe by any slight fault and should feel shame and repent. He should not take lightly any of the Tathagata's precepts. He should guard himself from slander and from showing dislike so as not to rouse people in their delusion to commit any offense or sin. Question: How should he practice patience? Answer: He should be patient with the vexatious acts of others and should not harbor thoughts of vengeance, and he should also be patient in matters of gain or loss, honor or dishonor, praise or blame, suffering or joy, etc. Question: How should he practice zeal? Answer: He should not be sluggish in doing good, he should be firm in his resolution, and he should purge himself of cowardice. He should remember that from the far distant past he has been tormented in vain by all of the great sufferings of body and mind.

Because of this he should diligently practice various meritorious acts, benefiting himself and others, and liberate himself quickly from suffering. Even if a man practices faith, because he is greatly hindered by the evil karma derived from the grave sins of previous lives, he may be troubled by the evil Tempter (Mara) and his demons, or entangled in all sorts of worldly affairs, or afflicted by the suffering of disease. There are a great many hindrances of this kind. He should, therefore, be courageous and zealous, and at the six four-hour intervals of the day and night should pay homage to the Buddhas, repent with sincere heart, beseech the Buddhas for their guidance, rejoice in the happiness of others, and direct all the merits thus acquired to the attainment of enlightenment.

If he never abandons these practices, he will be able to avoid the various hindrances as his capacity for goodness increases. Question: How should he practice cessation and clear observation? Answer: What is called "cessation" means to put a stop to all characteristics (lakshana) of the world of sense objects and of the mind, because it means to follow the samatha (tranquility) method of meditation. What is called "clear observation" means to perceive distinctly the characteristics of the causally conditioned phenomena (*samsara*), because it means to follow the vipasyana (discerning) method of meditation. Question: How should he follow these? Answer: He should step by step practice these two aspects and not separate one from the other, for only then will both be perfected.

THE PRACTICE OF CESSATION

Should there be a man who desires to practice "cessation", he should stay in a quiet place and sit erect in an even temper. His attention should be focused neither on breathing nor on any form or color, nor on empty space, earth, water, fire, wind, nor even on what has been seen, heard, remembered, or conceived. All thoughts, as soon as they are conjured up, are to be discarded, and even the thought of discarding them is to be put away, for all things are essentially in the state of transcending thoughts, and are not to be created from moment to moment nor to be extinguished from moment to moment; thus one is to conform to the essential nature of Reality (dharmata) through this practice of cessation. And it is not that he should first meditate on the objects of the senses in the external world and then negate them with his mind, the mind that has meditated on them.

If the mind wanders away, it should be brought back and fixed in "correct thought". It should be understood that this "correct thought" is the thought that whatever is, is mind only and that there is no external world of objects as conceived; even this mind is devoid of any marks of its own which would indicate its substantiality and therefore is not substantially conceivable as such at any moment. Even if he arises from his sitting position and engages in other activities, such as going, coming, advancing, or standing still, he should at all times be mindful of the application of expedient means of perfecting "cessation", conform to the immobile principle of the essential nature of Reality, and observe and examine the resulting experiences. When this discipline is well-mastered after a long period of practice, the ideations of his mind will be arrested.

Because of this, his power of executing "cessation" will gradually be intensified and become highly effective, so that he will conform himself to, and be able to be absorbed into, the "concentration (*Samadhi*) of Suchness". Then his defilements, deep though they may be, will be suppressed and his faith strengthened; he will quickly attain the state in which there will be no retrogression. But those who are skeptical, who lack faith, who speak ill of the teaching of the Buddha, who have committed grave sins, who are hindered by their evil karma, or who are arrogant or indolent are to be excluded; these people are incapable of being absorbed into the *Samadhi* of Suchness.

Next, as a result of this *Samadhi*, a man realizes the oneness of the World of Reality (*dharmadhatu*), i.e., the sameness everywhere and nonduality of the Dharmakaya of all the Buddhas and the bodies of sentient beings. This is called "the *Samadhi* of one movement". It should be understood that the *Samadhi* of Suchness is the foundation of all other *Samadhi*. If a man keeps practicing it, then he will gradually be able to develop countless other kinds of *Samadhi*. If there is a man who lacks the capacity for goodness, he will be confused by the evil Tempter, by heretics and by demons. Sometimes these beings will appear in dreadful forms while he is sitting in meditation, and at other times they will manifest themselves in the shapes of handsome men and women.

In such a case he should meditate on the principle of "Mind only", and then these objects will vanish and will not trouble him any longer. Sometimes they may appear as the images of heavenly beings or *Bodhisattvas*, and assume also the figure of the Tathagata, furnished with all the major and minor marks; or they may expound the spells or preach charity, the precepts, patience, zeal, meditation, and wisdom; or they may discourse on how the true *nirvana* is the state of universal emptiness, of the nonexistence of characteristics, vows, hatreds, affections, causes, and effects; and of absolute nothingness.

They may also teach him the knowledge of his own past and future states of existence, the method of reading other men's minds, and perfect mastery of speech, causing him to be covetous and attached to worldly fame and profit; or they may cause him to be frequently moved to joy and anger and thus to have unsteadiness of character, being at times very kind-hearted, very drowsy, very ill, or lazy-minded; or at other times becoming suddenly zealous, and then afterward lapsing into negligence; or developing a lack of faith, a great deal of doubt, and a great deal of anxiety; or abandoning his fundamental excellent practices toward religious perfection and devoting himself to miscellaneous religious acts, or being attached to worldly affairs which involve him in many ways; or sometimes they may cause him to experience a certain semblance of various kinds of *Samadhi*, which are all the attainments of heretics and are not the true *Samadhi*; or sometimes they may cause him to remain in *Samadhi* for one, two, three, or up to seven days, feeling comfort in his body and joy in his mind, being neither hungry nor thirsty, partaking of natural, fragrant, and delicious drinks and foods, which induce him to increase his attachment to them; or at other times they may cause him to eat without any restraint, now a great deal, now only a little, so that the color of his face changes accordingly.

For these reasons, he who practices "cessation" should be discreet and observant, lest his mind fall into the net of evil doctrine.

He should not be diligent in abiding in "correct thought", grasping nor attaching himself to anything; if he does so, he will be able to keep himself far away from the hindrance of these evil influences. He should know that the *Samadhi* of the heretics is not free from perverse views, craving, and arrogance, for the heretics are covetously attached to fame, profit, and the respect of the world. The *Samadhi* of Suchness is the *Samadhi* in which one is not arrested by the activity of viewing a subject nor by the experiencing of objects in the midst of meditation; even after concentration one will be neither indolent nor arrogant and one's defilements will gradually decrease. There has never been a case in which an ordinary man, without having practiced this *Samadhi*, was still able to join the group that is entitled to become Tathagatas.

Those who practice the various types of dhyana (meditation) and *Samadhi* which are popular in the world will develop much attachment to their flavors and will be bound to the triple world because of their perverse view that *atman* is real. They are therefore the same as heretics, for as they depart from the protection of their good spiritual friends, they turn to heretical views.

Next, he who practices this *Samadhi* diligently and wholeheartedly will gain ten kinds of advantages in this life. First, he will always be protected by the Buddhas and the *Bodhisattva*s of the ten directions. Second, he will not be frightened by the Tempter and his evil demons.

Third, he will not be deluded or confused by the ninety-five kinds of heretics and wicked spirits. Fourth, he will keep himself far away from slanderers of the profound teaching of the Buddha, and will gradually diminish the hindrances derived from grave sins. Fifth, he will destroy all doubts and wrong views on enlightenment. Sixth, his faith in the Realm of the Tathagata will grow. Seventh, he will be free from sorrow and remorse and in the midst of *samsara* will be full of vigor and undaunted. Eighth, having a gentle heart and forsaking arrogance, he will not be vexed by others.

Ninth, even if he has not yet experienced *Samadhi*, he will be able to decrease his defilements in all places and at all times, and he will not take pleasure in the world. Tenth, if he experiences *Samadhi*, he will not be startled by any sound from without. Now, if he practices "cessation" only, then his mind will be sunk in self-complacency and he will be slothful; he will not delight in performing good acts but will keep himself far away from the exercise of great compassion. It is, therefore, necessary to practice "clear observation" as well.

THE PRACTICE OF CLEAR OBSERVATION

He who practices "clear observation" should observe that all conditioned phenomena in the world are unstationary and are subject to instantaneous transformation and destruction; that all activities of the mind arise and are extinguished from moment to moment; and that, therefore, all of these induce suffering. He should observe that all that had been conceived in the past was as hazy as a dream that all that is being conceived in the present is like a flash of lightning, and that all that will be conceived in the future will be like clouds that rise up suddenly. He should also observe that the physical existences of all living beings in the world are impure and that among these various filthy things there is not a single one that can be sought after with joy.

He should reflect in the following way: all living beings, from the beginningless beginning, because they are permeated by ignorance, have allowed their mind to remain in *samsara;* they have already suffered all the great miseries of the body and mind, they are at present under incalculable pressure and constraint, and their sufferings in the future will likewise be limitless. These sufferings are difficult to forsake, difficult to shake off, and yet these beings are unaware that they are in such a state; for this, they are greatly to be pitied. After reflecting in this way, he should pluck up his courage and make a great vow to this effect: may my mind be free from discriminations so that I may practice all of the various meritorious acts everywhere in the ten directions; may I, to the end of the future, by applying limitless expedient means, help all suffering sentient beings so that they may obtain the bliss of *nirvana,* the ultimate goal.

Having made such a vow, he must, in accordance with his capacity and without faltering, practice every kind of good at all times and all places and not be slothful in his mind. Except when he sits in concentration in the practice of "cessation", he should at all times reflect upon what should be done and what should not be done. Whether walking, standing, sitting, lying, or rising, he should practice both "cessation" and "clear observation" side by side. That is to say, he is to meditate upon the fact that things are unborn in their essential nature; but at the same time he is to meditate upon the fact that good and evil karma, produced by the combination of the primary cause and the coordinating causes, and the retributions of karma in terms of pleasure, pain, etc., are neither lost nor destroyed.

Though he is to meditate on the retribution of good and evil karma produced by the primary and coordinating causes [i.e., he is to practice "clear observation"], he is also to meditate on the fact that the essential nature of things is unobtainable by intellectual analysis. The practice of "cessation" will enable ordinary men to cure themselves of their attachments to the world, and will enable the followers of the Hinayana to forsake their views, which derive from cowardice. The practice of "clear observation" will cure the followers of the Hinayana of the fault of having narrow and inferior minds which bring forth no great compassion, and will free ordinary men from their failure to cultivate the capacity for goodness. For these reasons, both "cessation" and "clear observation" are complementary and inseparable.

If the two are not practiced together, then one cannot enter the path to enlightenment. Next, suppose there is a man who learns this teaching for the first time and wishes to seek the correct faith but lacks courage and strength.

Because he lives in this world of suffering, he fears that he will not always be able to meet the Buddhas and honor them personally, and that, faith being difficult to perfect, he will be inclined to fall back. He should know that the Tathagatas have an excellent expedient means by which they can protect his faith: that is, through the strength of wholehearted meditation on the Buddha, he will in fulfillment of his wishes be able to be born in the Buddha-land beyond, to see the Buddha always, and to be forever separated from the evil states of existence.

It is as the sutra says: "If a man meditates wholly on Amitabha Buddha in the world of the Western Paradise and wishes to be born in that world, directing all the goodness he has cultivated toward that goal, then he will be born there." Because he will see the Buddha at all times, he will never fall back. If he meditates on the *Dharmakaya*, the Suchness of the Buddha, and with diligence keeps practicing the meditation, he will be able to be born there in the end because he abides in the correct *Samadhi*.

ENCOURAGEMENT OF PRACTICE AND THE BENEFITS THEREOF

As has already been explained in the preceding sections, the Mahayana is the secret treasury of the Buddhas. Should there be a man who wishes to obtain correct faith in the profound Realm of the Tathagata and to enter the path of Mahayana, putting far away from himself any slandering of the teaching of Buddha, he should lay hold of this treatise, deliberate on it, and practice it; in the end he will be able to reach the unsurpassed enlightenment.

If a man, after having heard this teaching, does not feel any fear or weakness, it should be known that such a man is certain to carry on the lineage of the Buddha and to receive the prediction of the Buddha that he will obtain enlightenment. Even if a man were able to reform all living beings throughout all the systems in the universe and to induce them to practice the ten precepts, he still would not be superior to a man who reflects correctly upon this teaching even for the time spent on a single meal, for the excellent qualities which the latter is able to obtain are unspeakably superior to those which the former may obtain.

If a man takes hold of this treatise and reflects on and practices the teachings given in it only for one day and one night, the excellent qualities he will gain will be boundless and indescribable. Even if all the Buddhas of the ten directions were to praise these excellent qualities for incalculably long periods of time, they could never reach the end of their praise, for the excellent qualities of the Reality (*dharmata*) are infinite and the excellent qualities gained by this man will accordingly be boundless. If, however, there is a man who slanders and does not believe in this treatise, for an incalculable number of aeons he will undergo immense suffering for his fault. Therefore all people should reverently believe in it and not slander it, for slander and lack of faith will gravely injure one as well as others and will lead to the destruction of the lineage of the Three Treasures.

Through this teaching all Tathagatas have gained *nirvana*, and through the practice of it all *Bodhisattva*s have obtained Buddha-wisdom. It should be known that it was by means of this teaching that the *Bodhisattva*s in the past were able to perfect their pure faith; that it is by means of this teaching that the *Bodhisattva*s of the present are perfecting their pure faith; and that it is by means of this teaching that the *Bodhisattva*s of the future will perfect their pure faith. Therefore men should diligently study and practice it.

Bibliography

Akira, Hirakawa, The Formation of the Panca-Sila in Early Buddhism, *World Fellowship of Buddhists Review* 32 (3): 8–23, 1995.

Barua, Dipak Kumar, *Viharas in Ancient India: A Survey of Buddhist Monasteries,* Calcutta: Indian Publications, 1969.

Cousins, L. S., Ethical Standards in World Religions: III. Buddhism, *The Exository Times* Vol. LXXXV, pp. 100–104, 1974.

Cousins, L. S., Good or Skilful? Kusala in Canon and Commentary, *Journal of Buddhist Ethics* 3:136–64, 1996.

Dharmasiri, G., *Fundamentals of Buddhist Ethics,* Antioch, CA.: Golden Leaves Publ. Co., 1989.

Frauwallner, E., *The Earliest Vinaya and the Beginnings of Buddhist Literature,* Rome: Istituto Italiano per il Medio ed Estremo Oriente, 1956.

Fu, C. W., and S. A. Wawrytko, eds., *Buddhist Ethics and Modern Society: an International Symposium,* New York: Greenwood Press, 1991.

Guenther, Herbert V., *Philosophy and Psychology in the Abhidharma,* Berkeley, Calif.: Shambhala, 1976.

Harvey, P., *An Introduction to Buddhism: Teachings, History and Practices,* Cambridge: Cambridge University Press, chap. 9, 1990.

Harvey, P., *An Introduction to Buddhist Ethics: Foundations, Values and Issues,* Cambridge: Cambridge University Press, 2000.

Harvey, P., *An Introduction to Buddhist Ethics: Foundations, Values and Issues*, Cambridge: Cambridge University Press, pp. 11-31, 2000.

Hinderey, R., *Comparative Ethics in Hindu and Buddhist Traditions,* Delhi: Motilal Banarsidass, 1978.

Jacobson, Nolan Pliny, *Buddhism, the Religion of Analysis.* London: Feffer & Simons, 1974.

Jayatilleke, K. N., *Ethics in Buddhist Perspective: Wheel Booklet no,*175/176. Kandy, Sri Lanka: Buddhist Publication Society, 1972.

Keown, D. (ed), *Contemporary Buddhist Ethics*, London: Curzon Press, 2000.

Keown, D., *The Nature of Buddhist Ethics*, London: Macmillan, 1992.

Keown, D., *Buddhism and Bioethics*, London: Macmillan; New York: St. Martin's Press, chap. 1, 1995.

Little, D. and S. B. Twiss., *Comparative Religious Ethics: A New Method,* New York: Harper and Row, 1978.

Mahasi Sayadaw, *Sallekha Sutta: A Discourse on the Refinement of Character*, Hinsdale, Il.: Buddhadharma Meditation Center, 1981.

McDermott, J. P., *Development in the Early Buddhist Concept of Kamma/Karma,* New Delhi: Munshiram Manoharlal, 1984.

Misra, G. S. P., *Development of Buddhist Ethics*, New Delhi: Munshiram Manoharlal, 1984.

Nhat Hanh, Thich, et al., *For a Future to be Possible: Commentaries on the Five Wonderful Precepts*, Berkeley, CA.: Parallax Press, 1993.

Nyanaponika, *The Roots of Good and Evil: Wheel booklet no,* 251/253. Kandy, Sri Lanka: Buddhist Publication Society, 1978.

Pardue, Peter, *Buddhism: A Brief Account.* New York: Macmillan, Social history, 1971.

Prebish, C. S., ed., *Buddhist Ethics: A Cross-cultural Approach*, Kendall/Hunt, 1992.

Whitehill, James, "Buddhism and the Virtues" in Keown, D. (ed) *Contemporary Buddhist Ethics*, London: Curzon Press, 17-36, 2000.

Saddhatissa, H., *Buddhist Ethics: Essence of Buddhism*, London: George Allen and Unwin, 1970.

Saddhatissa, H., *The Buddha's Way*, New York: Brazillier, Reprint, London: Allen and Unwin, 1985.

Varma, Vishvanath Prasad, *Early Buddhism and Its Origins.* Delhi: Munshiram Monaharlal, 1973.

Index

I

K

L

M

N

O

P